PSYCHOTHERAPY
FOR BETTER
OR WORSE

PSYCHOTHERAPY FOR BETTER OR WORSE

The Problem of Negative Effects

**Hans H. Strupp, Suzanne W. Hadley,
Beverly Gomes-Schwartz**

Jason Aronson, Inc.
New York, N.Y.

110373

Strupp, Hans H.
    Psychotherapy for better or worse.

    Bibliography: p.
    Includes indexes.
    1. Psychotherapy—Complications and sequelae.
I. Title. [DNLM: 1. Psychotherapy. 2. Iatrogenic disease.
WM420 S927 pe]
RC480.5.S77   616.8:914

ISBN: 0-87668-306-5

Library of Congress Catalog Number: 77-88413

Manufactured in the United States of America

Acknowledgments

The stimulus for the exploration reported in this book was provided by the National Institute of Mental Health, which provided support under Contract #278-75-0036 (ER). Even more important were the encouragement and support we received from Dr. Morris B. Parloff, Chief of the Psychotherapy and Behavioral Intervention Section of the Clinical Research Branch at NIMH. We gratefully acknowledge his substantive contribution to the planning and execution of our study.

Other members of the Vanderbilt University Psychotherapy Research Team who participated in many discussions and enriched our thinking were Dianna Hartley and Dr. Grady Blackwood. Dr. Stephen Armstrong, in addition to participating in many discussions, contributed an early draft of the summary tables in Appendix A.

Mrs. Brenda Merritt, our faithful secretary, typed numerous drafts and assisted in the preparation of the final manuscript. Mrs. Cathy Albert was the typist for the summary tables in Appendix A.

We are particularly indebted to scores of colleagues, both in the United States and England, who generously shared their ideas with us. We were frankly amazed by the interest our inquiry generated in them, and take the seriousness and thoughtfulness of their comments as evidence for the importance and timeliness of the topic. The names of those colleagues who consented to be identified are listed in Appendix B.

Contents

Chapter 5

Chapter 6

Appendix A

Appendix B

Appendix C

Authors of Letters
(Appendix C)

Chapter 1

The Problem

Psychotherapy is the art and science of relieving human suffering resulting from emotional conflicts and disturbances. Practitioners of psychotherapy are almost by definition dedicated to healing or ameliorating human suffering by psychological techniques. In modern jargon, psychotherapy is one of the "healing professions" and psychotherapists qualify as "health providers." Thus it is almost a contradiction in terms to raise the possibility that psychotherapy may have deleterious effects, that it may augment rather than alleviate the patient's suffering and distress. How can procedures aimed at healing produce increased suffering? How can interventions designed to help result in harm? As public debate and a growing literature attest, these are not idle questions. In fact, they are posed with greater frequency and urgency in our day than at any time in the past. What are the issues? What is the evidence? How can the problem be dealt with? This book is addressed to these questions.

Within the profession (we use *psychotherapy* and *psychotherapists* as generic terms without regard to the background, training, or professional affiliation of practitioners) it has long been known that some patients—once thought to be a relatively small minority—either fail to improve or actually deteriorate while in therapy or following its conclusion. In recent years, due in part to increasing consumer consciousness (see chapter 2 for a more detailed discussion of the factors involved), all activities of psychotherapists have come under closer scrutiny. What can psychotherapy do and how does it produce results? These are the fundamental issues. Both clinicians and researchers have typically focused their attention on the curative aspects of therapy; however, it is clear that any treatment capable of producing beneficial effects may also be capable of doing harm. To deny this possibility is tantamount to asserting that psychotherapy is not very potent under any circumstances. While some of its more vociferous critics have embraced this conclusion, we believe it is neither warranted on the basis of available evidence nor supported by clinical experience. The latter remains a valuable source of knowledge, at least until it is replaced by systematic research.

Today we witness a coalescence of seemingly disparate forces. Within the field of psychotherapy there is a heightened awareness of the possibility of negative effects, while in the public domain the proliferation of malpractice suits, aimed thus far primarily at medical practitioners but showing signs of extending to psychotherapists, is symptomatic of a serious problem. From both perspectives there is considerable urgency for a systematic analysis of the problem. Negative effects cannot be ignored nor can they remain shrouded in secrecy. For the good of the profession as well as that of the public, psychotherapists as well as researchers must face the issues squarely. The study of negative effects is both significant and timely.

DEFINITIONS AND CAUSES

At the outset we are confronted with a need to define our terms. What do we mean by *negative effects*? Some obvious instances—suicides, psychotic breaks—are universally regarded with opprobrium. But what of more complex changes in functioning? What of individuals who learn to behave more adaptively only at great cost to their creativity and happiness? What of individuals who shed repressive aspects of their life only to be overwhelmed by anxiety accompanying the loss of impulse control? Are these positive or negative therapy outcomes? The answer to such questions involves *decisions concerning the kinds of indicators accepted as evidence and the manner in which any change is valued*—as change for better or for worse. There is obviously less than unanimous agreement on such decisions, and an important part of our effort is to provide a framework within which questions may be posed and answers sought.

However a negative effect is identified or defined, of great practical significance are the factors contributing to such an outcome. Three primary classes of factors, acting singly or in combination, may be responsible for therapeutic change in general and negative effects in particular: (1) *environmental variables* (including the patient's interpersonal relationships with significant persons in his life and other variables in the social and cultural milieu within which he functions); (2) *patient variables* (including prominently the nature of the psychopathology, degree and chronicity of disturbance, intelligence, education, socioeconomic factors, motivation for change, etc.); and (3) *therapist variables* (including the therapist's personality as well as his therapeutic techniques, which are always intertwined).

Within these three major categories a wide variety of factors must be considered as potential sources of negative effects. To arrive at a better understanding of the general problem, we considered it important as part of our effort (1) to explore prevailing conceptions of negative effects and (2) to assemble a catalogue of likely causes. On both points, the views of prominent clinicians, researchers, and theoreticians are obviously highly relevant. To this end, we invited comments from a sizable sample of colleagues, many of whom were personally known to us. Their responses were incorporated into our analysis of definitions and causes presented in chapter 4. (The letters of those authors who granted permission for publication are reproduced as Appendix C.)

NEGATIVE EFFECTS
IN THE CLINICAL LITERATURE

As soon as Breuer and Freud (1893-1895) recognized that many persons who seek psychotherapy are suffering from neurotic disturbances involving intrapsychic conflict, the groundwork was laid for the introduction and subsequent elaboration of the concept of the "negative therapeutic reaction." Individuals manifesting such reactions, in order to avoid painful affect, defend the status quo (resistance) and thus unwittingly may seek to involve the therapist in an interpersonal struggle in order to defeat the therapeutic effort (negative transference). The crux of psychoanalytic therapy, as we know, consists in the therapist's dealing with the patient's resistances as manifested in the therapeutic situation and in his "handling of the transference," that is, skillful management of the patient-therapist relationship in order to achieve therapeutic goals. Thus, a negative therapeutic outcome may result (a) if the patient prevails in neutralizing or fending off the therapist's interventions by various defensive operations or (b) if the therapist, for a variety of reasons, allows this to happen, or—more unfortunately—actively promotes it. The net effect in both instances is the same: the patient remains unchanged or gets worse, and the reasons lie either in the patient's neurotic structure, which proves impervious to reasonable therapeutic efforts, or in deficiencies within the therapist. The latter may be divided into (1) deficiencies in technical skill, traceable to the therapist's inability to correctly identify and deal with the patient's defensive operations, and (2) emotional reactions to the patient as a person or to his defensive strategies. A deficiency of either type may create blind spots in the therapist or, interacting with his own unresolved problems, give rise to the well-recognized countertransference reactions, a problem to which a great deal of thought has been devoted by clinicians and theorists alike (for an overview of this literature, see Orr 1954).

To state the basic issue somewhat differently: A patient in psychotherapy may fail to improve or may even get worse. To answer the question, What factors are responsible?, one must turn to the analysis of variables in the patient, the therapist, or the vicissitudes of their interaction. To these Freud (1917) added counterproductive influences traceable to the patient's social milieu. In this connection, he spoke with particular vehemence about members of the patient's family who, frequently for neurotic reasons of their own, actively interfere with the therapeutic effort. He likened this problem to family members looking over the surgeon's shoulder in the operating room. While undoubtedly real and highly important, we will not pursue these latter factors because of their elusiveness and idiosyncratic character.

Since in subsequent chapters of this book we will deal in detail with patient and therapist factors responsible for negative therapeutic outcomes, we will confine ourselves here to brief references to the pertinent clinical literature.

Patient factors. As already noted, the large literature on transference and resistance covered in all standard textbooks of psychoanalytic psychotherapy (e.g., Greenson 1967) is germane to the discussion of patient variables potentially responsible for negative therapeutic effects. While nonanalytic authors of psychotherapy have devoted a certain amount of space to this problem (e.g., Rogers 1951), the incisiveness of the psychoanalytic literature, because of its sharp focus on the dynamics of the patient-therapist interaction, remains unequaled.

In one of his last papers, "Analysis Terminable and Interminable," Freud (1937) addressed himself, as he had on numerous previous occasions, to conditions limiting the success of psychoanalytic therapy. Importantly, he identified constitutional factors, the effects of early traumas, malformations in the patient's ego, and, he added, an unconscious sense of guilt. Previously, he had spoken of the repetition compulsion, the patient's unconscious tendency (attributed to the death instinct) to perpetuate the search for neurotic goals by neurotic means. Greenson (1967), for example, deals extensively with these problems, including his own emphasis on the therapist's too-frequent failure to analyze the patient's negative transference (pp. 236-237).

Therapist factors. It was not long after the inception of modern psychotherapy that the therapist's personality was identified and implicated as a potential factor in therapeutic failure. Introducing the term *countertransference*, Freud (1910) gave clear recognition to variables in the therapist that might exert an adverse influence upon the course and outcome of therapy, together with a proposal for counteracting their effect:

We have become aware of the 'counter-transference,' which arises in him [the therapist] as a result of the patient's influence on his unconscious feelings, and we are almost inclined to insist that he shall recognize this countertransference in himself and overcome it. Now that a considerable number of people are practicing psycho-analysis and exchanging their observations with one another, we have noticed that no psycho-analyst goes further than his own complexes and internal resistances permit [an interesting but as yet untested hypothesis] and we consequently require that he shall begin his activity with a self-analysis and continually carry it deeper while he is making his observations on his patients. Anyone who fails to produce results in a self-analysis of this kind may at once give up any idea of being able to treat patients by analysis. [pp. 144-145]

For the researcher in psychotherapy it is of interest to note that Freud stressed the impact of the therapist's personality on the reliability of his clinical observations and the necessity of calibrating the therapist as a clinical instrument perhaps even more than the impact of his personality on the "purity" of his therapeutic influence. (See Strupp 1973, chapter 15, for a fuller discussion of this issue.)

Since Freud's time a voluminous literature on countertrans-ference has sprung up. However, agreement on a precise definition has been far from unanimous, with conceptions ranging from transient unconscious attitudes on the part of the therapist to "the whole of the analyst's attitudes and behavior toward his patient" (Little 1951, p. 32). There has also been less than complete consensus on how countertransference reac-tions are to be handled. Nonetheless, authors seem to agree that countertransference reactions represent potential if not actual interferences with the course and outcome of therapy. In short, it has been recognized that regardless of any technique he may use, the therapist's personality may have an

adverse effect on the patient. Conversely, there has been
increasing recognition that, apart from the fact that the patient
imbues his relationship to the therapist with unresolved
problems from his past (transferences), there is always a "real"
relationship, based on their present-day interaction as adults.
Greenson (1967) spoke of the "realistic *and* genuine relationship between analyst and patient" (p. 217), characterizing the
optimal therapist attitude as one of acceptance, tolerance,
compassion and trust—a far cry from Freud's conception of
the analyst as a "blank screen." As we shall see in subsequent
chapters, therapist factors of various kinds loom as a powerful
force in therapeutic outcomes, both positive and negative.

Since much of the information about negative therapeutic
reactions and countertransference problems comes from
patients who have been unsuccessful with one therapist and
enter therapy with a second (sometimes more), considerable
caution must be exercised in interpretation. It is obvious that
data deriving from such "reanalyses" are frequently confounded by inaccuracies and distortions in the patient's
reports and, of course, are further influenced by complications
in the patient's relationship with the current therapist.
Probably a more reliable source of information is supervisors'
observations of therapists in training. In either event, it is easy
to commit the *post hoc ergo propter* fallacy when one tries to
explain the occurrence of a therapeutic failure.

NEGATIVE EFFECTS AND
THE RESEARCH LITERATURE

A comprehensive review of the empirical literature cited in
support of the "deterioration hypothesis" (Bergin 1971,
Lambert, Bergin, and Collins 1977) provides less than
compelling evidence that a significant proportion of patients
experience negative effects from psychotherapy, nor do these

studies yield reliable information about the factors in the therapy experience which might have contributed to the observed negative effects (see chapter 3). This does not mean—we hasten to add—that negative effects are not a serious problem. The clinical literature and therapists' own experiences amply document that some patients, albeit perhaps a small minority, manifest a lasting negative reaction to psychotherapy—which alone is sufficient justification for studying in great detail how and why such reactions occur. The lack of clear-cut evidence for negative effects in the contemporary research literature is primarily due to methodological flaws in many of the studies cited in support of the contention. Since this problem is a part of the larger issue of psychotherapy outcomes in general, a brief discussion of the state of the outcome literature seems in order.

On the positive side, clinicians and investigators have abandoned such simplistic formulations as "Does psychotherapy do any good?" and instead have moved toward clarifying and confronting the complex issues involved in studying the patient-therapist relationship and its consequences for therapy outcome (Bergin and Strupp 1972). How does change in psychotherapy come about? What is the nature of these changes? What factors in patient, therapist, technique, and environmental circumstances further or impede change? How can we match patient and therapist for maximal therapeutic gain? Is one therapeutic technique more effective than another? If so, what are the unique characteristics of such techniques? Are therapeutic changes predominantly a function of the psychotherapist's personality, apart from any technique he might use? Is modern psychotherapy intrinsically different from faith healing? Is psychotherapy nothing but a giant placebo? These are some of the important questions which have been addressed by researchers over the years.

Although there are as yet no definitive studies of psychotherapy outcomes, a small number of studies qualify as approximations. These studies allow the conclusion that under particular circumstances we can be much more certain than in the past that psychotherapy is more than a placebo (Bergin 1971, Meltzoff and Kornreich 1970) or the "purchase of friendship" (Schofield 1964). Serious collaboration between clinicians and researchers in certain areas (e.g., in the treatment of depressions) and systematic comparisons between treatment modalities under reasonable specified conditions have been carried out with considerable success (Sloane et al. 1975, DiLoreto 1971). Systematic study of such thorny problems as how and why one patient improves whereas another gets worse is obviously difficult and slow; however, it is an absolute necessity if the field is to advance.

At present, the great complexity of the subject matter and the youth of psychotherapy research do not permit us to say how positive *or* negative therapy effects are achieved. We shall deal at greater length with much needed improvements in psychotherapy research in chapter 6. For the present, however, it seems appropriate to note that research has created a number of beachheads, despite the seemingly insurmountable problems in methodology and conceptualization. There remains an urgent need for systematic and rigorous research— a challenge that must be met in the years to come.

NEGATIVE EFFECTS IN THE CONTEXT OF THERAPY OUTCOME IN GENERAL

The problem of *negative effects* (a term we have adopted in preference to *deterioration*, the former appearing to us a more accurate description of *therapy-induced* changes for the worse) is, as we have suggested, an integral part of the issue of psychotherapy outcome and, more broadly, of psychotherapy's effectiveness. Improvement and deterioration are two sides of the same coin: If we succeed in defining more stringently and in assessing more precisely what constitutes change for the better, we will have also achieved a clearer understanding of what constitutes change for the worse.

The evaluation of change in psychotherapy, as clinicians and researchers have come to appreciate (for an excellent analysis, see Bergin 1971), is a difficult undertaking. In the first place, the measures used (clinical observations in particular) are fraught with shortcomings in terms of reliability and validity, and there is a grave potential for bias from a variety of sources. However, the problem is not simply one of assessment and measurement, important as these issues are. We must realize that in the final analysis we are concerned with *judgments*—based on clinical observations, psychological tests, reports by significant others, etc.—that a patient has changed for the better, for the worse, or that there has been no change. Such judgments are always made with reference to a metric or a standard and unless such guideposts are stringently defined and generally accepted, disagreements and polemics will continue. Moreover, since we are dealing with variegated aspects of human functioning and performance, rather than physical properties, subjective elements in judgment are impossible to eliminate—a further obstacle to consensus.

Finally, we must acknowledge the influence of such variables as the social milieu, the culture, diverse conceptions of psychopathology, mental health and human values, all of which detract from the reliability and validity of judgments of mental health and psychotherapy outcome. Chapter 5 includes an analysis of these issues which, we believe, leads to a better appreciation of the obstacles impeding consensus, and suggests an improved approach.

FORMAT OF THE BOOK

The present analysis of the problem of negative effects in psychotherapy is structured around the following issues:

1. Is there such a phenomenon as a negative effect in psychotherapy?
2. If the answer is yes, how may a negative effect best be defined and what is the empirical evidence of negative effects?
3. What factors may contribute to negative effects?
4. How can inquiry into the problem best be pursued?

Chapter 2 presents an overview of the problem, relating the current interest in negative effects to the social, political and philosophical milieu of psychotherapy. In chapters 3 and 4 we focus on the psychotherapy field itself with an analysis of empirical studies and the views of contemporary experts concerning definitions and causes of negative effects. In chapter 5 we describe the intimate relationship between the problem of negative effects and the broader issues of psychotherapy outcome and mental health evaluations. A conceptual model elaborating this relationship is described and the implications of the model for psychotherapy research are presented. Finally, in chapter 6 we recapitulate the issues, both those broader in scope and those more specifically related to negative effects. The major findings of our investigations into the issues are described and their theoretical, educational, and clinical implications explored.

Our aim throughout has been to examine historical and contemporary approaches to the problem of negative effects, while simultaneously considering the implications of these approaches for the future. More importantly, we have attempted to deal comprehensively with the specific problem of negative effects in psychotherapy while at the same time giving adequate consideration to the more general social, philosophical, and political issues which are inextricably involved.

Chapter 2

Psychotherapy Under Attack

As we have demonstrated in chapter 1, the problem of negative effects in psychotherapy is inextricably interwoven with the problem of psychotherapy outcomes in general—a topic that created controversy almost from the moment modern psychotherapy made its appearance in the late 1800s. Freud's theoretical formulations as well as his claims of having devised an effective form of psychological treatment unleashed a storm of criticism that was apparently fueled as much by strong emotional reactions as by healthy skepticism. Freud initially tended to attribute the critics' skepticism and vituperation to their "resistances" to psychoanalysis, commenting wrily that "psychoanalysis brings out the worst in people." Eventually it became apparent that the demand for hard empirical evidence, particularly with respect to therapeutic claims, could not be dismissed in so cavalier a fashion, and Freud himself began to address the problem in earnest, despite the fact that he continued to hold "statistics" in considerable disdain. In the middle decades of our century, and well into our time, psychotherapy researchers have devoted themselves seriously to the task of bringing modern methods of clinical and behavioral science research to bear upon the issue of psychotherapy's effectiveness, their efforts resulting in slow but steady advances. Most recently, legislators, insurance companies, and consumers, for different but equally valid reasons have begun to demand from the mental health professions clear-cut answers to the extraordinarily difficult and complex questions concerning what psychotherapy does and how it does it. Thus, it seems important to take a closer look at some of the reasons behind contemporary society's critical view of psychotherapy.

1. Lack of specification of treatment and its effectiveness. It is clear that if psychotherapy, of whatever variety, is presented to the public as a valid treatment modality, that is, if therapy is claimed to ameliorate problems in living or psychopathology, however defined, it is incumbent upon those who advance such claims to specify: (a) the nature of the problem or problems psychotherapy is supposed to help; (b) the conditions under which it is helpful; (c) the kinds of changes or improvements that may reasonably be expected; (d) the operations necessary to bring about the change; and (e) perhaps somewhat further down the road, the advancement of reasonable theoretical formulations to explain psychotherapy's modus operandi. Each of these requirements entails careful definition of variables, the description of measurement or assessment operations, and the ruling out of alternatives, for instance, the possibility that the observed changes are "spontaneous," due to factors unrelated to the treatment under investigation.

In this connection, it is noteworthy—although frequently overlooked—that Freud delineated rather stringently the range of applicability of the psychoanalytic technique, by which he meant essentially classical analysis:

You know already that the field of application of analytic therapy lies in the transference neuroses—phobias, hysteria, obsessional neurosis—and further, abnormalities of character which have been developed in place of these illnesses. Everything differing from these, narcissistic and psychotic conditions, is unsuitable to a greater or less extent. It would be entirely legitimate to guard against failures by carefully excluding such cases. This precaution would lead to a great improvement in the statistics of analysis. [Freud 1933, p. 155]

In the ensuing discussion (pp. 155-157) Freud pursued these ideas by pointing out that often analysis must precede diagnosis, and when a patient is rejected after a period of trial analysis he "has his revenge by adding to our list of failures," perhaps even by writing books on psychoanalysis himself. He also defended the length of many analyses by calling attention to the severity of the problems to be treated. While time-consuming, even the treatment of character disorders often yields satisfactory results. At any rate, Freud concluded modestly yet proudly, psychoanalysis is one among many methods of treatment, "though, to be sure, *primus inter pares.*"

As already noted, Freud was subjected to critical attack as soon as he presented psychoanalysis as a legitimate treatment modality to a skeptical public. Thus he was forced to deal with issues of therapeutic effectiveness and the justification for expenditures of time and money in therapy. In a revealing passage, which also speaks to the issue of negative effects from psychotherapy, he said:

This presents a gloomy prospect for the effectiveness of psycho-analysis as a therapy—does it not?—even though we are able to explain the great majority of our failures by

attributing them to external factors. Friends of analysis
have advised us to meet the threatened publication of our
failures with statistics of our successes drawn up by
ourselves. I did not agree with this. I pointed out that
statistics are worthless if the items assembled in them are
too heterogeneous; and the cases of neurotic illness which
we had taken into treatment were in fact incomparable in
a great variety of respects. Moreover, the period of time
that could be covered was too short to make it possible to
report on many of the cases: they concerned people who
had kept both their illness and its treatment secret, and
their recovery had equally to be kept secret. But the
strongest reason for holding back lay in the realization
that in matters of therapy people behave highly
irrationally, so that one has no prospect of accomplishing
anything with them by rational means. A therapeutic
novelty is either received with delirious enthusiasm—as,
for instance, when Koch introduced his first tuberculin
against tuberculosis to the public—or it is treated with
abysmal distrust—like Jenner's vaccination, which was in
fact a blessing and which even today has its irreconcilable
opponents. There was obviously a prejudice against
psycho-analysis. If one had cured a severe case, one might
hear people say: 'That proves nothing. He would have
recovered on his own account by this time.' And when a
woman patient, who had already passed through four
cycles of depression and mania, came to be treated by me
during an interval after an attack of melancholia and
three weeks later started on a phase of mania, all the
members of her family—and a high medical authority,
too, who was called in for consultation—were convinced
that the fresh attack could only be the result of my
attempted analysis. Nothing can be done against
prejudices. . . . [Freud 1917, p. 461]

While Freud was undoubtedly justified in asserting that there was a prejudice *against* psychoanalysis, his own writings—and more importantly the claims of his followers who advocated "a widening scope" of psychoanalysis (Stone 1954)—may be seen as an equally strong prejudice *for* psychoanalysis. Furthermore, Freud's description of the "delirious enthusiasm" with which new treatment modalities tend to be greeted has a remarkably modern ring. Unfortunately, psychotherapists themselves have often set the stage for the "attacks" on psychotherapy by excessive, unsubstantiated claims regarding its applicability and potency.

At any rate, neither Freud nor therapists of later generations were able to make much headway in answering the problem of effectiveness in terms of the stringent specification of conditions we have spoken of above. In fact, it has become clear only in recent years that advancements in the evaluation of psychotherapy or any other treatment are contingent upon greater specificity. In the absence of highly specific information concerning the nature of the treatment for which change is sought and the precise quality of the changes achieved, it remains possible to argue that psychotherapy "on the whole" or "in general" is either highly effective, moderately effective, or ineffective. For many years, answers to questions concerning psychotherapy's effectiveness have been further confounded by the absence of adequate control groups and insufficient attention to other methodological considerations. Gradually, however, these caveats are being heeded by researchers, and it may be expected that in the foreseeable future more decisive answers will be forthcoming.

2. Proliferation of therapies. When modern psychotherapy came into existence toward the end of the nineteenth century—and reaching back into earlier history—neurotic problems that brought patients to a specialist were considered "nervous diseases." In other words, the problems were considered analogous to a medical illness whose course was either stemmed or ameliorated. In favorable circumstances, the patient achieved a "cure" or he underwent "spontaneous remission." Residues of this conception are, of course, still found in our time, and claims for reimbursement from insurance companies—to cite one example, are handled on this basis. However, when neurotic problems gradually came to be viewed as "problems in living," a new approach was necessary. Attacks on the "medical model" gained momentum with the arguments of writers like Szasz (1961), who identified the concept of mental illness as a "myth."

A further change in conceptions was ushered in by the emergence of a host of "new" therapies which no longer addressed themselves to emotional illness or disturbances but which dealt with philosophical and existential problems, man's place in the world and its attendant anxieties and dilemmas. Humanistic psychology and the human potential movement, among others, broadened the notion of treatment to include "training," "personality growth," "self-realization," "self-actualization," and "self-awareness." Furthermore, the teachings of Eastern religions attracted many followers in the United States who embraced meditation, yoga, etc. as means toward peace of mind and heightened self-awareness. Even within the mold of "traditional" therapies, innumerable variations began to occur. One author (Harper 1975) identified well over one hundred "systems."

If "treatment" merges with "training," if neurotic disorders become indistinguishable from existential anxieties, if emotional suffering is traced (as in so-called radical therapy) to oppressive social conditions, what has happened to such time-honored concepts as "treatment," "cure," "improvement" or "deterioration"? What remains of the meaning of such terms as "patient," "therapist," and "therapy"? If seemingly "normal" persons expose themselves to an encounter group led by a "trainer" or "facilitator," the "experience" ostensibly structured for the purpose of helping people "get in touch with their feelings," and if—as happens in a number of cases—some of these people subsequently require hospitalization or psychiatric treatment, can one speak of "deterioration," or "a negative effect"? More to the point, should such unfortunate occurrences be charged against the effectiveness of "psychotherapy"?

The point to be made is that the boundaries between "treatment" and a host of "growth experiences" have become increasingly obscure, and it is unclear what conditions the latter are designed to "improve." Similar comments, of course, apply to such latter-day developments as Erhard seminars training, transcendental meditation, assertiveness training, transactional analysis, and many others. Since very frequently "traditional" methods of psychotherapy become intermixed with a variety of "new" techniques (exercises, games, etc.), often in the hands of the same practitioner, it has become increasingly difficult to make meaningful statements about specifiable "treatments" or "treatment outcomes." Furthermore, if the objectives and outcomes of these procedures are unclear, what can be said about the qualifications of individuals who are instrumental in their application? Is it appropriate to call them either "therapists" or "mental health professionals"?

The major mental health professions (psychiatry, psychology, and social work) have attempted to address these problems through their respective codes of ethics which prescribe standards for responsible conduct on the part of their members. In addition, licensing and certification laws enacted by the majority of states provide a measure of regulation to protect the public. Nonetheless, because of the enormous difficulties encountered in defining terms, criteria, and standards, many untrained or poorly trained individuals remain free to offer a wide range of "services" to an unwary public, thus inflicting damage on consumers as well as on the reputation of responsible practitioners.

3. Third parties. As long as individuals seek growth, enlightenment, therapy, or whatever for their personal needs, and as long as they pay for the services or training opportunities from their own funds, judgments of "effectiveness" remain highly personal and there can be little quarrel except in instances where misrepresentations are made and individuals in one way or another come to grief. This has indeed occurred, and continues to occur with some frequency. Thus, the demand for better forms of regulation or quality control is being heard, and governmental agencies are devoting attention to the matter, for example, the Clinical Research Branch of the National Institute of Mental Health, which stimulated the efforts resulting in this book. Consumer advocate groups, like Ralph Nader's Public Citizen, Inc. have likewise expressed their concern.

The greatest impetus for evaluation and quality control has come from insurance carriers whose policies frequently provide benefits for treatment of emotional disturbances, and from proponents of national health insurance, which for several years has been debated by the U.S. Congress. All ask the question: Who is treated by whom, for what conditions, and with what results? A challenge is posed to all individuals who provide "mental health services" for a fee, and who assert—in a variety of ways—that their services are socially useful and contribute to their clients' mental health. Like pharmaceutical companies, psychotherapists are being asked to provide evidence that their product is beneficial and largely free of harmful side effects. What kind of evidence is demanded, and how can it be supplied?

It is clear that neither testimonials from clients nor claims by the service providers—both useful in a limited way—can carry the weight. What is called for is the most objective evidence possible, which in turn points to the need for systematic research under controlled conditions. In this domain, clinical investigators who have the requisite skills—which means primarily research psychologists—can make a significant contribution.

While solid empirical evidence demonstrating the effectiveness of psychotherapy under particular conditions will certainly go a long way in answering troublesome questions, it is doubtful that scientific evidence alone will suffice. Psychotherapy touches upon philosophical, moral, and religious convictions; it evokes prejudices and other resistances, and in various other respects it is experienced by many people as a threat. Freud discussed the problem on numerous occasions (including the passage quoted above). However, he committed the logical error of attributing *all* questions about the effectiveness of psychotherapy to the questioner's internal resistances, so that *any* request for scientific evidence came to be defined as a "neurotic problem" in those who raised the issue. Many of Freud's followers took a similar position. Obviously, this approach does not answer the real questions, which indeed exist. It is also clear, however, that no single study or series of studies, no matter how meticulously executed, will silence all opposition. For one thing, scientific evidence in this field, because of the multiplicity of interacting variables, can hardly be conclusive; for another, when scientific evidence conflicts with deeply held beliefs and values, resistance to accepting the scientific evidence may never be fully overcome. Finally, since the issues of psychotherapy and its outcomes are thoroughly intertwined with the values cherished by a society, society has a strong voice in deciding what is "normality" or a "desirable" therapy outcome. It may be anticipated that the basic questions will be with us for a long time to come.

Psychotherapy is currently under attack from many quarters, and mental health practitioners are challenged by society to justify the value of their services and the "cost effectiveness" of their product. The problem of patients coming to grief in psychotherapy and experiencing negative outcomes, as we have attempted to show, must be viewed in a broader context than has been traditionally employed. For all these reasons (and others) the time is ripe for a systematic analysis of what is surely one of the important social problems of our time.

Chapter 3

Empirical Evidence

Beginning in the mid-1960s Bergin (1963, 1966, 1971) attempted to demonstrate that in several studies of psychotherapy outcome, differences between treated and control patients had been obscured because the treated group contained both negative and positive changers. Since that time the issues of whether the psychotherapy experience might exacerbate as well as ameliorate psychic distress and with what frequency this deterioration might occur have been of wide concern. Clinicians have been generally willing to acknowledge that some patients occasionally change for the worse during the course of treatment (Hoch 1947). Instances of negative effects among various types of patients have been chronicled in case reports, for example, among psychosomatic patients treated with cathartic techniques (Lowry 1970, Mittelman 1947); psychotics (Davison 1969, Ludwig et al. 1969) and anorectics (Bruch 1974) treated with behavioral techniques; and anxious, acutely psychotic young adults treated with family therapy (Guttman 1973). However, controlled psychotherapy research in which the issue of negative effects has been directly addressed is limited.

Following the original formulation of the deterioration hypothesis—that changes for both better and worse are reflected in greater variability of outcome criterion scores among therapy as opposed to control patients—Bergin and his colleagues have compiled a set of psychotherapy outcome studies (1) to support the hypothesis of greater variability of changes among therapy patients, and (2) to demonstrate that subgroups of treated patients evidence decrements in personality adjustment or social functioning following therapy. Basing their observations upon data from forty-eight studies (forty-two psychotherapy outcome studies, six follow-up studies of untreated patients), Lambert, Bergin, and Collins (1977) have concluded that negative effects in psychotherapy routinely occur with varying frequency among many types of patients treated by a variety of therapists with a variety of techniques. Furthermore, they have suggested that maladaptive changes from pre-therapy to post-therapy or to follow-up are induced by the therapy experience, particularly by the influence of the therapist.

Several critics of the deterioration hypothesis (Braucht 1970, Gottman 1973, May 1971) have questioned the validity of interpreting greater change score variance among experimental patients as evidence of deterioration and have noted methodological flaws in the studies originally cited as providing evidence of the deterioration effect (Bergin 1966). However, the bulk of the literature presented in support of the deterioration hypothesis in later papers (Bergin 1971, Lambert, Bergin, and Collins 1977) has not been critically examined. The present review was undertaken to determine whether the empirical data adequately demonstrate that maladaptive changes in psychotherapy patients were induced by the therapy experience, or more particularly, by some aspect of the therapist's behavior. Since the review by Lambert, Bergin, and Collins (1977) was comprehensive, we have restricted our analysis to studies cited in their paper.

A number of criteria for conducting methodologically sound research on the effectiveness of psychotherapy have been proposed (cf. Bergin 1971, Fiske et al. 1970, Luborsky, Singer and Luborsky 1975, Strupp and Bergin 1969). In general, the shortcomings in design which have occurred most often in psychotherapy research are of two varieties: (1) inappropriate selection of therapists, patients or treatment modalities which compromise the generalizability of results, and (2) methodological flaws which compromise interpretation of the findings. If an investigator who wished to examine the effects of insight oriented therapy utilized volunteers from introductory psychology courses as patients and relatively inexperienced graduate students as therapists, his results would not necessarily provide information about the efficacy of insight oriented techniques as practiced by qualified, experienced therapists with patients experiencing sufficient distress to seek treatment. This problem in selecting representative samples can be compared with other flaws in methodology which limit interpretation of the research findings. For example, if hospitalized patients in a treatment group received, in addition to psychotherapy, varying doses of ataractic drugs or electro-convulsive therapy (ECT), it is not possible to determine whether any positive changes which occurred were attributable to psychotherapy, to one of the other concurrent interventions, or to some unique interaction of the various treatment modalities.

It is difficult to specify which kind of deficiency (nonrepresentative selection or methodological flaw) has greater repercussions for the validity of research findings. The value of results from a carefully designed, rigorously controlled research project may be jeopardized if the clients are student volunteers rather than real patients (DiLoreto 1971). Conversely, the value of data assessing changes among genuinely disturbed patients in long-term treatment with trained analysts may be seriously limited by the absence of data from an untreated but otherwise comparable control group (Aronson and Weintraub 1968).

After critically reviewing the psychotherapy outcome studies cited as providing evidence of therapy- or therapist-induced deterioration (Lambert, Bergin, and Collins 1977), we have concluded that nearly all of the studies are marred by multiple flaws, both in selection of samples and in methodology. This is not to suggest that negative effects in psychotherapy do not occur, but that interpretations based on the reported findings must be carefully qualified. Rather than criticize each study separately, we have chosen to specify a number of types of errors or deficiencies which compromise the validity of data from psychotherapy outcome research and to identify studies falling into each category (see Appendix A for a summary of the data).

PROBLEMS OF GENERALIZABILITY

Definition of psychotherapy. To determine whether the psychotherapeutic experience can precipitate negative effects, it is necessary to arrive at some definition of psychotherapy, preferably one which sufficiently distinguishes therapy from other helpful human interventions and from somatic treatments of emotional problems. Such distinctions are often difficult to make. At what point does "group therapy" become "sensitivity training"? The dividing lines are vague, and hence decisions about what is and what is not psychotherapy must be somewhat arbitrary. For the purposes of this review, a traditional definition of psychotherapy has been accepted:

> Psychotherapy can be defined as a psychological process occurring between two (or more) individuals in which one (the therapist), by virtue of his position and training, seeks systematically to apply psychological knowledge and interventions in an attempt to understand, influence and ultimately modify the psychic experience, mental function and behavior of the other (the patient). This form of interaction is distinguished from other relationships between two people by the formality of the therapeutic agreement (whether explicit or implicit), the specific training, skill and experience of the therapist, and the fact that the patient (either voluntarily or by coercion) has come to the therapist seeking professional therapeutic help. [Dewald 1964, p. 156]

Accordingly, we propose to exclude interventions such as social services, where the professional provides direct assistance in manipulating environmental pressures; encounter groups or sensitivity training, where presumably adequately functioning individuals seek personal growth or learning experiences; hospital milieu programs; or treatments which are primarily somatic (e.g., brief interviews during psychoactive drug treatment).

Utilizing the foregoing (or a comparable) definition of psychotherapy, treatment interventions in a number of studies cited in the deterioration literature cannot be legitimately called psychotherapy. In two research programs identified as "delinquency prevention" projects (Berleman and Steinburn 1967, Powers and Witmer 1951), the treatments primarily involved delivery of social services. The counselors made home visits, intervened with other agencies to help the client and his family meet environmental needs (e.g., obtain eyeglasses, welfare services, medical attention) and offered varying degrees of friendship and support. In a third project with delinquent and predelinquent boys (Stuart and Lott 1972), although the description of treatment is meager, it seems likely that it involved social services as well as behavior modification. The electrosleep techniques utilized in the Feighner, Brown, and Olivier (1973) study represent somatic rather than psychological treatment. Although some of the group methods applied in the Lieberman, Yalom, and Miles (1973) research might be encompassed in a traditional definition of psychotherapy, the manner in which the group experiences were presented—an educational experience for which academic credit was awarded—raises serious questions whether the results would be applicable to group therapy in the context of a psychiatric clinic or counseling center.

In several studies, some of the patients received traditional psychotherapy, but the therapy was only one facet—in some cases a minor facet—of a comprehensive rehabilitation program (Fairweather et al. 1960, Kringlen 1965, Ling, Zausmer, and Hope 1952, Masserman and Carmichael 1938). When a variety of treatments are offered in varying quantities, it is impossible to determine how psychotherapy influenced outcome. (Further discussion of this issue follows in the section on confounded treatment.)

It seems reasonable to assume that the therapeutic experience must have an impact in order to produce relatively enduring changes (either negative or positive), as contrasted with transitory shifts in moods or feelings. If the amount of therapeutic contact is very limited, the relationship between behavioral or personality changes in the patient and the nature of the therapeutic intervention becomes tenuous. It is quite possible for patients to experience almost immediate symptom reduction following a single interview (cf. Frank et al. 1959, Malan et al. 1968); however, it is unclear whether such changes should be attributed to the therapeutic interaction itself or to potent nonspecific factors (Frank 1973) resulting in the patient's expectation that help is forthcoming, thus reviving hope and boosting morale.

The hypothesis that the treatment experience, particularly the relationship with the therapist, contributed to an exacerbation of the patient's condition cannot be adequately tested in studies in which the therapeutic contact was very limited (a maximum of six sessions, Gottschalk, Mayerson, and Gottlieb 1967; five hours, Paul 1966, 1967a; one to ten sessions, Volsky et al. 1965). The argument that such brief therapy experiences caused deterioration is even less convincing when comparisons with control groups (drop-outs from treatment, Gottschalk, Mayerson, and Gottlieb 1967; untreated or placebo treatment patients, Paul 1966, 1967a) reveals a greater incidence of negative changes among the controls than among the experimental patients.

In addition to the studies in which the identification of the interaction as psychotherapy was questionable or where the short duration of treatment raised questions whether any meaningful association between patient status and the therapeutic intervention existed, there are a few studies in which the ingredients of treatment were incompletely specified so that "psychotherapy" could have included a wide variety of interactions (Mink and Isaksen 1959, Warne, Canter and Wiznia 1953).

Selection of therapists. One of the perennial problems in psychotherapy research involves the selection of representative therapists (Luborsky, Singer, and Luborsky 1975). Because trainees are usually more readily accessible than experienced professionals, they have often been utilized as therapists in outcome research. While inexperienced or nonprofessional therapists often carry major responsibilities for service delivery in community mental health centers or psychiatric hospitals, research findings based solely upon the

therapy performed by untrained or partially trained novices
cannot be generalized to psychotherapy as practiced by fully
qualified, experienced mental health professionals. In more
than one-third of the psychotherapy studies cited as evidence
of deterioration effects, either all of the therapists were
inexperienced—paraprofessionals (Carkhuff and Truax 1965,
Powers and Witmer 1951); medical students (Uhlenhuth and
Duncan 1968); psychology graduate students (DiLoreto 1971,
Garfield and Bergin 1971); psychiatric residents (Gottschalk,
Mayerson, and Gottlieb 1967, Imber et al. 1968, Koegler and
Brill [brief and longterm therapy] 1967, Rosenbaum,
Friedlander, and Kaplan 1956, Rosenthal 1955, Truax et al.
1966)—or results from trainees and more experienced
therapists were combined rather than analyzed separately
(Fairweather et al. 1960, Feifel and Eells 1963, Rogers and
Dymond 1954, Stuart and Lott 1972). In the single study
which compared results obtained by experienced and
inexperienced therapists (Cartwright and Vogel 1960), the
experience criterion (more than six previous clients) was so
lenient that trainees in other research projects (e.g., Garfield
and Bergin 1971) had had more contact with patients than
some of Cartwright and Vogel's "experienced" therapists.

In order to demonstrate that therapists have induced
deterioration, basic information about the attributes of the
therapist is essential. Ideally, the psychotherapy researcher
should collect information about the therapist's personality
characteristics and behaviors in the therapy setting, as well as
basic data on training and experience (Fiske et al. 1970).
However, in more than one third of the cited studies, the
authors did not report variables as basic as the number of
therapists involved in the research (Barron and Leary 1955,
Horwitz 1974, Koegler and Brill [brief and long-term therapy]
1967, Rosenbaum, Friedlander, and Kaplan 1956, Rosenthal
1955, Weber, Elinson, and Moss 1965) and their training or

experience (Henry and Shlien 1958, Jonckheere 1965, Kringlen 1965, Ling, Zausmer, and Hope 1952, Masserman and Carmichael 1938, Mink and Isaksen 1959, Sager, Riess, and Gundlach 1964, Truax 1963, Volsky et al. 1965, Wispé and Parloff 1965).

Selection of patients. If the psychotherapy researcher wishes to generalize his findings to a population of patients broader than the subjects in his study, he must exercise care in selecting a sample that is representative of a circumscribed patient category (e.g., female depressives, hospitalized acute schizophrenics) or of a more general classification (e.g., outpatient neurotics). Perhaps the most obvious requirement for selection of an appropriate patient sample is that the research subjects are genuinely distressed individuals seeking psychotherapy as a means of alleviating some of their problems (Luborsky, Singer, and Luborsky 1975). The value of the research findings for predicting treatment outcome among real patients is severely limited if research "patients" are junior high school students who are placed in counseling regardless of whether they wish to receive treatment (Mink and Isaksen 1959), or if they are college student volunteers recruited from the classroom (DiLoreto 1971, Paul 1966, 1967a, 1968) or given academic credit for participation in the research program (Lieberman, Yalom, and Miles 1973). As the latter have suggested, many participants entered the encounter groups "to experience, to satisfy curiosity, to test out, to meet people" (p. 326), rather than to fulfill psychotherapeutic goals.

The representativeness of the patient population is also at issue when research patients are in some sense "volunteers" from a larger population of prospective subjects. In the case of retrospective surveys of patients who completed therapy several years prior to the investigation (Feifel and Eells 1963, Kringlen 1965, Imber et al. 1968, Sager, Riess, and Gundlach 1964, Saslow and Peters [untreated patients] 1956, Strupp,

Wallach, and Wogan 1964), the patients who chose to respond to a questionnaire or to be interviewed may have differed along important psychological dimensions from those who did not participate. It is insufficient to demonstrate that the respondents did not substantially differ on demographic variables from nonrespondents or from the general clinic population, since the factors which predisposed one former patient to participate in the study and another to refuse may have been more complex. Some patients may have answered a questionnaire because they wanted to convey their satisfaction, while others may have responded to ventilate residual hostilities about an unsatisfactory treatment experience. With return rates as low as 53% (Sager, Riess, and Gundlach 1964), it is impossible to predict what results might have been obtained if more complete data had been available.

The absence of data from patients who dropped out of treatment, failed to complete the experimental measures, or who for some other reason were excluded from the data analysis, is not generally as great a threat to the representativeness of the patient sample as is a low response rate in a follow-up survey. However, the possibility exists that the experimental patients constituted a biased sample in studies where the proportion of missing data was relatively large (29% "lost data," Carkhuff and Truax 1965; 22% dropouts, Cartwright and Vogel 1960; 26% dropouts, Fairweather et al. 1960—final N's not reported, so it is unclear whether the 25 subjects lost from the study were replaced, or whether data analysis was performed with a reduced N; up to 64% missing data for some analyses, Powers and Witmer 1951; 46% dropouts, Rogers and Dymond 1954; 22-34% missing data on individual outcome measures, Stuart and Lott 1972) or where the research patients represented a small, specially selected sample, rather than a random one from the treatment population (Ricks 1974, Rosenthal 1955). The suggestion that patient samples were biased does not imply that genuine negative effects may not have occurred in some proportion of the patients, but rather that the frequency of negative effects cannot be adequately assessed when data are available only for a potentially biased subset of patients from a larger treatment population. Indeed, in research where high drop-out rates challenged the representativeness of the final sample, some of the patients who terminated prematurely may have been negative changers. The frequency of negative effects actually may have been underestimated.

While chronic schizophrenic patients are certainly appropriate subjects for studies of psychotherapy outcome, the interpretation of negative changes among such patients is complicated by the nature of their psychological disturbance. Since schizophrenia is often marked by a continuous deteriorative course (Langfeldt 1969), it is difficult to distinguish decrements in functioning which were precipitated by the therapeutic experience from those expectable during the course of the psychiatric illness. In studies in which chronic schizophrenics represented all or a substantial proportion of the sample (Carkhuff and Truax 1965, Fairweather et al. 1960, Masserman and Carmichael 1938, Rogers et al. 1967, Truax 1963), it is unclear whether any observed negative changes were precipitated by the therapy experience or whether the therapy was not effective in interrupting a deteriorative course. The results of Fairweather et al. (1960)—that chronic patients in various forms of therapy changed in maladaptive directions (on MMPI scales K, Pd, Simon's Scale of Inner Maladjustment) while similar control patients did not change at all—support the notion that therapy may have exacerbated the patients' conditions. However, equivalent or greater frequencies of negative changes on global improvement indices among control, as compared to treated patients in studies by Carkhuff and Truax (1965), and Rogers et al. (1967), and in similar studies of group therapy with schizophrenics (Feifel and Schwartz 1953, Sacks and Berger 1954) not included in the Lambert, Bergin, and Collins (1977) review suggest that in some cases the nature of the patient's illness may have accounted for the negative changes.

Similarly, when results from neurotic and psychotic patients were combined rather than analyzed separately (Gottschalk, Mayerson, and Gottlieb 1967, Koegler and Brill [brief therapy] 1967, Rosenbaum, Friedlander, and Kaplan 1956), it is difficult to distinguish negative effects which may have been due to the treatment experience from those which represent a deteriorative disease course.

METHODOLOGY AND DESIGN ISSUES

Lack of appropriate control groups. In order to demonstrate that psychotherapy has produced some effects above and beyond those attributable to maturation, environmental factors, or traumatic life events, psychotherapy researchers generally have attempted, based on demographic and/or diagnostic criteria, to compare changes in experimental and control patients, from pre- to post-treatment. Patients who sought treatment but were not immediately taken into therapy (wait-list controls), or who participated in some treatment progran which did not include psychotherapy (e.g., hospital milieu) have often been utilized as control subjects. Surely, true "untreated" control groups are virtually impossible to implement (Fiske et al. 1970, Strupp and Bergin 1969). The patient may perceive placement on a waiting list as either therapeutic ("Help is forthcoming") or anti-therapeutic ("I have been neglected or abandoned"). Control patients may seek informal counseling from friends, clergy or medical doctors during the course of the waiting period. Nonetheless, it is essential that the experimenter provide some comparison group if he wishes to assert with any degree of certainty that either adaptive or maladaptive changes were attributable to the psychotherapy experience.

However, in approximately half the studies cited as evidence of therapist-induced deterioration, no control or comparison groups were included (Aronson and Weintraub 1968, Feifel and Eells 1963, Garfield and Bergin 1971, Horwitz 1974, Imber et al. 1968, Jonckheere 1965, Koegler and Brill [brief therapy] 1967, Kringlen 1965, Ling, Zausmer, and Hope 1952, Masserman and Carmichael 1938, Rosenbaum, Friedlander, and Kaplan 1956, Rosenthal 1955, Sager, Riess, and Gundlach 1964, Strupp, Wallach, and Wogan 1964, Truax et al. 1966, Uhlenhuth and Duncan 1968, Weber, Elinson, and Moss 1965); or data relevant to negative changes were not available for the control group (Stuart and Lott 1972, Varble and Landfield 1969). In several additional studies the control groups were not composed of comparable patients who had been randomly assigned to a no-treatment group, a wait list, or an alternative treatment but included instead such groups as "normal" college students demographically similar to the patients (Rogers and Dymond 1954, Varble and Landfield 1969); college students nominated by their friends as potential candidates for encounter groups (Lieberman, Yalom, and Miles 1973); patients who refused treatment or terminated prematurely (Gottschalk, Mayerson, and Gottlieb 1967, Stuart and Lott 1972); psychologists who had never sought treatment (Wispé and Parloff 1965); and boys with less serious disturbances than those in the experimental group (Berleman and Steinburn 1967).

Although studies of the natural course of a psychiatric syndrome or follow-ups of subjects who did not receive psychotherapy provide some information on the frequency of "naturally occurring" deterioration, samples from these studies cannot be considered control groups allowing comparisons with treated patients in other studies. In some cases the subjects never sought treatment (Agras, Chapin, and Oliveau 1972, Subotnik 1972), while in others the subjects consulted a physician (Endicott and Endicott 1963, Giel, Knox, and Carstairs 1964, Jurjevich 1968), sometimes apparently for medical problems (Saslow and Peters 1956), or a psychiatric clinic, but did not receive psychotherapy. Note that two studies (Kringlen 1965, Masserman and Carmichael 1938) listed in the "no-treatment group" category by Lambert, Bergin, and Collins (1977), were considered confounded treatment studies in this paper because, in some cases, patients received "supportive" therapy as part of the hospital regimen. In the Endicott and Endicott (1963) study all patients were placed on a waiting list. It was unclear in the other studies of those who sought but did not receive treatment whether they failed to follow through with treatment recommendations, were not considered amenable to psychotherapy, or were promised treatment at a later time. If they did not receive psychotherapy because they refused treatment or because they were considered unsuitable candidates, comparisons with psychotherapy patients, even with demographically and diagnostically similar patients, are particularly inappropriate.

Confounded treatments. When patients simultaneously receive a variety of treatments (psychotherapy, ECT, drugs, vocational counseling), it is impossible to isolate the effects of any one treatment unless the study includes controls for each treatment variable and each possible combination of treatments (May 1968). When one is treating hospitalized or severely disturbed patient populations, the potential for confounded treatment is especially high because of the ubiquitous use of ataractic drugs with these patients. In studies where psychotherapy patients received varying doses of psychoactive drugs (Fairweather et al. 1960, Gottschalk, Mayerson, and Gottlieb 1967, Jonckheere 1965, Koegler and Brill [brief therapy] 1967, Kringlen 1965, Rogers et al. 1967,

Rosenbaum, Friedlander, and Kaplan 1956, Carkhuff and Truax [probably] 1965, and Truax 1963), or "sedatives" (Ling, Zausmer, and Hope 1952, Masserman and Carmichael 1938, Warne, Canter, and Wiznia 1953), the assessment of negative effects is problematic, particularly when the outcome criteria were global judgments. The "worse" status could reflect extrapyramidal symptoms as well as exacerbation of psychological conflicts. Even when the outcome criteria were more specific, one could not determine whether any observed changes were due to therapy, drugs, other somatic treatments, or a unique interaction of treatment modalities.

Similarly, when patients received both ECT or insulin shock and psychotherapy, some of the observed negative effects could have reflected adverse side effects of shock treatment as well as negative effects due to the psychotherapy (Kringlen 1965, Ling, Zausmer, and Hope 1952, Rosenbaum, Friedlander, and Kaplan 1956).

Problems with outcome criteria. Assessment of therapeutic change is a complex issue. The low correlations among outcome criteria found in several multivariate assessments of the effects of psychotherapy (cf. Cartwright, Kirtner, and Fiske 1963, Garfield, Bergin, and Prager 1971) suggest that change is not a unitary process and that outcome should be assessed from multiple perspectives (see chapter 5 for a discussion of this issue). However, in much of the previous psychotherapy research, the primary assessment of outcome has been the therapist's global rating (pre-therapy versus post-therapy status or degree of change). Such global ratings are susceptible to numerous biases (Fiske et al. 1970). The therapist's perceptions of change may be influenced by either excessively positive or negative attitudes toward the patient, strong ego involvement in the case, defensiveness, or a variety of other biasing factors. Furthermore, therapists or clinicians utilizing global scales may differ in their frames of reference, especially when the criteria for judging improvement or deterioration are not clearly specified. The interpretation of what constitutes "worse" status is unclear in studies where the primary criterion for assessing deterioration was a global judgment of improvement, functioning or psychological health (Giel, Knox, and Carstairs 1964, Horwitz 1974, Jonckheere 1965, Koegler and Brill [brief therapy] 1967, Kringlen 1965, Ling, Zausmer, and Hope 1952, Masserman and Carmichael 1938, Rosenthal 1955, Rosenbaum, Fried-lander, and Kaplan 1956).

Even greater interpretive problems are posed by global evaluations in which "unchanged" and "worse" are combined into one category (Cartwright and Vogel 1960, Endicott and Endicott 1963, Feifel and Eells 1963, Imber et al. 1968, Rogers et al. 1967, Sager, Riess, and Gundlach 1964, Truax et al. 1966). If a patient fails to show improvement, it does not necessarily follow that he has been harmed by the psychotherapy experience. Similarly, if a patient reports he did not benefit from therapy (Koegler and Brill [long-term therapy] 1967, Strupp, Wallach, and Wogan 1964), this does not indicate that therapy was necessarily detrimental. Examination of several studies in which patients were separately categorized as "unimproved" and "worse" suggests that the statistic of deterioration may have been artificially inflated by including unimproved patients in the negative effects category (e.g., inclusion of unchanged patients increases the percentage from 4% to 14% in Giel, Knox, and Carstairs 1964; from 9% to 19% in Jonckheere 1965; from 1% to 7.4% in Rosenbaum, Friedlander, and Kaplan 1956).

In addition to global ratings, the studies cited in support of the negative effects hypothesis have utilized a variety of outcome indices. In some cases, standard instruments with demonstrated reliability and validity as indices of psychopathology and changes in psychiatric status, such as the MMPI, were employed (Barron and Leary 1955, Fairweather et al. 1960, Garfield and Bergin 1971, Rogers et al. 1967, Volsky et al. 1965). In a number of projects, however, either the reliability or the validity of major outcome indices is questionable.

Questions about the reliability of a particular instrument arise when one or more raters are required to make complex judgments, particularly when the judgments relate to intrapsychic states. It is impossible to determine the reliability of ratings when they are all made by a single judge (TAT mental health rating, Cartwright and Vogel 1960, Rogers and Dymond 1954; affective complexity, Henry and Shlien 1958; terminal adjustment, "harmed by treatment," Powers and Witmer 1951; TAT variables, Rogers et al. 1967). Although data from a judge's reratings of the same cases at a later date have been cited as evidence of reliability in some studies (Endicott and Endicott 1963, Henry and Shlien 1958, Rogers and Dymond 1954, Rogers et al. 1967), such rate-rerate methods are inappropriate (Tinsley and Weiss 1975). Reratings may be contaminated by recall of the original judgments. Even more importantly, the extent to which the ratings are replicable by other judges cannot be assessed. Similarly, reliability, in the sense of replicability, cannot be determined if a variety of raters each rate different patients (e.g., therapists' global outcome ratings; ratings in Aronson and Weintraub 1968, Carkhuff and Truax 1965).

When multiple judges rate the same cases, interrater reliability can be assessed through a number of statistical procedures (Tinsley and Weiss 1975). If the investigator did not report reliability data, however, the reader does not know the degree to which the judges concurred in their evaluations and is unable to assess the stability of the measures (e.g., for ratings of "sleep, anxiety, depression and level of social adjustment," Feighner, Brown, and Olivier 1973; for improvement ratings, Rosenthal 1955; for therapist "conditions" and outcome ratings, Truax 1963).

The replicability of findings is questionable in studies where there were major discrepancies among judges in the ratings of outcome indices (change in problem solving, defensiveness and anxiety, Jewell 1958, reported in Volsky et al. 1965) or of hypothesized correlates of outcome (therapist "conditions," Rogers et al. 1967, Truax et al. 1966). Furthermore, low reliability levels (which indicate considerable error in measurement) limit the validity of a measure (Nunnally 1967). If a group of raters consistently did not agree on the level of ego strength evidenced by patients, it is unclear precisely what variables the resulting ratings were measuring, particularly if average or composite scores were used.

The reliability, and consequently the validity, of an outcome measure is questionable in studies where judgments of improvement of change were based primarily upon information from routine case files (e.g., Ling, Zausmer, and Hope 1952). As some investigators who have used this technique noted (Saslow and Peters 1956, Warne, Canter, and Wiznia 1953), the quantity and the quality of information available from old records is highly variable. By using such files, the data base for making ratings varies from one patient to the next. In some cases the data from old files may have been insufficient for deriving reasonable conclusions about the patient's status.

The validity of an outcome measure is also at issue if the relationship between the variables which the outcome measure is tapping and the types of changes in behavior or personality predicted by theories of psychotherapeutic movement is unclear. For instance, Wispé and Parloff's (1965) assumption that constructive personality change should be correlated with increased scholarly publication is questionable. The psychologist-patient may not have regarded research or writing productivity as a problem area. In cases where productivity was an issue, decreased quantity of publications may actually have been a positive rather than a negative outcome for a patient whose complaints involved a compulsive need to achieve.

In general, the validity of an outcome instrument is suspect if the rationale underlying its use can be challenged, and if results obtained with the measure show little statistical association with more conventional indices of outcome. For instance, the use of change in the degree of correlation between "self" and "ideal self," as assessed by Q-shorts or similar instruments, as a criterion of personality integration (Fairweather et al. 1960, Rogers and Dymond 1954, Varble and Landfield 1969) can be criticized on these grounds. The expectation is reasonable that a patient who gained a greater sense of self-awareness and self-acceptance through therapy would report increased congruence between the way he saw himself and the way he wished to be. However, the absolute magnitude of the self-ideal correlation, as well as changes in the degree of correlation from pre- to post-therapy, may be influenced by a number of variables. As Butler and Haigh (1954) noted, high correlations may reflect defensive responding or poor reality testing, particularly among psychotic patients. Conversely, greater openness in recognizing inadequacies or admitting weaknesses as a consequence of therapy may reduce the self-ideal correlation. Finally, small fluctuations in the magnitude of a correlation may be due to random error in measurement (which reduces the stability of the correlation coefficient), rather than to real changes in self-concept. The possibility that the relationship between increased self-ideal correlation and therapeutic outcome is not straightforward is further attested by Butler and Haigh's finding that subjects who were dichotomized into greater versus lesser improvement categories on independent outcome criteria were not distinguishable on the measure of change in self-ideal correlation; and by Varble and Landfield's (1969) finding that increases in self-ideal discrepancy were *more frequent* among patients rated as "improved" by independent judges, than among those who showed minimal improvement or no change.

The validity of Henry and Shlien's (1958) TAT-derived measure of affective complexity can be challenged on similar grounds. The rationale that improvement during psychotherapy is correlated with increased willingness to describe dual or ambivalent affect states in TAT stories is based upon vague theoretical premises and data from only one published study of the acculturation of Navaho children (Henry 1947). In addition, the authors reported that data from a variety of other outcome measures, including Q-sort adjustment scores, therapists' and clients' ratings, attrition rates and percentages of patients seeking supplemental therapy after the completion of the research, were essentially contrary to the results obtained with the TAT measure.

In most of the psychotherapy studies, the assessment of negative effects was based upon the frequency with which patients were rated as worse or showed changes in directions which were, by a priori standards, considered maladaptive. In a few studies, greater change score variance among experimental, as contrasted with control patients, was the primary criterion of negative effects (Barron and Leary 1955 as reinterpreted in Cartwright 1956, Carkhuff and Truax 1965, Fairweather et al. 1960, Mink and Isaksen 1959, Powers and Witmer 1951, Rogers and Dymond 1954, Volsky et al. 1965). Interpretation of larger variance as evidence of deterioration is based upon the premise that therapy patients change in both positive and negative directions, while control patients evidence very little change. However, as Gottman (1973) has demonstrated and Lambert, Bergin, and Collins (1977) have acknowledged, interpretation of greater change score variance as evidence of deterioration may be statistically inaccurate. For example, the difference in variance of changes between experimental and control patients which Cartwright (1956) reported, in his reanalysis of the Barron and Leary (1955) data, was probably influenced by greater variance among therapy patients *prior* to treatment.

Finally the notion that the direction of adaptive change is similar for all patients has been challenged (Braucht 1970, Fairweather et al. 1960, Gottman 1973). As Jewell (1958, cited in Volsky et al. 1965) demonstrated, for some patients greater defensiveness or greater anxiety may be therapeutically desirable goals.

"Relapse" versus "deterioration." A necessary, but not sufficient, criterion for demonstrating that the psychotherapy experience has exacerbated a patient's difficulties is evidence of negative changes from pre- to post-therapy or "worse" functioning at the conclusion of therapy. If the patient shows no change or even positive movement at the conclusion of psychotherapy, but exhibits decrements in functioning at a later follow-up evaluation, should the negative changes from post-therapy to follow-up be attributed to the therapy process? Conceivably, negative changes following therapy might represent the long-term consequences of a destructive therapy experience. Alternatively, such negative changes might also be viewed as "backsliding" or "relapse," particularly if the initial changes during therapy are in a positive direction. Surely, therapy cannot be said to have been notably effective if patients cannot maintain their improvements after therapy ends. However, there is a major conceptual distinction to be made between therapy-induced deterioration and "relapse," which may be due to environmental factors (e.g., renewed or increased stresses).

Thus, in studies where the negative changes occurred only from post-therapy to follow-up (Berleman and Steinburn

1967, Henry and Shlien 1958) or where a number of patients changed in a positive direction from pre- to post-therapy and then declined (Q-sort self-ideal correlation, Rogers and Dymond 1954), interpreting these changes as therapy-induced deterioration is questionable. In studies which presented changes from pre-therapy to follow-up rather than from pre- to post-therapy, it is not possible to distinguish deterioration from relapse (Imber et al. 1968, Ling, Zausmer, and Hope 1952, Paul 1967a, 1968). Indeed, Paul (1967a) specifically refers to negative changes in speech behavior during the two year follow-up period as "relapses."

WHAT CONCLUSIONS CAN BE DRAWN FROM THE DATA?

A tabular listing of the various shortcomings and deficits of each study cited in support of the deterioration hypothesis reveals that only one research project (Sloane et al. 1975a, 1975b) is free from shortcomings in selecting patients, therapists, or treatment modalities, and from flaws in methodology and experimental design which limit interpretation of the findings (see Appendix A). Results from this (1975a) study indicate relatively low rates (3-6%) of negative change among outpatients suffering from neurotic difficulties and personality disorders who were treated by experienced psychotherapists and behavior therapists. These rates are similar to those of untreated wait-list patients (3-6%).

Given the inadequacies of the remaining psychotherapy outcome studies, what conclusions about the prevalence or causes of negative effects can be drawn? Clearly, the potential for negative effects in psychotherapy cannot be denied. Both clinicians and researchers accept the idea that psychotherapy may exacerbate as well as ameliorate psychic distress (see chapter 4; also, Frank 1967, Matarazzo 1967, Truax 1967).

The issue here is not whether negative effects occur, but whether the frequency or the determinants of negative change are explicated by the available empirical literature.

Despite the various flaws in the research which seriously impede definitive conclusions, some suggestions about correlates of negative outcome can be derived from the literature. Data from several studies suggest that the frequency of negative effects may vary with patient diagnosis (Fairweather et al. 1960, Feighner, Brown, and Olivier 1973, Jonckheere 1965, Sager, Riess, and Gundlach 1964), and that patients of borderline status may be more likely to decompensate in therapy (Aronson and Weintraub 1968, Horwitz 1974, Weber, Elinson, and Moss 1965).

Indications that negative outcomes may be related to therapists' attitudes and behaviors are present in several studies. Patients' retrospective evaluations of their therapy experiences (Feifel and Eells 1963, Strupp, Wallach, and Wogan 1964) indicate that poor outcome, and possibly negative outcome, may be related to the quality of the therapeutic relationship.

In the Ricks (1974) study, information derived from case files of boys treated with psychotherapy during late childhood or early adolescence who were later diagnosed schizophrenic, and of similar boys who made more adequate adjustments in adulthood indicated that therapists' techniques and interpersonal styles might have had a bearing upon the long-term adjustment of these patients. Comparison of the records from a subsample of cases seen by two therapists revealed that one had far fewer patients who later evidenced schizophrenic symptoms, and that techniques of the more and the less successful therapist could be contrasted clearly. While these findings are weakened by the nonrandom selection of a subset of cases from each therapist and by the use of therapists' notes, gleaned from old files, as the sole measure of the therapeutic interaction, the data offer some fascinating insights into the nature of facilitative therapeutic interventions with severely disturbed boys.

Although retrospective studies of the therapeutic relationship offer some suggestions about qualities that might contribute to positive or negative outcomes, the most appropriate test of the hypothesis that the therapist induces deterioration lies in direct analysis of the therapeutic interaction. Unfortunately, only in very few studies were sufficient measures of the therapeutic interaction collected to permit analysis of the relationship between therapeutic interaction and negative outcomes.

Measures of therapy process derived from client-centered theory were utilized in several research programs. In one study, Truax (1963) obtained strong support for the hypothesis that low levels of therapist-offered empathy, warmth and genuineness are predictive of negative outcomes. In several other studies, however, the relationship between the three therapeutic conditions and outcome was either equivocal (Rogers et al. 1967, Truax et al. 1966) or clearly not significant (Garfield and Bergin 1971). Furthermore, critiques of the conceptualization and application of the scales for assessing therapeutic conditions, particularly accurate empathy, indicate that the results obtained with these scales must be viewed with considerable caution (Blackwood 1975, Chinsky and Rappaport 1970, Lambert, Bergin, and Collins 1977, Rappaport and Chinsky 1972).

The Lieberman, Yalom, and Miles (1973) research represents an excellent approach to the study of negative effects in encounter groups. Extensive process data from direct observations of the groups were available. The criteria for determining which subjects might have been harmed by the encounter group experience were explicit. "Casualties," that is, subjects whose decrements in functioning were attributable to the group experience were distinguished from "negative changers," those cases where attribution of casuality was less clear. The only major limitation of this research in explaining the causes of negative effects in *psychotherapy* was that the treatment was not psychotherapy and the subjects were not patients. The study of negative effects in encounter or experiential groups is significant, particularly in light of anecdotal accounts and data which suggest the high potential for destructive interactions in such groups (Cooper 1975, Fromme, Jones, and Davis 1974, Hartley, Roback, and Abramowitz 1976). However, are the factors which contribute to negative change in encounter groups and in psychotherapy the same? Without equally soundly designed studies of negative effects in psychotherapy, this question cannot be answered.

The available empirical data suggest hypotheses about what might cause negative effects and avenues for future research. However, the previous research is inadequate to convincingly demonstrate the frequency with which patients are harmed by their psychotherapy experiences or the reasons underlying deterioration. Further investigation of the problem of negative effects in psychotherapy is crucial. In our society, where mental health professionals are increasingly being held accountable for their results by health insurance companies, by the patient-consumer, and by the general public, better understanding of when and how psychotherapy can harm is essential.

Chapter 4

Opinions of
Psychotherapy Experts

In an effort to determine contemporary views on definitions and causes of negative effects in psychotherapy, a survey of expert clinicians, theoreticians, and researchers was undertaken. Letters were sent to approximately 150 experts, representing a wide range of theoretical orientations, soliciting their opinions.

Approximately seventy responded to our request. (A complete listing of these respondents appears as Appendix B. The letters of those authors who granted permission for publication are reproduced as Appendix C.) Their answers were often detailed and thoughtful, indicating a keen interest in the general subject of negative effects. Taken as a whole, the responses represent a spectrum of contemporary thinking of some of the best minds in the field of psychotherapy. This chapter describes the responses in the context of our organization and discussion of the common significant themes.

IS THERE A PROBLEM
OF NEGATIVE EFFECTS?

Among the experts in psychotherapy who responded to our letter, there was virtually unanimity that there is a real problem of negative effects in psychotherapy. The frequency of occurrence was judged as moderate by some, whereas others, for example Spitzer, suggested that "negative effects in long-term outpatient psychotherapy are extremely common." On the other hand, there were some noteworthy dissents. One respondent felt there is little evidence for negative effects of therapy, noting that although most clinicians are able to cite experiences they have had with patients who appeared to deteriorate during treatment, he believes there is no persuasive evidence that the negative effects which appeared were due to the psychotherapy itself. Similarly, an operant oriented expert expressed reservations about the reality of negative effects, stating that he himself does not think too seriously about negative effects in psychotherapy because "that idea gives the therapist more power and influence than he has."

The issue of negative effects as a result of psychotherapy is intimately related to the question of the potency of psychotherapy per se, as many of our respondents noted. Cohen, for example, stated that "we had better be able to speak of getting worse in psychotherapy," or else we cannot speak of a patient getting better. Will commented similarly that psychotherapy "cannot in any sense be 'neutral,' " while Prague noted that "if psychotherapy can't do harm it is the only therapy in medicine so blessed." There is a consensus that if it is possible for psychotherapy to produce beneficial effects, it must be capable, at least theoretically, of producing negative effects as well.

The foregoing consensus was qualified, however, in the sense that all of the experts proceeded to list various limitations, definitions, and conditions. Many elaborated on what a negative effect *is not*. Liberman noted that a negative effect is not the same as the temporary deterioration which is an inevitable part of some forms of psychotherapy. In a similar vein, Marks and a number of other respondents noted that we must distinguish between normal and expected regressions from psychotherapy which are temporary, and real or lasting negative effects.

Ford suggested that we must determine whether an observed negative effect is indeed the product of a therapeutic intervention or merely an event independent of that intervention which may coincide in time. He went on to discuss the time issue in general terms, noting that it is important to make decisions about the temporal proximity of a negative effect to the termination of therapy. Thus, the most clear-cut negative effects are "those that appear immediately in temporal relationship with the psychotherapy," (Gottschalk) although there can, in addition, be delayed adverse effects. Atthowe spoke of this issue in terms of short-term versus long-term goals of psychotherapy. In his opinion, it is fulfillment of long-term goals which is most critical for ultimate judgments of treatment outcome, but these goals may not be correlated with short-term measures.

Marks provided a concise but comprehensive definition of a negative effect as "a lasting deterioration in a patient directly attributable to therapy." This definition is quite similar to that adopted in this book (see page 91).

Multiple Perspectives on Psychotherapy Evaluation

Having dealt with the issue of negative effects in general terms, many respondents went on to consider conceptual issues relevant to the problem. Mahoney, speaking from the perspective of his interest in therapeutic ethics, urged that we examine the basic premises and the prime goals of therapy (e.g., Is it true that the "satisfaction" of the "customer" is the primary criterion by which therapy shall be evaluated?). Ford stressed that the identification of a negative effect from psychotherapy is basically a value judgment which depends heavily on the value reference of the person or persons making the judgment. A similar comment was made by Gurman, who noted that the judgment of a treatment's effects as positive or negative depends on the evaluative perspective chosen as most valid. It is thus incumbent upon researchers to evaluate therapy-related change in the patient from a variety of perspectives.

Krasner spoke of the growth in importance of the study of negative effects which, in his view, is related to the shift from the medical to the social-educational model of psychological functioning and psychotherapy. He added that the assessment of behavior changes resulting from psychotherapy must include an assessment of the consequences of those changes for the client, for the people in his life, and for the therapist: "Issues of negative effects must now be considered within this broader issue of values (what is good behavior for an individual and for society)."

Of course, discrepancies are likely to exist among judgments of outcome made from different perspectives, for example, those made by a therapist, and those made by the patient (Weintraub). Judgments from these perspectives may include two kinds of negative effects—(1) those generally harmful to the patient and (2) those harmful to the attainment of the goals of therapy which "may or may not include harm to the patient." Weintraub cited as an example of the latter outcome the "transference cure." An identical effect may be viewed by the therapist as positive or negative depending on his strategies and goals in therapy. Further, in more general terms, effects may be viewed as positive or negative by others, depending on the impact of the patient's behavior upon them.

The latter issue is particularly salient in family therapy where assessments must include changes in the patient's relationships with others as well as changes in those significant others to whom the patient relates (Gurman). Speaking from her experience as a child therapist, Kessler cited examples illustrating this. Psychotherapy with children may create behavioral or loyalty conflicts with the parents; the latter, as a result of having a child in therapy, may come to feel alienated, helpless, or guilty over their performance as parents.

Abse gave a vivid clinical description of an adult patient who became hostile and sadistic toward his family, and whose therapy outcome he therefore considers definitely negative. Nonetheless, the patient was judged a therapeutic success by others who knew him, including some of Abse's colleagues, largely on the basis of his achievement in the business world. For Abse, this patient represented a clear-cut example of the discrepancies among evaluative perspectives, and he summarized the lesson learned from this patient as follows: "The identifiable psychiatric syndrome following intensive analytic work may be succeeded by personality malfunctioning vis-a-vis other people, though adapted to 'sick' aspects of our present society."

Divorce resulting from an individual's therapy experiences is one of the most-clear-cut examples of the multiple perspectives issue. Ann Appelbaum described the dilemma which typically surrounds such situations and offered suggestions as to how such outcomes should be evaluated:

> A person who has lived for some years as a conventionally good wife and mother at the price of suppressing her hatred for an unloving, emotionally limited and intellectually inferior husband, and who as the result of psychotherapy becomes aware of her own needs for love and stimulation, enters into an affair and

eventually divorces her husband—is she "worse" or
"better"? Would her children have been better off had she
lived out the marriage at least until they grew up so as to
provide them a stable home? I think the answer to this
would depend on the kind of life the woman would be able
to create for herself and her children after the divorce, and
the extent to which her awareness and acceptance of her
own emotional needs went hand in hand with a growing
capacity for concern and a growing capacity to take into
account the needs of others as well as of herself.

It is obvious from the foregoing examples that the issues we
deal with in our discussion of the tripartite model of
therapeutic outcomes (see chapter 5) are increasingly salient
for therapists today. Numerous therapists agree that therapy
outcomes cannot be evaluated in isolation, nor from a strictly
intrapsychic perspective; and they rarely can be viewed as
absolutely positive or negative. As noted earlier, a number of
interested parties are demanding a voice in evaluating therapy
outcome, and this is particularly true in the case of negative
effects. Judgments of therapy outcome, whether positive or
negative, will depend heavily on the perspective of the
evaluator.

Assessing the Outcome of Psychotherapy

How then shall we measure therapy outcome in general, and
negative effects in particular? Ford stressed the need for
analytic precision and a sophisticated conceptual approach to
the problem. He suggested that in the early stages of research
one might "conceptually canvass and try to explicate the value
frameworks within which such judgments might be made and
to elaborate the alternatives."

Any judgment of therapy outcome obviously must be
centered on the patient. Roback noted that the determination

of a negative effect from psychotherapy requires initially a "comprehensive understanding of the patient," which leads to the question of the dimensions in which a patient shall be evaluated. Changes in target symptoms are commonly used as a measure of therapeutic effectiveness. Lieberman, for example, reported "numerous" instances of patients "doing worse" on the basis of an assessment of target problems. However, as Orne notes, evaluating a patient in terms of target symptoms may not be altogether appropriate to the study of negative effects since "the patient who gets worse does not usually do so in terms of the target symptoms." As an alternative, reminiscent of Freud's maxim, Orne suggested that patients should be evaluated in terms of their ability to enjoy work, love, and play and to successfully cope with the usual stresses of life. Marks advocated a problem oriented approach to the study of negative effects, noting that adequate evaluations of therapeutic effectiveness must specify the problems being treated and "the precise criteria for outcome during, at the end of, and subsequent to treatment."

Marks's stress on measures *throughout* the course of therapy was reiterated by Liberman who suggested repeated and continuous measures of behavior and affect over the course of therapy. Hersen, stressing a single case research strategy, urged repeated measurements of both targeted and non-targeted behaviors as essential for the identification of negative effects. With respect to the problem of identifying causative factors, Hersen suggested that only a functional analysis of therapy will enable us to draw conclusions about such factors. Thus, there emerges a consensus that measures of the effectiveness of psychotherapy must be made at repeated intervals.

Further, many respondents urged that psychotherapy be evaluated in a comprehensive, multifaceted sense. Will, for example, suggested that one must evaluate the overall effect of example, suggested that one must evaluate the overall effect of therapy on the patient's personality; it is conceivable that the effect of therapy on only one aspect of the personality might be judged as negative, while the overall judgment might be that therapy had led to a positive outcome.

Fiske suggested a multiple criterion approach to the problem. Similarly, Atthowe urged that measurements be multidimensional, and Stephen Appelbaum proposed the use of an algebraic sum by which the overall effectiveness of therapy would be evaluated.

WHAT CONSTITUTES A NEGATIVE EFFECT?

Exacerbation of Presenting Symptoms

Gottschalk spoke of the "worsening" of presenting symptoms, and Rhoads described "the increase in symptoms corresponding to heightened resistance or defensiveness." Such exacerbations are particularly noteworthy if they result in hospitalization or institutionalization (Berlin). Other examples include "exacerbation of suffering" or the generalization of symptoms to new areas (Wolpe); decompensation in a patient who had previously exhibited equilibrium (Greenson, Weiner); or the development of a harsher superego and more rigid personality structure (Strupp). Specific indicators of exacerbated symptoms included the following:

—Depressive breakdown, severe regression, destructive acting out (Malan)
—Increased anxiety, hostility, self-downing, behavioral shirking, inhibition (Ellis)
—Paranoia (Will)
—Fixing of obsessional symptoms, exaggeration of somatic difficulties, extension of phobias (Salzman)
—Increased guilt or confusion, lowered self-confidence (Lazarus)

—Lower self-esteem, diminished capacity for delay and impulse control (Goldberg)
—Worsening of phobias

Appearance of New Symptoms

Rhoads noted that a negative effect may occur when a psychic disturbance is manifested in a less socially acceptable form than had been the case previously, for example, a shift from somatic complaints (which might elicit sympathy from others) to paranoia. Miller suggested that new symptoms may be due to substitution, that is, the classical case of a new symptom developing when another, which had fulfilled some imperative need, is blocked without a suitable available alternative.

Obviously, any of those listed above as instances of exacerbation could also arise as part of a novel symptom configuration. In addition, the following were mentioned as examples which might be judged as negative therapeutic results:

—The erosion of solid interpersonal relationships, and decreased ability to experience pleasure (Weintraub)
—Severe or fatal psychosomatic reactions (Ann Appelbaum)
—Withdrawal, regression, rage, dissociation
—Acting out (Marmor, May)
—Drug or alcohol abuse, criminal behavior (Gottschalk)

The most extreme manifestations of new symptomatology are suicide and psychotic breaks. Suicide was identified repeatedly as the most clear-cut example of a negative effect, particularly if the patient was not noticeably suicidal at the beginning of therapy (Greenson). Insensitive handling of patients with suicidal tendencies may provoke overt attempts at self-destruction. Knapp, for example, described the case of a therapist who refused to recognize the depth of his client's depression, interpreting her behavior as stubbornness. When she made her third serious suicide attempt and missed an appointment with the therapist, it was only at his supervisor's insistence that a visit was made to the home where the woman was found in a deep stupor as the result of a barbiturate overdose.

Suicide, as Dyrud observed, is not necessarily a negative effect of psychotherapy, particularly with a suicide-prone patient with whom one takes a calculated risk in attempting therapy. Farberow notes that when suicide does result from psychotherapy, it is most likely to occur as the result of a "burned out" syndrome in the therapist, due to the repeated and exhausting demands of seriously depressed and suicidal patients. This may become a particularly grave problem for formerly hospitalized patients who have alienated the hospital staff by their demanding behavior and thus may feel there is no haven to which they may return when suicidal urges recur, as they often do.

Psychotic breaks resulting from psychotherapy were also frequently mentioned as a clear-cut negative effect. Matarazzo noted that such an occurrence would most typically be due to ego disintegration brought on by therapy.

Misuse/Abuse of Therapy

Less obvious perhaps than the exacerbation of presenting symptoms or the appearance of new symptoms is a negative effect which was often mentioned and which we have chosen to term the patient's "misuse/abuse" of therapy. This phenomenon may take a number of forms. Will, for example, described the substitution of intellectualized insights for other obsessional thoughts in patients, as in a patient who appears to benefit from therapy in the sense of achieving and internalizing therapeutic insights, but who may in fact be merely substituting these insights for earlier obsessional thoughts.

Marmor identified a phenomenon observed in some patients which he described as "utilization of a psychotherapeutic experience ... to rationalize feelings of smugness, superiority over others, or utilizing 'insights' to aggressively comment on other people's behavior." Many former patients exhibit this "symptom" as an undesirable by-product of some therapies. Even the mental health professional may be a "victim," as witness the example cited by Friedman of a professional in training who, after several years of analysis, "declared that she no longer found anything in common with people who weren't analyzed, or any pleasure in their company."

Psychological jargon may also be directed toward oneself, functioning as an " 'alibi' for certain actions or lack of action" (Endicott). More generally, for some patients therapy may become an end in itself. Ann Appelbaum put it this way: "Therapeutic work begins to assume priority over other tasks and goals. . . . being a good patient comes to assume priority higher than that of living life to the fullest." Stephen Appelbaum described a similar phenomenon in which therapy becomes a substitute for action, thereby reinforcing passivity in the patient's life. Lazarus commented that such an outcome is likely when therapists teach their patients to become preoccupied with intrapsychic phenomena instead of solving their problems.

As Franz Alexander (Alexander and French 1946) and others have noted previously, intensive psychotherapy carries with it a multiplicity of dangers, one of which is inadequate regard for the patient's intentionality or will. The analytic therapist's persistent search for unconscious determinants of behavior may stifle constructive action in the outside world, where therapy must come to fruition. Unless the therapist remains alert to this problem, the patient may, in Salzman's words, have an "endless and interminable therapeutic experience and fail to change while verbalizing insights and formulas of living."

Meehl described a similar phenomenon of patients becoming so focused on "wonders of their psyche and its internal connections" that they lose the willingness and disposition to examine their ethical and philosophical commitments. In Meehl's view, this examination of one's basic life commitments is essential to healthy living and the loss of this disposition is related to therapy's tendency to "downgrade the work of the intelligence and to classify almost any rational examination of either external reality or value commitments as being mere intellectualization."

Most of the foregoing abuses of psychotherapy are particularly likely to occur in the context of analytic or insight-oriented therapy. However, the more radical therapies have other drawbacks. Salzman voiced the opinion that participation in such organizations as est and marathon groups, particularly for excessive periods of time, encourages belief in the irrational as a comfort, by which the patient hopes to avoid more painful confrontation with the realities of life.

Undertaking Unrealistic Tasks or Goals

If, as a result of some aspect of the psychotherapeutic intervention, the patient feels constrained to undertake or pursue goals for which he is ill-equipped and which, therefore, place great strain on his psychological resources, a negative effect may result. Similarly, excessive stress may be experienced by the patient who feels called upon to act prematurely in the outside world.

Such situations may arise from a patient's intense wish to please the therapist (Ann Appelbaum), which in turn is related to excessive dependency on the therapist, discussed previously. It is also possible that some therapists may actively push individuals into facing challenges for which they are ill-prepared (Davison).

Stephen Appelbaum attributed this form of negative outcome to the value judgments which communicate an expectation that the patient must live up to some grand ideal. And he noted further that "it is not writ in stone that all people should conform to middle class values, and many patients would be well advised to stay out of them."

Similarly, Ellis discussed the increase of "irrational ideas" within the patient during the course of therapy—for example, one must be loved all the time, must do very well in all achievements (he is no good if he does poorly), or must have immediate gratification.

Whether such outcomes are due to a wish to please the therapist, or the inculcation of unachievable ideals, they often result in increased instances of failure, accompanied by guilt, anxiety, and pain.

Loss of Trust in Therapy and the Therapist

As a result of one or more of the foregoing adverse influences, or because of failure to change at all, a patient may come to experience a sense of disillusionment with therapy and the therapist.

This disillusionment may be manifested in various ways. One respondent, for example, discussed "wasting" the patient's resources when he is not helped by his therapist—resources which might have been better utilized by another therapist or in another form of therapy. Yorke, with special reference to psychoanalysis, noted that "it is not so much a question of adverse response as a waste of time, skills, resources, [and] money" which constitutes negative effects in analysis. Moreover, a patient may become discouraged from seeking more effective forms of therapy—what Lazarus called "hardening in . . . negative attitudes toward future help."

A severe negative outcome is exemplified by loss of confidence in the therapist which generalizes (Rhoads) to disillusionment with any form of human relationship (Will).

Perhaps even more serious is the general loss of hope which a patient may experience as a result of not succeeding in therapy. Bieber spoke of this as a sense of "futility" and Davison added that this futility is all the more severe because of the initial hopes raised in any patient entering therapy. Meehl poignantly described this situation:

> When a patient finally comes to a point of seeking professional help for his functional incompetence or subjective distress, and goes and spills his guts to a psychotherapist and takes time and money to do it, it means, even among most intellectuals, a certain amount of ego threat, from having to admit his failure to cope on his own, and the whole business about labeling oneself as "mentally aberrant" and the like. Then, when the patient finds that, despite what he perceives as his own cooperative behavior in paying the fee and showing up and talking and so forth, he doesn't get better, this result is experienced by many people as a *nearly catastrophic removal of a background source of hope*, an "ace in the hole" that they had carried around (sometimes for years). . . .

WHAT FACTORS ARE PROMINENTLY ASSOCIATED WITH NEGATIVE EFFECTS IN PSYCHOTHERAPY?

In discussions of negative effects it is often difficult to identify what is cause and what is effect, and at times we may face a semantic problem. In psychoanalysis, for example, becoming dependent upon the therapist is seen as a sign of progress because it may facilitate resolution of the transference neurosis. Instead of "acting out" in the outside world, the patient now enacts his problems with the therapist, and if all goes well he may resolve them in this interaction. For complex reasons, however, the patient may come to cling tenaciously to the therapist and the therapy may become interminable. Is this the therapist's fault or are we dealing with a "negative therapeutic reaction"? These factors may interact, leading to further complications. While we are aware of these cause-effect complexities, we shall wherever possible attempt to relate negative effects to specific causative factors.

Inaccurate/Deficient Assessment.

Earlier we noted that determination of the presence of negative effects requires an initial comprehensive understanding of the patient (Roback). Further, several correspondents stressed that "the best safeguard against adverse effects is a thorough diagnostic assessment" (Yorke).

Problems in this area may include either inadequate or erroneous assessments of the patient (Palmer). The consequence may be mismatching or misapplication of therapies to particular patients. Positing "mismatching" as a factor in negative effects presumes, of course, "that we know which therapies fit which problems" (Palmer), which is not always the case.

What should such an assessment include? The following specific assessment areas were mentioned by our respondents:

—Ego functions (Nemiah)
—A *general baseline*, including the patient's age and current tasks, diagnosis, state of his capacities, family history and life situation (Freedman)
—Natural history of the patient's difficulties (Orne)
—"The functional value of the psychopathology . . . which kinds of symptoms serve useful needs in overall adjustment" (Orne)

Deficient or mistaken assessments may lead to a number of adverse developments. For example, the therapist may "probe more deeply than the patient is capable of tolerating, and hence ... provoke untoward regressions" or else he may not "work intensively enough, and thus cheat the patient of the possibility of experiencing as much change for the better as he is capable of" (Ann Appelbaum). Bordin observed that certain temporary regressions may be expected during the course of therapy and that patients with minimal resources of strength will be able to weather these temporary periods of stress. Some patients, however, may lack these resources, and deficient assessments may fail to identify these vulnerabilities.

Goldberg discussed the prevailing trend away from diagnostic assessment, holding it responsible for an increased incidence in misdiagnosis. For example, the practice of treating hysteriform and overly ideational borderline schizophrenics as high ego strength neurotics is a flagrant mistake which has resulted from this incidence of misdiagnosis.

Therapist Variables

The therapist himself was one of the most often cited sources of negative effects in psychotherapy. Roback's statement is typical: "Most *prominent* factors leading to negative treatment effects are therapist variables." More specifically he implicated "poor clinical judgment." Similar views were expressed by Gottschalk and by Fiske who observed that "any overall negative effect is due to the fallibility of the therapist." Fiske went on to say that even when the therapist himself is not *directly* contributing to negative effects in psychotherapy, he should be able to tell when the treatment or some other variable *is* producing negative effects. He should then be able and willing to take appropriate countermeasures.

Major therapist variables discussed fell into two broad categories, the first being deficiencies in training and skills, resulting in part from poor training facilities and "the development of delivery systems which do not require the maximum background in the biomedical and psychological sciences" on the part of practitioners (Salzman). Goldberg likewise noted deficiencies in training and supervision, which result in the delivery of inadequate professional services. Deficiencies in the therapist's skill may produce particularly severe negative effects in dealing with borderline patients due to the therapist's stimulating the release of primitive aggression without quite knowing how to deal with it in psychotherapy. Such negative effects may be exacerbated by the therapist who masochistically participates in the patient's acting out.

Part of the problem with training in the mental health field, of course, is simply the relative lack of knowledge within the field itself. What is not known cannot be taught and, as Salzman observed, "The total picture of human behavior and its neurophysiological and biochemical correlates has yet to be established." Similarly, after laying the blame for negative effects at the doorstep of fallible therapists, Fiske noted that, "more charitably, negative effects are due to our limited knowledge about treating persons."

Several respondents observed that the contribution to negative effects in psychotherapy resides in what Bordin termed a "*complex* of ignorance and inappropriate personality." Engel suggested that negative effects may be caused by an ill-trained or incompetent person or by "one who abuses his position." The second important variable which may contribute to negative effects is the therapist's personality.

Incompatibility between the patient's and therapist's personalities may contribute to negative effects in psychotherapy (Wolberg). Even more ominous are the problems posed by certain noxious personality traits in the therapist. Ellis identified three such characteristics—ignorance or stupidity, incompetence, and the "need to exploit the patient." Roback described therapists whose personalities have an adverse effect on therapy as "unable to utilize their intellect and acquired knowledge in therapeutically productive ways. . . . [C]linical decisions are based on their own personality needs (although perhaps theoretically rationalized)." He listed "sadomasochism, voyeurism, and faddism" as examples of personality traits in the therapist which may have an adverse effect on therapy.

Additional deleterious personality attributes mentioned by respondents include:

—Coldness, obsessionalism—"anything goes as long as 'analyzing' is happening" (Ann Appelbaum)
—Excessive need to make people change (Ann Appelbaum)
—Excessive unconscious hostility, often disguised by diagnosing the patient as "borderline" or schizophrenic (Fine)
—Seductiveness, lack of interest or warmth (Marmor)
—Neglect, pessimism, sadism, absence of genuineness (Betz)
—Greed, narcissism, dearth of self-scrutiny (Greenson)

As we shall see, the variety of factors discussed here may adversely influence therapy in a number of ways, including deleterious effects on the relationship with the patient (English), and misuse of therapeutic techniques. It is also possible for a well-meaning therapist, with the unconscious motivation of enhancing his own personal and professional self-esteem, to inadvertently overemphasize his assets (Holmes). For the present, we note in passing Ann Appelbaum's general comment that pathology or deficient skills in the therapist may lead to inadequate recognition of transference manifestations, premature uncovering of unconscious conflicts without provision of concomitant support, or both.

Patient Qualities

Certain patient variables may, of course, also contribute to negative effects in therapy. Low or absent motivation—especially in patients who feel "sentenced to treatment"—strongly suggests a poor prognosis (Goldberg). As noted previously, patients with low ego strength or deficient psychic resources may be poor candidates for certain kinds of therapy and indeed may prove vulnerable to psychotic breaks as a result of the uncovering process. Adequate diagnosis at intake should provide better identification of high risk patients before therapy is undertaken.

Adequate assessment might also help to identify patients with a masochistic character structure, which was identified by several respondents as a potential contributor to negative effects in therapy (Gottschalk). Such patients do not feel comfortable when functioning well. Other patients may experience guilt due merely to the fact that the therapist provides concern and understanding. Special psychotherapeutic techniques based on careful diagnostic assessment might forestall such negative outcomes.

Finally, it is important to note, as Castelnuovo-Tedesco observed, that some neurotic patients are "prone to disappointment and . . . have a special talent for seeking it (and finding it) even as they yearn for deliverance from it." Such patients inevitably may be disappointed with their experience in psychotherapy, regardless of what the therapist may do or say.

Misapplication and Deficiencies of Technique

Over and above any contribution made by the therapist's personality, negative effects may result from errors in technique. Lazarus, for example, described "seemingly responsible practitioners who never deviate from the specified ethical norms but who nevertheless harm rather than help many of the people who consult them." The implication here is that these apparently well-meaning individuals are nonetheless noxious to their patients due to the manner in which they apply therapeutic principles and techniques.

Numerous and varied examples of mistakes in the practice of therapy were cited. These statements appeared to be based on strong sentiments exemplified by Dyrud: "Negative effects must be linked to the therapist's error—either inappropriate technique or misapplication." Orne described as potentially deleterious the use of *any* technique which undercuts symptoms that function for the patient's adjustment, in the absence of the development of alternative coping mechanisms. In a general sense, Greenson identified as a potential contributor to negative effects any therapy which "dehumanizes" the patient.

False assumptions concerning the scope and potency of therapy. This is a fundamental issue, relating to the most basic premises therapists hold about themselves and their therapy. Problems may arise when the therapist entertains assumptions of omniscience (Salzman), or when he believes himself to be "God" (Davison). Therapy by its very nature can be "meddlesome" (Prange), that is, it may send a message to the patient, "you're not okay."

An additional problem is that therapy is not able to solve all ills. As Zubin noted, "The omnipotent view of therapy in being able to improve adjustment in general . . . is beyond the scope of therapeutic intervention today." The negative effect potential arises when the patient is simultaneously given messages of "you're not okay" coupled with "therapy can solve anything." Such a patient may come to entertain or perpetuate unrealistic expectations and goals for himself in therapy and when these are not achieved fall prey to disillusionment and loss of faith in therapy and therapists.

Problems with the goals of therapy. The problem most frequently mentioned relative to therapeutic goals concerned failure to discuss, describe, or even acknowledge the reality of goals per se (Weintraub, Freedman). Another respondent called attention to therapeutic goals that are too "abstract," as well as failure by therapist and patient to reach mutual agreement on the goals of therapy. Many of our respondents strongly expressed the view that "some sense of direction is necessary. The patient's realistic hopes need to be distinguished from his fantasies" (Goldberg).

Further problems may arise when the goals of therapy are not in the patient's best interest (Davison), as when the goal of therapy is directed toward "fusion" with others or requiring directives from others (Betz). The latter observed that although the achievement of such goals may provide some immediate gratification to the patient, it will in the long run have a negative effect, particularly in terms of perpetuating the patient's dependence.

Finally, problems may be created by a therapist who sets up goals which exceed the patient's capabilities or who fosters expectations of speedy progress beyond the patient's capabilities. Knapp related an example of a therapist who, acting out some of his *own* wishes, urged a divorce on his patient, with destructive consequences (including the development of alcoholism). Friedman described a patient for whom the imposition of the therapist's values had even more grave consequences:

The worst consequence I have personally seen was in a man with a process-type schizophrenia, who had seriously and continuously loosened associations, and very great difficulty keeping track of the elementary procedures of daily life. His expressed interest in becoming a physician was enthusiastically welcomed by a group psychotherapist who was culturally and ideologically sold on upward mobility, and who encouraged his group to challenge the patient to implement his ambition, and simultaneously strip away his rationalizations and ways of maintaining his self-esteem. He decompensated, became catatonic and required hospitalization.

These patients exemplify a negative effect described earlier—the emergence of guilt and lowered self-esteem (and for these particular individuals, the development of serious psychiatric symptoms) as a result of their being urged to attempt life tasks for which they were ill-prepared.

Misplaced focus of therapy. There was a consensus among respondents that there is a fundamental problem in determining whether psychotherapy should focus primarily on the patient himself and his inner workings, or be externally directed toward significant others and toward society. Palmer stressed the environmental emphasis, faulting psychotherapy which is devoted entirely to the inner man, for it is only by awareness of environmental stresses that the patient will be helped to evaluate these stresses realistically. Similarly, Atthowe saw a problem in therapy which fails "to involve the patient's environment in his treatment"; he spoke not only of enlisting the cooperation of institutions and significant others in treating the patient, but also urged comprehensive treatment of the relevant social community systems.

Others argued against a form of "determinism" which presumes that "the focus of difficulty lies with parents, society, others, and not within the individual's own resistances to change" (Salzman). Meehl took a similar tack, faulting therapy which focuses on "anything and everything" instead of problem behaviors, such as drinking, procrastination, etc., which may have brought a person to psychotherapy. Meehl put the case well:

> I have known quite a few people . . . who have spent many hours in intensive psychotherapy and who have in fact learned a good deal about themselves . . . who are still pretty ineffective or unhappy individuals, in large part because they are persisting in overt behavior of a destructive or ineffective kind. For such persons it would require some kind of massive brainwashing for them to stop feeling unethical or incompetent, for the simple reason that they are *in fact*, by any usual standards of ethics or of vocational, financial, family and sexual performance, doing things that are wrong, inept, or both.

The thrust of this argument is that one can spend a great deal of time and energy in psychotherapy which will nonetheless remain relatively ineffectual both in changing behavior and alleviating distress because the therapeutic focus is displaced from "behavior and will" (Salzman), to insights, interpretations, and the like. We shall presently deal with the problem of insight at greater length. For the present, we note that the kind of outcome described by Meehl may readily lead to the feelings of disillusionment and loss of hope identified previously as a particularly pervasive negative effect of psychotherapy.

Mismatch of technique to the patient. We have previously called attention to the need for adequate assessment and diagnosis, as well as problems which may result from failure to identify patient characteristics that militate against a positive therapeutic outcome. Inadequate assessment may also contribute to "mismatching" of therapy to the patient, with even greater potential for negative effects (Greenson).

Malan urged that patients be assigned to a form of psychotherapy appropriate to both the nature and the degree of their disturbance, particularly to "exclude from very deep-going psychotherapy those patients who have not the strength to bear it." More generally, he stated that "it is the failure to match therapy to the patient's disturbance that is most likely to lead to negative effects." Others affirmed that it is quite possible for therapy to have negative effects even when skillfully conducted, if it happens to be inappropriate for the particular patient in question (Engel).

What specifically are mismatches in psychotherapy? What kinds of therapy may be actually harmful if applied to a particular kind of patient? Nemiah observed that psychoanalytically oriented insight therapy can be "actively harmful" when it is applied to either borderline patients, in which case it may promote regressive transference, angry acting out or manipulation; or to patients with psychosomatic symptoms, where the focus on fantasies and feelings may be incomprehensible to the patient with the result that he may either give up therapy or show an exacerbated somatization. Knapp vividly described just such a situation:

In the late 1940s we were just beginning to learn about the psychotherapy of patients with severe psychosomatic disease, particularly ulcerative colitis. We saw numerous instances of patients who were encouraged to express their emotions. They got enormously involved with therapists, poured out beautiful material, and became steadily worse. Several of them died.

Knapp went on to observe that soon thereafter there developed an awareness of such "ill-advised" interventions and the "need for sensitive supportive therapy with such sick individuals." In a similar vein, Garfield noted that a negative effect may occur when a therapist attempts to uncover repressed material which is very threatening to the patient and which he is uncapable of assimilating—a likely outcome when the patient is not sufficiently well integrated to handle the uncovering process.

Weintraub discussed problems that may accompany attacking the defenses of patients with particularly fragile egos and defense structures. Prange foresaw problems if the therapist allies himself with id mechanisms when this is inappropriate (as is true with many adolescents). With respect to behavior treatments, Davison discussed problems in aversion therapy. This form of therapy may be counterproductive with some homosexuals, by feeding into the patient's pathology and need for punishment.

Technical rigidity in therapy. Problems resulting from the mismatch of therapy to the patient may be exacerbated if the therapist adheres rigidly to a particular form of therapy (Palmer) or to the theoretical prescriptions of one individual (Greenson). Most of the respondents who discussed rigidity of technique related it to the therapist's insecurity. Salzman, for example, observed that "when the therapist is rigid, inflexible, insecure, and essentially a technician following rules of procedure," the process of therapy itself may become "an obsessional ritual."

The consequences of therapeutic rigidity bode ill for the patient because his individual characteristics and needs may not be given sufficient consideration (Will). Excessive rigidity may also force the patient into submission to a preestablished procedure (Fine), or may encourage him to perform certain "standard" behaviors (aggressiveness, bluntness) which conform to the therapist's definition of mental health (Friedman). Additional problems may arise when a therapist's rigidity prevents him from shifting to other modes of treatment, even when it is clear that the original treatment of choice is inappropriate for the patient involved (Atthowe). One behavior therapist observed that in behavior therapy (as well as in all other forms), rigidity and strict adherence to technique restricts the therapist's ability to understand the patient and his problems, with potentially adverse consequences for the patient-therapist relationship and the therapeutic outcome.

Overly intense therapy. Any or all of the mistakes discussed here may be aggravated by therapy which is overly intense (e.g., "pushing too much" or getting too close to the patient when he is unable or unwilling to tolerate such proximity [Orne]). Paul spoke of "coming on too strong" to the patient, particularly in terms of overly specific advice or tasks. Garfield discussed the issue of intensity in terms of particularly fragile patients who may be pushed too hard to reveal themselves while being unable or unwilling to relax their defenses.

Misuse of interpretations or insight therapy. Misuse of interpretations in psychotherapy was frequently mentioned as a factor contributing to negative effects. Generally, the problems related to misuse of interpretations appear to fall into two major categories. The first of these includes problems in focusing discussed earlier. Thus, therapy may fail to achieve a proper "balance between internal investigation and utilization of life resources for energy, pleasure, and integrity of function," which according to Freedman leads to the development of many "half persons" impaired in their real development and growth. The problem here is excessive diversion of critical personality resources and energies from growth into internal investigation. We have discussed this issue previously in terms of therapy becoming an end in itself.

Even more directly related to the issue of inappropriate

focus in therapy are interpretations which are so "predominantly 'transference-centered' that they distort or minimize the impact of reality factors in the patient's life" (Marmor). Such interpretations may contribute to a pervasive denigration of the patient's sense of autonomy, responsibility, and self-esteem—a trend which in Salzman's view characterizes much of psychotherapy today. The reason given by this respondent is that much of psychoanalytic training and therapy still focuses on interpretation as the *key factor* in effecting change.

Malan noted in particular the potential for negative effects in the analyst's tendency to interpret apparent "getting better" as a "flight into health" to avoid continuing therapy. In Malan's opinion, such improvement may at times represent considerably more than merely a flight into health and "even if it is a patient is sometimes able to make use of it as a point of growth. Keeping the patient in therapy may bring back his symptoms without the final outcome of resolving them."

Particularly severe problems may result from destructive interpretations or from critical interpretations made before genuine trust and rapport have developed between patient and therapist (Marmor). Dollard observed that the mere revelation of a patient's problems in the course of psychotherapy may increase his adjustment difficulties in everyday life. The problem may become especially acute, of course, with borderline or psychotic patients where the "ill-conceived utilization of uncovering or insight oriented approaches" may have decidedly negative effects.

At a minimum, interpretations may arouse anxiety. As Wolpe noted, interpretations may convey an implicit message to the patient of "basic abnormality." At its most extreme, this may lead to an "excessively deep and terrifying awareness of the person's primitive longings and/or of the actual discrepancies between legitimate and instinctual needs and their likelihood of satisfaction in reality" (Ann Appelbaum).

These misuses of interpretations are particularly likely to have negative consequences when they are presented without adequate follow-up or opportunities for working through—in Bellak's terms, "analysis without sufficient synthesis." The proper use of interpretations requires skill in timing, tact, and "buffering." Failure to exercise these skills may result in a patient with a "battered self-concept" (Meehl).

Meehl also expressed the opinion that it is better sometimes for people not to know too much about themselves and their relationships to others: "I had never seen any really convincing theoretical argument which shows that it is *always* a good thing to 'have insight'." Thus, even when the therapist is skillful, and "uncovering" psychotherapy may be indicated in a particular case, the patient still may emerge from treatment with his self-concept further impaired. Since defects in self-esteem are almost a defining characteristic of patients in psychotherapy, such an outcome must be viewed as extremely unfortunate and clearly indicative of a negative effect.

Dependency-fostering techniques. Greenson observed that any form or aspect of therapy which makes the patient "an addict to therapy and the therapist" is undesirable. We have already observed that techniques which encourage interminable self-exploration to the exclusion of behavioral change and at the expense of the patient's intentionality may have these consequences. While the therapist may not actively encourage the patient's dependency, he may fail to take appropriate measures to counteract it—with equally unfortunate results (Hollender).

Problems in the Patient-Therapist Relationship

Negative effects in psychotherapy may arise from or become exacerbated by problems in the rapport between the therapist and patient. In general, "too little" or "too much" rapport instead of an intermediate optimal level is implicated

(Atthowe). The instance of poor rapport most often cited by our respondents was faulty handling of the manifestations of countertransference. Palmer reiterated the traditional view—a therapist should not underestimate his own reactions to a patient, but rather assess them honestly and deal with them constructively. The therapist must also be on guard against countertransference problems that extend beyond the patient to his environment—for example, to the parents of disturbed children (Berlin).

A major source of difficulty relating to the patient-therapist interaction was termed by Langs "interactional neurosis." He called for intensive study of both the conscious and unconscious interaction between patient and therapist to understand precisely how this neurosis develops and in what ways it may adversely affect the progress of psychotherapy. Luborsky similarly described the therapist's failure to recognize the patient's "conflictual relationship theme" and the more serious problem created if the therapist unwittingly "fits in" with the theme.

Hostile countertransference by the therapist toward the patient may assume a number of deleterious forms, including the following (Goldberg):

—Prevention of the establishment of a working alliance
—Lack of respect for the patient's pain
—Failure to allow the patient to experience choices
—Aggressive assault on the patient's defenses
—A disappointed attitude toward the patient and his progress

For a variety of reasons—including hostile countertransference—some therapists may fail to maintain minimally necessary professional distance (Weintraub). Several respondents mentioned the therapist's exploitation, manifested as seductiveness, as the most blatant example of this problem. Therapists' sexual involvement with their patients is currently a "hot issue" in the news media and most recently has led to a number of lawsuits. The consequences of such liaisons are almost invariably negative, including occasional suicides. Rhoads, for example, described the case of a female patient who committed suicide at her psychiatrist's cabin following their sexual involvement and his subsequent rejection of her.

A number of respondents stressed the importance of making the patient-therapist relationship explicit in order to deal with developing problems and to forestall the development of difficulties.

Communication Problems

Fundamental problems which may contribute to or aggravate other negative effects, particularly those relating to the therapeutic relationship, pertain to difficulties in patient-therapist communication. Problems may arise if the therapist is unable to communicate his ideas clearly or fails to determine whether the patient is comprehending adequately what has been said (Bieber). On the patient's side there is a great potential for problems when distortions, omissions, or falsifications in his communications to the therapist occur and go uncorrected (Roback). A particular problem with patient communications was noted by Berlin in his discussion of the nonverbal communication of disturbed children and the need for the therapist to understand and respond appropriately to these communications.

Problems Unique to Certain Forms of Therapy

Behavior therapy. Behavior therapy has long been the target of criticism, particularly from proponents of other forms of therapy. Symptom substitution is one of the most often mentioned negative effects attributed to behavior therapy. From the psychoanalytic perspective, Abse noted that behavior therapy "has so many possibilities of negative effects, not the least being that some people best treated analytically are seduced along the lines of their resistance to change."

A major advantage of many of these techniques is their great potency for the rapid modification of behavior. This same advantage, however, simultaneously creates a greater potential for abuse. In a case described by Knapp, a woman with hysterical leg paralysis was "partly bullied, partly tricked" into walking by the use of a particularly crude and forceful form of behavior modification. The patient walked out of the hospital but returned that night with two arteries slashed in a major suicide attempt.

Even among the adherents of behavior therapy, there is a recognition of special problems that may result from this form of treatment. A general problem is increased behavioral feedback, which while an integral y, may at times lead to the reinforcement of inappropriate responses. When this happens, problem behaviors may actually show an increase during baseline or extinction periods before treatment is introduced. Further, when contingencies are reversed in order to demonstrate the efficacy of treatment in reducing negative behaviors, there will of necessity be an increase in these behaviors. Other problems may accompany hierarchical steps toward therapeutic goals which are too large or which are undertaken at too rapid a pace for the patient to achieve success (Liberman). Finally, one behavior therapist observed that the main contributor to negative effects in behavior therapy is failing to engage the patient in the "here and now"— suggesting concern with the *lack of relationship* during the strict technical application of behavior modification techniques.

Radical (confrontational/tactile) therapies. Many of the

more radical forms of therapy are relatively young, and thus there has been little opportunity for data on their effects to be accumulated. However, some evidence is beginning to accumulate and a number of respondents indicated they have questions or concerns about these therapies. Ellis, for example, minced no words in referring to certain "misleading and idiotic theories of psychotherapy."

Many of these therapies are group-based. Davison observed that with groups in general there is a danger of inadequate assessment and attention to the needs and vulnerabilities of individual members. Furthermore, there is the problem of charismatic group leaders whose potential for impact upon the group members is great. Yalom, one of the few workers who has published evidence of negative effects associated with such group leaders (Lieberman, Yalom, and Miles 1973), observed that there may be a further problem with time-limited groups or encounter groups in which the patient does not have sufficient time to work through issues of discomfort and distress confronting him at the time the group terminates.

Bellak referred to problems of "excessive awareness" brought about by some encounter groups as well as excessive repression due to "stupid value judgments" by the therapist and other group members. Similarly, another respondent noted problems of increased feelings of alienation or depression in some group members. In its most extreme form, these negative effects may lead to decompensation of very disturbed individuals (Bieber).

Miscellaneous

Finally, respondents mentioned several general mistakes which, regardless of the context or form of therapy in which they occur, are clearly to be avoided. Among these are: breaches in confidentiality (Weintraub); prolongation of therapy when an impasse is reached; refusal of the therapist to refer a patient to another therapist or another form of therapy if the present situation is not productive (Weintraub); and, finally, labeling which becomes "either an excuse and/or a reason for repeated failures" (Lazarus).

CONCLUSIONS

It is clear that negative effects of psychotherapy are ovewhelmingly regarded by experts in the field as a significant problem requiring the attention and concern of practitioners and researchers alike. The responses to our survey show that these experts are prepared to point the way for investigators by specifying criteria of negative effects and possible causative factors.

The traditional and relatively obvious identifying criterion of an increase in the number and/or the severity of problems was mentioned by most respondents. Many went on, however, to describe certain less obvious, but nonetheless real indicators of negative effects including the patient's abuse or misuse of therapy; ill-fated attempts by the patient to overreach his capabilities; and, as a result of any or all of these more specific negative effects, disillusionment with the therapist or with therapy in general.

The list of factors which may conduce to negative effects in psychotherapy was lengthy. Deficiencies in *assessment* were described by many as one of the most fundamental contributory factors, leading to a variety of problems stemming from a failure to identify borderline patients and others for whom psychotherapy may pose serious risks.

A wide range of patient and therapist *personality* qualities was identified as problematical, along with the obvious but extraordinarily serious problem of deficiencies in the therapist's *training*. By far the greatest number of factors cited fell under the general heading of misapplications or deficiencies in technique. In particular, the misuse of interpretations and insight therapy came in for severe criticism. At a minimum, the misuse of interpretations may promote an unhealthy imbalance in the patient's life, diverting his energies into the pursuit of insight as an end in and of itself. At its worst, the misuse of interpretations and faulty efforts to produce "insight" may be patently destructive of the patient's psychological well-being. (A complete listing of identifying criteria of negative effects and potential contributory factors mentioned by our respondents appears in tables 4-1 and 4-2.)

Perhaps the most compelling finding of the survey was strong support of the need for systematic research into the problem of negative effects. There were repeated references to the issue as "important," "intriguing," and "exciting." A number of respondents expressed their pleasure at the fact that a systematic study of negative effects was underway and offered additional assistance and cooperation. Others indicated they themselves had recently been thinking or writing about the problem of negative effects. The spirit of these experts was perhaps best summed up by Orne who observed that, "The issues . . . are as important as they are difficult. It certainly is time for someone to bite the bullet and seek to address the matters empirically. I wish you luck!"

Table 4-1

WHAT CONSTITUTES A NEGATIVE EFFECT?

Exacerbation of Presenting Symptoms

1. *"Worsening"*—increase in severity, pathology, etc.

2. *Generally*, may take form of (or be accompanied by):

   a. exacerbation of suffering
   b. decompensation
   c. harsher superego or more rigid personality structure

3. *Specific* examples of symptom exacerbation:

—depressive breakdown
—severe regression
—increased self-downing
—increased behavioral shirking
—increased inhibition
—paranoia
—fixing of obsessional symptoms
—exaggeration of somatic difficulties
—extension of phobias
—increased guilt
—increased confusion
—lowered self-confidence
—lower self-esteem
—diminished capacity for delay and impulse control

Appearance of New Symptoms

1. *Generally*, may be observed when:

a. psychic disturbance is manifested in a less socially acceptable form than previously
b. symptom substitution where a symptom which had fulfilled an imperative need is blocked

2. *Specific* examples:

—erosion of solid interpersonal relationships
—decreased ability to experience pleasure
—severe or fatal psychosomatic reactions
—withdrawal
—rage
—dissociation
—drug/alcohol abuse
—criminal behavior
—suicide
—psychotic breaks

Patient Abuse or Misuse of Therapy

1. Substitution of intellectualized insights for other obsessional thoughts

2. Utilization of therapy to rationalize feelings of superiority or expressions of hostility toward other people

3. Therapy becomes an end in itself—a substitute for action

4. Fear of "intellectualization" prevents patients from examining their ethical and philosophical commitments

5. Participation in more radical therapies encourages belief in the irrational in order to avoid painful confrontations with realities of life

6. Sustained dependency on therapy or the therapist

Patient "Over-Reaching" Himself
1. Two forms:

   a. undertaking life tasks (marriage, graduate school, etc.) which require resources beyond those of the patient
   b. undertaking life tasks prematurely

2. May be related to:

   a. intense wishes to please the therapist
   b. inculcation of inachievable middle-class "ideals"
   c. increased "irrational" ideas

3. May result in any or all of the following:

   a. excessive strain on patient's psychological resources
   b. failure at the task
   c. guilt
   d. self-contempt

Disillusionment with Therapy and/or the Therapist
1. May appear variously as:

   a. wasting of patient's resources (time, skill, money) which might have been better expended elsewhere
   b. hardening of attitudes toward other sources of help
   c. loss of confidence in the therapist, possibly extending to any human relationship
   d. general loss of hope—all the more severe for initial raising of hopes which may have occurred at onset of therapy

Table 4-2

WHAT FACTORS ARE ASSOCIATED WITH NEGATIVE EFFECTS?

Inaccurate/Deficient Assessment
1. Assessment must include:

   a. ego functions
   b. general baseline
      1. age
      2. diagnosis
      3. state of capacities
      4. life situation
   c. natural history of difficulties
   d. functional value of psychopathology

2. Assessment deficiencies may lead to:

   a. probing more deeply than the patient can tolerate
   b. failing to work intensively enough—thus cheating the patient of experiencing as much change as he is capable of

Therapist Variables
1. Deficiencies in training or skills—related in part to limited knowledge within the field itself

2. Personality factors:

   a. need to exploit the patient
   b. sado-masochism
   c. voyeurism
   d. faddism
   e. coldness
   f. obsessionalism
   g. excessive need to make people change
   h. excessive unconscious hostility
   i. seductiveness
   j. pessimism
   k. absence of genuineness
   l. greed

m. narcissism

n. dearth of self-scrutiny

Patient Qualities

1. Low or absent motivation

2. Low ego strength

3. Masochism—"feeling bad" because in some respects is doing well

Misapplications/Deficiencies of Technique

False assumptions concerning the scope and potency of therapy. Particularly, the assumption that therapy is all-powerful and the therapist all-knowing

Mistakes with therapeutic goals. (1) Failing to discuss or acknowledge reality of goals per se (2) Failing to reach *mutual* agreement on goals (3) Goals which are not in the patient's best interest (4) Too demanding goals—or too rapid progress toward goals.

Misplaced focus. (1) Focus exclusively on "the inner man"—failure to involve environment in treatment of the patient *or* to treat problem aspects of the environment (2) Focusing on anything and everything except problem behaviors of the patient and his will to stop them

Mismatch between therapy and the patient. *Examples* include: (1) Insight therapy applied to borderline or psychosomatic patients (2) Attacking the defenses of fragile patients (3) Therapist allying himself with id mechanisms when dealing with adolescents (4) Aversion therapy which satisfies patient's "sick" need to be punished

Technical rigidity. (1) *Generally*, considered to result from the therapist's insecurity (2) May have any or all of the following adverse effects:

a. failure to take into account patient's individual needs

b. forces patient to submit to pre-established procedure

c. inability or unwillingness to shift mode of treatment

d. decreased understanding and thoughtfulness

Overly intense therapy. (1) Getting too close to the patient (2) Too specific advice or tasks (3) Pushing the fragile patient to reveal himself

Misuse of interpretation or insight therapy. May take form of:

1. *Imbalance* between insights or interpretations and other processes of therapeutic change

   a. diversion of patient's resources into pursuit of insights
   b. predominance of transference-centered interpretations to the exclusion of reality factors

2. *Destructive interpretations*

   a. at a minimum, may arouse anxiety through conveying message of "basic abnormality"
   b. adverse effects likely when insufficient follow-up, analysis without sufficient synthesis

Dependency-fostering techniques. Includes failure to recognize and head off development of overly intense dependency

Problems with the Patient-Therapist Relationship
1. Too much or too little rapport

2. Countertransference (especially due to underestimating one's reactions to the patient) may have any or all of these effects:

   a. prevention of working alliance
   b. lack of respect for the patient's pain
   c. failure to allow the patient to experience choices
   d. aggressive assault on the patient's defenses
   e. disappointed attitude toward the patient and his progress

3. Failure to maintain professional distance—especially sexual involvement with the patient

Communication Problems
1. *Therapist*—inability to communicate clearly *and* to determine if patient is comprehending what was said

2. *Patient*—distortions, omissions, and falsifications in communications to the therapist

Problems Unique to Special Forms of Therapy
1. *Behavior Therapy*

  a. symptom substitution
  b. reinforcement of inappropriate responses by behavioral feedback
  c. increase in negative behaviors during baseline or extinction periods
  d. too large or too rapid hierarchical steps toward therapy goals
  e. failure to engage the patient in the here and now

2. *Radical Therapies* (especially in group context)

  a. inadequate assessment and attention to individuals
  b. charismatic, but destructive group leaders
  c. time limitations may prevent some individuals from working through distress
  d. excessive awareness
  e. "stupid" value judgments
  f. depression and feelings of alienation

Miscellaneous Problems which May Occur in Any Form of Therapy
1. Breaches in confidentiality

2. Prolongation of therapy when an impasse is reached (refusal to refer patient elsewhere)

3. Labeling—especially when it becomes an excuse/reason for repeated failures

Chapter 5

A Tripartite Model

The extensive literature on conceptions of mental health (see, for example, Jahoda 1958, for a comprehensive discussion) and the voluminous literature on outcome criteria in psychotherapy (cf. Bergin and Garfield 1971, Strupp and Bergin 1969) demonstrate the absence of a consensus as to what constitutes mental health and consequently, how changes resulting from psychotherapy are to be evaluated. The reality of this state of affairs vis-à-vis psychotherapy outcomes in general has become clear to us as we have pursued an analysis of the specific problem of negative effects in psychotherapy. For present purposes, we shall define a negative effect in psychotherapy as a worsening of a patient's condition attributable to his having undergone psychotherapy. We further postulate that a negative effect must be relatively lasting, which excludes from consideration transient effects (e.g., temporary sadness or anxiety contingent upon separation from the therapist at termination) and random fluctuations due to momentary life stress and intercurrent events. Excluded also are instances in which psychotherapy produces no change in the patient. Thus, in order for us to speak of a negative effect in psychotherapy, there must be evidence of adverse changes in the patient's condition (in relation to his *status quo ante*) directly attributable to, or a function of, the character and quality of the therapeutic experience or intervention to which he has been exposed.

It may readily be seen that a definition of "worsening" is the fulcrum upon which the problem of negative effects in psychotherapy turns. Since a judgment of "worse" is always made in relation to an implicit or explicit standard, which also presupposes a definition of the meaning of "better," it is clear that *the problem of what constitutes a negative effect is inextricably interwoven with a definition of mental health.* This is the case because any form of psychotherapy or behavior modification is designed to move the patient toward a particular ideal, standard, or norm, and the procedures and techniques utilized in a given form of therapy are instruments for accomplishing that purpose. Furthermore, we have concluded that only by considering multiple perspectives will it be possible to derive a truly comprehensive definition of mental health and meaningful evaluations of psychotherapy outcomes.

Consider the following: Do assessments of change in self-concept have anything in common with observations of overt behaviors, as in the treatment of a snake phobia? If, following psychotherapy, a patient manifests increased self-assertion coupled with abrasiveness, is this good or a poor therapy outcome? If, as a result of therapy, a patient obtains a divorce, is this to be regarded as a desirable or an undesirable change? A patient may turn from homosexuality to heterosexuality or he may become more accepting of either; an ambitious, striving person may abandon previously valued goals and become more placid (e.g., in primal therapy). How are such changes to be evaluated?

The difficulties inherent in evaluating psychotherapy outcome are exacerbated by the fact that problems in living which bring patients to psychotherapists are no longer necessarily viewed as "illness" for which psychotherapy is prescribed as "treatment." In increasing numbers, patients enter psychotherapy not for the cure of traditional "symptoms" but (at least ostensibly) for the purpose of finding meaning in their lives, for actualizing themselves, or for maximizing their potential.

MULTIPLE PERSPECTIVES TO BE CONSIDERED

In our pluralistic society the term "mental health" has assumed a multiplicity of meanings. If conceptions of mental health are fuzzier than ever, how can we determine whether a particular intervention has led to improvement, deterioration, or no change? Unless we make certain assumptions and develop a generally acceptable set of criteria concerning mental health, it is more or less meaningful to speak of "improvement" or a negative effect from psychotherapy. Further, in deriving these criteria, it is essential that we consider the social and cultural ramifications of therapy-induced change, the patient's place in society, his stage of life, and the general context within which he functions.

In other words, we are commending to practicing psychotherapists and researchers the value of taking into account the vantage points of those who judge mental health and therapy-induced change, including the values brought to bear on these judgments. To further the inquiry, we have developed a tripartite model which takes account of three major vantage points from which a person's mental health may be judged. Similar models have been described previously, most notably by Parloff, Kelman, and Frank (1954). The present discussion demonstrates the value of this model for describing changes which may result from psychotherapeutic interventions, and for highlighting the difficulties inherent in judgments of these changes. Thus, in the present chapter we propose to raise major questions pertaining to the evaluation of psychotherapy's effectiveness, and to describe a framework within which answers may be sought. An important aspect of the latter effort is our attempt to delimit those areas of inquiry which psychotherapy researchers can profitably address and those they cannot, and to explain why this is so.

Three major interested parties are concerned with definitions of mental health: (1) *society* (including significant persons in the patient's life); (2) the *individual patient*; and (3) the *mental health professional*. Each of these parties defines mental health in terms of certain unique purposes or aims it seeks to fulfill and consequently, each focuses on specific aspects of an individual's functioning in determining his mental health.

1. *Society* is primarily concerned with the maintenance of social relations, institutions, and prevailing standards of sanctioned conduct. Society and its agents thus tend to define mental health in terms of behavioral stability, predictability, and conformity to the social code.

The reaction of many mental health professionals to the inclusion of society as a bona fide evaluative agent of mental health and psychotherapy outcome is often less than enthusiastic. In part, this response arises from therapists' rejection of the noxious image of psychotherapy as an instrument of social control (Kittrie 1971, Szasz 1970) and the implication that its practitioners are thus either the agents of or accountable to social and political authorities. In part, the response may arise from therapists' concern that agents of society are not sufficiently knowledgeable and sensitive to the intricacies of the individual. But like it or not, it is clear that society has been and is increasingly involved in assessments of mental health and psychotherapy.

The historical involvement of society in mental health evaluations which is based on its needs to maintain order has increased markedly in recent years with the trend toward third party payments for mental health care. A patient who pays for his own therapy is certainly at liberty to structure the goals of that therapy to suit his own needs and he can spend as much time in therapy as his bank account allows. Such an individual is, in a most personal and subjective sense, the ultimate judge of the treatment outcome. But as insurance companies or the taxpaying public have begun to foot the bill, issues of treatment have become translated into issues of accountability. Aldrich (1975) has described the changing scene from the perspective of the practicing psychiatrist:

> As long as Jones paid me for his psychotherapy or friendship, or however he wanted to use the time I sold him, it was none of Smith's business. But when Smith's taxes or insurance premiums began to contribute to my fee, Smith's interest in what I was doing with Jones increased. In other words, Smith now expects me to be accountable—and in terms that he can understand. [p. 509]

The debate over national health insurance is only the most obvious and recent example of the growing interest of society in defining mental health and in developing sound criteria for evaluating psychotherapy outcomes. The issues were squarely joined in a recent meeting of mental health professionals and congressional proponents of the national health insurance package. While the mental health professionals decried simplistic assessments of mental health and psychotherapy outcome, the politicians responded, "We need facts, not messages" (Quality psychiatric care vs. political realities 1976). Thus, at present, matters stand at an impasse.

2. The *individual client* evaluating his own mental health uses a criterion distinctly different from that used by society. The individual wishes first and foremost to be happy, to feel content. He defines mental health in terms of highly subjective feelings of well-being—feelings with a validity all their own. Some individuals will experience contentment coincident with behavioral adaptation and there will thus be agreement by the individual and society that he is mentally sound. But the agreement is, nonetheless, between *independent* evaluations made from different vantage points, and it is quite conceivable that an individual may define himself as mentally sound quite independent of society or the mental health profession's opinion.

3. Most *mental health professionals* tend to view an individual's functioning within the framework of some theory of personality structure which transcends social adaptation and subjective well-being (although clinical judgments of another's mental health are often significantly influenced by these latter two criteria). The professional thus defines mental health largely with reference to some theoretical model of a "healthy" personality structure which may on occasion result in a diagnosis of mental health or pathology at variance with the opinion of society and/or the individual.

The most comprehensive and ambitious model of mental functioning is psychoanalytic theory (e.g., Rapaport 1960), including prominently such concepts as drives, defenses, and ego structures. For present purposes we need not concern ourselves with the evolution of the system or its complexities. It is important, however, to note in general the advantages of positing some form of mental structure within which a person's subjective feeling-states and behavior gain meaning.

Rapaport formulates the construct of structure as follows:

> Structures appear as *independent variables* wherever individual differences in behavior, under (relatively) constant motivation and stimulation are studied: for instance, in the comparative study of symptoms in various neuroses, and in the studies of individual differences in perception. . . .
>
> Structures as *intervening variables* are common place in clinical observation. They account for the lack of one-to-one relationship between motivations and behavior. Defensive structures countermand motivations and replace them by derivative motivations (as, for instance, in reaction formation). Controlling structures direct and channel motivations, as in delay- and detour-behavior and in the choice of substitute goals. . . .
>
> It is less easy to conceive of structures as *dependent variables*, though they appear as such in processes of structural change, including those of learning. In so far as psychoanalysis as therapy achieves its goals of changing existing structures, in at least some of the observations made in therapy, structures appear as dependent variables. . . . [p. 71]

In conclusion Rapaport notes, "Any limitation on the choice of variables seems to result in a limited range of observables and observational methods, and it is the dearth of methods which is probably the major obstacle to bridging the gap between psychoanalysis and academic psychology and between the various schools of psychology" (p. 72).

By introducing the construct of structure—not necessarily the psychoanalytic conception—into the present discussion we assert that more may be involved in assessments of psychotherapy outcome than changes in the person's feeling state and/or behavior. For example, it is one thing to observe that following therapy a previously anxious and shy male asks a girl for a date (overt behavior); one may also inquire whether he is now happier than he was previously (well-being). It is quite another matter to determine the extent to which any observed behavioral and affective changes have become a part of a generalized disposition to deal differently with women, or to determine the *quality* of the experience—whether, for example, a rigid defensive structure has been replaced by a more modulated approach in interpersonal relations. Empirical studies of therapy outcomes have rarely dealt with these topics. To be sure, judgments concerning an individual's personality structure are inferential, and they are influenced by reports of his behavior, descriptions of his feeling-state, etc. (A possible exception is the evaluation of structure made on the basis of the Rorschach test, which is assumed to be free from such influences unless the clinician gathers collateral information from the subject, which indeed he often does.)

Models of psychological strcture vary considerably both in content and in the degree of inference involved in the observations and assessments derived from them. Indeed, some mental health professionals prefer not to invoke such models at all, but to focus their attention primarily on observable behaviors and/or feeling-states. For many others, however, a model of psychological structure and functioning provides the modus operandi of their therapeutic interventions and thus, assessments based on such models comprise a significant aspect of a comprehensive evaluation of each individual.

IMPLICATIONS OF DISCREPANT VANTAGE POINTS

It follows from the preceding discussion that the divergent vantage points described may result in different definitions of "mental health" and consequently, in discrepant evaluations of a given individual's functioning and performance. Table 5-1 describes the goals and values pertinent to each of the three perspectives on mental health, as well as the measures related to each frame of reference. It is seen that each person's mental health may be judged differently, depending on whether society, the individual himself, or a mental health professional makes the judgment. Correspondingly, a given individual is regarded as being in need of professional help to the extent that he deviates from the standards and values governing each of the vantage points.

No conflict of judgment arises as long as each dimension is considered in isolation. Thus, as long as an individual functions well in society and conforms to its conventions, he is generally not seen by society as suffering from a mental illness or disturbance, and consequently, he is not perceived as requiring professional help; similarly, an individual regards himself as mentally healthy as long as he experiences a genuine sense of well-being and happiness; and the mental health professional perceives no problem requiring his attention as long as the individual's personality structure is intact (this leaves out of account such instances as normal grief reactions and other transient conditions for which some form of "supportive psychotherapy" or "counseling" is often undertaken).

Evaluations of an individual's functioning often are made from one of these perspectives. In some cases, for specific narrowly defined purposes, such evaluations are adequate; however, it is clear that if one is interested in a *comprehensive* picture of the individual, evaluations based on a single vantage point are inadequate and fail to give necessary consideration to the *totality* of an individual's functioning. A single-minded emphasis on performance and conformity to societal expecta-

Table 5-1

Primary Perspectives on Mental Health

Source	Standards/Values	"Measures"
I. Society	Orderly world in which individuals assume responsibility for their assigned social roles (e.g., breadwinner, parent), conform to prevailing mores, and meet situational requirements	Observations of behavior, extent to which individual fulfills society's expectations and measures up to prevailing standards
II. Individual	Happiness, gratification of needs	Subjective perceptions of self-esteem, acceptance, and well-being
III. Mental Health Professional	Sound personality structure characterized by: Growth, development, self-actualization, integration, autonomy, environmental mastery, ability to cope with stress, reality-orientation, adaptation	Clinical judgment, aided by behavioral observations and psychological tests of such variables as self-concept, sense of identity, balance of psychic forces, unified outlook on life, resistance to stress self-regulation, ability to cope with reality, absence of mental and behavioral symptoms, adequacy in love, work, and play, adequacy in interpersonal relations

tions is best illustrated by the function of mental health professionals in totalitarian societies, such as the Soviet Union or Communist China, although even our own society is not free from the charge that "mental illness" is at times merely a label by which society attempts to deal with those who deviate from sanctioned behavior. On the other hand, exclusive concern with the individual's feeling-state is a clear-cut example of what currently has become known as "the new narcissism" (Marin 1975), characterized by the individual's disregard for societal expectations and the necessary balance of personality forces (impulse control and other ego functions) that characterizes the standpoint of many mental health professionals. Finally, the preoccupation with intrapsychic forces and mechanisms to the exclusion of other aspects of a person's functioning is a caricature of the psychoanalyst whose excursions into metapsychology bear little relation to a patient's real life, and for whom psychotherapy has become an end in itself, a way of life, rather than a vehicle for change.

Table 5-2 is designed to call attention to the implications of mental health judgments from the three major perspectives: *society*, which bases its judgments largely on the adaptive qualities of behavior (*B*); the *individual* who bases his judgments on his sense of well-being (*W*); and the *mental health professional*, whose judgments are grounded in the assessment of psychological structure (*S*). Thus, a comprehensive evaluation of any individual must take account of the BWS configuration. It will be seen that only in categories 1 and 8 is there perfect agreement among the three "interested parties" that the person is either mentally healthy or so seriously disturbed as to require the services of a mental health professional. All other categories entail some conflict in mental health judgments, which we shall consider below.

Table 5-2

Implications of Divergent Perspectives on Mental Health

Category	Adaptive Behavior (Society) B	Sense of Well-being (Individual) W	Personality Structure (Professional) S	Judgment of "Mental Health"		
				Society	Individual	Professional
1	+	+	+	HH	HH	HH
2	+	−	+	H	L	H
3	+	+	−	H	H	L
4	+	−	−	H	L	L
5	−	+	+	L	H	H
6	−	−	+	L	L	H
7	−	+	−	L	H	L
8	−	−	−	LL	LL	LL

H = High; HH = Very high
L = Low; LL = Very low

The tripartite model suggests that the three dimensions of a person's functioning (behavior, sense of well-being, and inferred psychological structure) should be considered *simultaneously* in evaluating his mental health and any changes related to psychotherapy. Of course, in the final analysis, the evaluation of any psychotherapy outcome will be essentially a value judgment. What is highlighted by the tripartite model is the importance of considering fully and simultaneously the *multiple values* which may be brought to bear on such judgments.

Table 5-3 presents the eight possible combinations of positive and negative poles of the three mental health indicators along with composite sketches of individuals falling into each of the categories. The eight configurations identified are, for purposes of discussion, the most extreme possible cases. Gradations between the positive and negative poles are certainly possible, and indeed, more likely. Each category is a potential therapy outcome state. The relevant question here is: How shall each of these eight outcomes be judged—as a positive or as a negative effect? In the following pages, we turn to a consideration of this question. We shall deal with the issue at some length because it is the core of the problem under consideration.

TREATMENT OUTCOMES EXEMPLIFIED

We have selected for detailed discussion four of the eight possible outcome states described in table 5-3. Categories 1 and 8 are excluded from discussion because, regardless of the evaluative perspective, they are considered clear-cut instances of a positive and negative outcome perspective. Categories 2 and 6 are excluded for the sake of efficiency inasmuch as they are infrequently encountered as therapy outcome states. The four remaining categories—3, 4, 5, and 7—will be discussed in terms of the most common intake states, for as we have noted,

Table 5-3

**The Tripartite View of
Mental Health and Therapy Outcomes**

Category (Configuration)		Mental Health Status
1.	B+W+S+	Well-functioning, adjusted individual, optimal "mental health"
2.	B+W–S+	Basically "healthy" person; troubled by dysphoric mood, perhaps due to minor trauma affecting self-esteem, temporary reverses, discouragement, loss, grief reaction
3.	B+W+S–	May have fragile ego (borderline condition, schizoid personality, etc.) but functions well in society and feels content. Underlying psychotic process may be present, but defenses may be reasonably effective
4.	B+W–S–	Similar to (3), but affect may be labile or dysphoric. Has basic ego weakness, but functions adequately in society
5.	B–W+S+	Society's judges person's behavior as maladaptive (e.g., unconventional life style), but his sense of well-being and personality structure are sound
6.	B–W–S+	Similar to (2), except that social performance is considered maladaptive. Example: As part of a grief reaction, person may withdraw, give up job, etc.
7.	B–W+S–	Person with ego defects; psychopaths, character disorders, conversion reactions *(la belle indifférence)*, individuals who have poor reality testing and poor insight
8.	B–W–S–	Clearly "mentally ill"

therapy outcome can only be judged as positive or negative relative to a known intake state. While our discussion will be centered on the three aspects of functioning in combination, we shall note particularly those instances in which consideration of only one aspect in isolation (i.e., evaluating an individual from only one perspective) might lead to discrepant opinions of therapy outcome. Finally, we shall offer our judgment as to whether each outcome state represents a positive or negative psychotherapeutic effect.

Outcome category 3 (B+W+S-). As noted in table 3, a person in this category emerges from psychotherapy well-adapted to his social role and feeling comfortable within himself, but is judged by the mental health professional as suffering from ego defects (e.g., brittle defenses, characterological distortions, deficient impulse control).

Such a person may have entered psychotherapy feeling anxious, depressed, lonely, etc. (W-). Therapeutic interventions may have boosted the individual's morale and perhaps increased his self-esteem, resulting in a self-report of positive outcome. Assuming, however, that there were initially serious ego defects (S-), which would lead most mental health professionals to diagnose psychopathology of varying degrees, the observed change in feeling-state would be seen by them as "symptomatic improvement" without any significant radical or permanent change. Short-term, "supportive," or "relationship" forms of psychotherapy, perhaps administered by an inexperienced therapist, lay counselor, etc., might produce such an outcome. Similarly, participation in a sensitivity training program, encounter weekend, and the like might give rise to changes in the person's feeling-state (from W- to W+), but such changes might be short-lived. Whether changes in subjective well-being are seen as consequential clearly depends on the perspective of the judge. In the present instance, the changes in feeling-state, because they were not accompanied by positive structural modifications, would not be regarded by many mental health professionals as having great significance, although the individual might value them highly.

It is also possible that prior to therapy a patient exhibited behavioral deficits (e.g., poor job performance, academic underachievement, phobias that might interfere with his ability to earn a living, etc.). In this case, observations of the person's changed behavior (from B– to B+) would lead to a judgment, particularly by agents of society, of positive therapeutic outcome.

With respect to the dimension of inferred structure, one possible situation is that in which the person was found to have marked ego defects prior to entering therapy (S–), and these remained unchanged during therapy. Most mental health professionals would rate such a lack of change as a therapeutic failure. Their judgments of negative outcome would thus be discrepant with judgments of positive outcome made by the individual (based on a greater sense of happiness) and by society (based on more adaptive behavior). Such discrepancies are particularly likely concerning category 3 outcomes and may contribute to the view of some lay people that therapy is an esoteric luxury which seeks a mythical ideal of psychological integration and functioning. Society wants the individual to function smoothly in his social context; the individual wishes to feel content; and, partly because of an inability to assess factors beyond immediately observable behavior or feelings, neither sees the usefulness of therapy beyond the attainment of these goals.

Many mental health professionals, as discussed previously, hold the view that behavioral adjustment and feeling-states are not therapeutic ends in themselves, but are reflections of the individual's underlying psychological structure. It would thus be their opinion that any B– to B+ or W– to W+ changes observed in category 3 individuals are likely to be superficial and temporary.

In the event that the category 3 patient's psychological structure had changed from positive to negative or from mildly to strongly negative, most mental health professionals (including the authors) would rate the patient as having deteriorated; as we have seen, however, from the standpoints of society and the individual himself there would be judgments of therapeutic improvement. An illustration of this outcome would be a person who entered some form of highly directive therapy aimed at the modification of maladaptive behavior such as nail biting or insomnia. As a result of therapy, the individual might learn to master the problem and concomitantly experience a greater sense of well-being. Such a person would be rated by himself and society as improved. The therapist would likewise consider the therapy a success. However, a more dynamically oriented or otherwise broadly trained mental health professional might judge that the patient had achieved the behavioral changes at the cost of increased rigidity and compulsivity (S+ to S–). This, in turn, might render the patient more susceptible to exacerbations (e.g., depression) at a later period in his life. Such outcomes are by no means uncommon, and they may occur as functions of training programs in assertiveness, self-control, etc. In the early days of behavior therapy modification of the symptom that brought patients to therapy was usually considered a sufficient criterion of improvement. In recent years, however, many behavior therapists have adopted a broader view which takes into account the patient's overall life adjustment.

The implications of such an outcome—judged by society as positive and perceived by the mental health profession as negative—are considerable, particularly with reference to public policy and decisions relating to governmental support of mental health programs. Governments are most likely to fund mental health programs and agencies whose goal is restoration of the individual to effective social functioning, as opposed to the goal of long-term psychological restructuring. The individual patient, by the same token, will probably be motivated to continue therapy only as long as he is experiencing some psychic distress. Thus, only to the extent that therapists can demonstrate the relevance of sound psychological structure to *long-lasting* effective behavior and subjective well-being will there be consensus on what constitutes mental health and how it is best attained.

Category 4 (B+W–S–). Therapeutic outcomes in this category are essentially a variant of those described for category 3, the only difference being that the patient's self-reported feeling-state following therapy is one of unhappiness and discontent. As is true of all the configurations discussed here, the patient may have entered therapy in category 8—with negative evaluations of his behavior, feeling-state, and psychic structure. If so, a category 4 outcome would be judged a therapeutic success by society (B+) although the individual has remained unhappy (W–) and his psychological structure has remained unchanged (S–). Such an outcome is most likely when therapy is overly attentive to society's demands and fails to deal adequately with the patient's personal needs.

It is also possible that at intake the patient was experiencing no feelings of distress and manifested a B–W+S– (or less likely, a B–W+S+) configuration. It is highly unlikely that a person would *voluntarily* enter therapy feeling positive about himself (W+), although there are a number of instances in which a behavioral deficiency may be identified by society which the individual does not perceive as a problem. Examples of this kind include: a teacher referring a child for therapy because of unruly behavior in the classroom, a psychopath or sexual offender referred for treatment by a court of law, a wife who insists that her husband undergo therapy if their marriage is to continue. In each instance the patient himself may be relatively unmotivated for therapy; that is, he sees no need for change.

By contrast, society diagnoses a problem and attempts to force the individual to change against his will. The mental health professional may concur with society that the individual manifests psychopathology (S-), particularly if on closer examination it is inferred that, contrary to his self-defined feeling-state (W+), the individual is on a deeper level unhappy and suffering, his self-reported contentment based on defensive operations like denial.

Clearly, if an individual entered therapy with a fairly sound psychological structure and a sense of well-being, although a nonconformist in behavioral terms, and emerged a behavioral conformist with feelings of unhappiness and an impaired psychological structure, we would judge his outcome to be a negative effect. Further, if the person's psychological structure remained unchanged from an originally negative state and if behavioral conformity was achieved at the price of lessened subjective well-being, we would judge this to be a negative effect.

The B+W-S- outcome is particularly likely to occur when behavior is modified without consideration for its adaptive function in the patient's life. If nonconforming behavior meets important defensive needs, and the patient is then deprived of those behaviors, such modifications may have important negative repercussions for his feeling-state or psychological structure, which the individual himself and many therapists would consider a negative effect. Examples are overeating, which may meet important intrapsychic needs, or self-induced starvation where the refusal to take nourishment may be the manifestations of a deep-seated conflict rather than merely a "bad habit." Category 4 outcomes may be brought about in such cases by crude or coercive attempts at behavior modification. While the patient's behavior may have become more adaptive and conforming, there may be increases in feelings of negativism and the patient may feel betrayed by the therapist and, indirectly, by society. The concomitant resentment may be associated with depression, renewed or exacerbated interpersonal conflicts, and a sense of estrangement and unhappiness.

Another therapy blunder which might lead to outcomes of the B+W–S– type is exemplified by a therapist who encourages the patient to undertake new tasks or roles in life (e.g., marriage or higher education) for which he is insufficiently prepared and which require deployment of nonexistent psychic resources or energies which must be diverted from other areas of life. If the patient then fails at these tasks, we may anticipate such adverse consequences for his subjective well-being as guilt and depression, which almost certainly have reverberations in his psychological structure.

In summary, a category 4 outcome is particularly likely where modification of behavior is the primary goal of therapy. Since in our view the psychotherapeutic enterprise should be aimed at helping the individual to achieve an optimal balance between the demands of society, his own desire for contentment, and "professional" conceptions of sound intrapsychic structure, we would regard most outcomes of this type, particularly those which involve W+ to W– and/or S+ to S– changes, as clear-cut negative effects.

Category 5 (B–W+S+). Individuals with this configuration emerge from therapy with behavioral deficits (as judged by society), but they perceive themselves as happy and content, and mental health professionals would rate their psychological make-up as sound. If an individual begins therapy with behavioral, affective, and structural deficits (B–W–S–) and at termination is found to be happy (W+) and sound in psychological structure (S+), the patient himself and most mental health professionals (including the authors) would see such a patient as having benefited from psychotherapy, regardless of whether his overt behavior has changed. It is even possible that the patient's behavior might change from B+ to B–, yet because of his W– to W+ and S– to S+ changes, he would still be evaluated from the above perspectives as showing overall improvement. Such an assessment, however, would probably be tempered by a value judgment concerning the nature of the behavioral deficits. Under these circumstances the therapist's judgment of the patient's status might be equivocal, depending on the degree to which the therapist himself subscribes to prevailing societal standards of acceptable behavior.

To illustrate: Suppose a person following therapy decides to dissolve what previously was seen as a functioning marriage (B+) and obtains a divorce (B–). Society would predictably view such an outcome as a negative effect. Society would enter a similar judgment if a latent homosexual came to adopt homosexuality as a life style; or if, as a result of therapy, an individual decided to give up a lucrative job and retire to a life of contemplation, abandon responsibility for his family and begin to draw welfare checks.

Less drastically, a person might continue his social responsibilities in the areas of vocation and family, but he might become freer to express himself sexually, a result of therapy which society might judge as promiscuity, and thus a negative outcome. This is the kind of situation Freud envisaged when he said that following psychoanalysis, once a person's repressions are resolved (S– to S+), he would accept himself more fully (W– to W+), but also might become sexually more liberated and expressive. With respect to the latter change, Freud commented that it should be a matter of indifference to the analyst whether the patient's new life style clashed with the standards of society (Freud, of course, was speaking of Vienna in the Victorian era). In this situation, based on the affective and structural components, the patient as well as the analyst would rate the therapy outcome as highly favorable despite the fact that society, judging the patient's behavior, might disapprove. The fact that some therapists view psychotherapy not as a means of making the patient conform to the establishment, but as a humane approach for liberating the individual from the shackles of social convention and his own internalized repressions sets the stage for a clash among judgments of therapy outcome. Recently we have witnessed similar disagreement between adherents to conservative mores and standards of conduct that glorify competitiveness and productivity (in an economic sense) on the one hand, and those who strive for liberation, self-actualization, and personality "growth" on the other. The examples of therapy outcome considered here illustrate vividly the potential for such clashes among judgments of outcome, depending on the judge's viewpoint and values.

The issue is drawn most sharply for the mental health professional in public service (e.g., a psychiatrist working in a state mental hospital, prison psychologist, etc.). Such professionals are generally regarded as agents of society which has delegated to them the treatment and "cure" of troublesome individuals. In practice if not in theory this frequently means inducing these people to abandon their deviant ways and become productive members of society. On the other hand, the therapist in private practice may enjoy the luxury of taking a more laissez-faire attitude toward his patients' overt behavior. Nonetheless, for most therapists it may prove exceedingly difficult to separate, even in their own minds, society's values, the patient's unique personality, and the therapist's own position as both a mental health professional and a member of society.

Category 7 (B–W+S–). An individual entering therapy with deficits in all three aspects of functioning would be considered an example of a category 7 outcome if following therapy he experiences feelings of well-being, but is judged by

society to have persisting behavioral deficits, and by the
mental health professional as continuing to manifest psychopathology of varying degrees. These outcomes are typical
where therapy may have dealt with the individual's sense of
hopelessness, demoralization, diminished self-esteem, and the
like, but where changes in the behavioral realm and more
fundamental changes in character structure are conspicuous
by their absence. As noted earlier, such narrowly defined
outcomes are frequent in brief psychotherapy, supportive
psychotherapy, crisis intervention, or in any of a wide variety
of experiences, such as encounter groups, sensitivity training,
etc., in which the person experiences increments in well-being
and contentment (which are typically short-lived) but where
little else has changed.

The patients in many psychotherapy outcome studies in
which results are based solely on self-reports, such as Q-sorts
between "real" and "ideal" self, are typical instances of
apparent category 7 outcomes. In the absence of data on
behavioral observations and more penetrating psychodiagnostic studies of these patients, the question of whether
changes in behavior and psychological structure have
occurred cannot be answered; but it is precisely cases of this
kind that lead both society and mental health professionals—
albeit for different reasons—to the judgment that supportive
or brief psychotherapy is of limited utility, and that changes in
subjective well-being resulting from such therapies are
unimpressive or trivial. If the individual's well-being and
contentment are of paramount concern, improvements in this
domain may be seen as quite important; if, on the other hand,
concern for the individual's happiness is overriden by
emphasis on society's standards of performance, or standards
of adequate personality functioning, then therapeutic interventions resulting in B–W+S– outcomes are by definition
inconsequential.

Another likely intake state is the B+W–S– configuration, that is, individuals who meet their social responsibilities but feel anxious and depressed and suffer from neurotic disturbances. This is the case of the typical neurotic patient whose inhibitions and intrapsychic conflicts, coupled with profound unhappiness (often in contrast to a seemingly comfortable set of external circumstances), lead him to seek professional help. If such an individual shows the category 7 outcome (B–W+S–), he would quite likely be regarded by society as an example of a negative effect of psychotherapy, although based on his enhanced sense of well-being he would probably judge therapy to be successful.

Therapist-judged deterioration would be manifested most likely by further decompensation from an S– intake state. Such situations, coupled with an individual's experiencing a sense of contentment, are probably relatively rare in intensive psychotherapy, but might result from the patient's wish to escape therapy (in which case the sense of well-being might be self-deceptive or misleading in other respects). Other possibilities include conversion to a new "faith" (meditation, yoga, Christian Science, etc.). In contemporary society, outcomes from many experiences that the individual regards as "therapeutic" or "self-actualizing" are instances of this kind— their value clearly dependent on the extent to which they "turn him on." By contrast, both society and most mental health professionals, although for different reasons, tend to reject such experiences as trivial.

Individuals having therapy outcomes of the B–W+S– variety, regardless of their initial status, may be persons with little insight and low motivation for self-exploration and serious work on their characterological problems, such as psychopaths or court-referred criminals. Such individuals may be viewed by society as being in need of psychotherapy or behavior modification (because their performance fails to meet acceptable standards) but they are judged as poor candidates for psychotherapy by mental health professionals.

CONCLUSIONS

In summary, the tripartite model analysis of mental health and psychotherapy evaluation points to a number of significant issues with ramifications for clinical, research, and public policy decisions. Of particular note are the following:

1. The same individual may simultaneously be judged as mentally healthy or mentally ill and, correspondingly, his therapeutic experience may be judged as positive or negative depending on *who* is evaluating the patient.

2. These differences in evaluation arise from the vested interests each judge brings to the evaluative task. Acknowledging these differences does not necessarily negate the validity of evaluations made from any one perspective, but rather emphasizes the unique values inherent in each. Furthermore, by acknowledging the reality of the differences, we have highlighted those instances in which a clash of values and, thus, a conflict in evaluations of mental health and psychotherapy outcome is most likely to occur.

3. One implication of our discussion is that judgments made from a single perspective must clearly be recognized as such; accordingly, their limited usefulness must be acknowledged. Failure to consider this principle adequately in the past has had extremely unfortunate consequences, particularly in debates concerning the effectiveness of psychotherapeutic interventions. Because psychotherapy outcomes have been judged by a wide variety of criteria, the research literature as a whole remains in a seriously confused state, which precludes comprehensive statements or conclusions. Since little or no comparability across studies exist, the urgent question being pressed by the public—Does psychotherapy work?—goes

unanswered. (For present purposes we ignore problems of methodology and other deficiencies in published studies, which have received ample attention, e.g., Strupp and Bergin 1969, Paul 1967b, Fiske et al. 1970).

4. *A truly adequate, comprehensive picture of an individual's mental health is possible only if and when the three facets of the tripartite model of functioning—behavior, affect, and inferred psychological structure—are evaluated and integrated.* This conclusion has important implications for the practicing clinician. Most generally, it implies that therapy must be planned, implemented, and evaluated with full consideration for the *totality* of its impact on the patient's personal and social life. For psychotherapy researchers, this means that assessments of therapy outcomes must be comprehensive, that is, tap all three areas of functioning. Equally important, assessments must be based wherever possible on standardized, generally accepted criteria of "good functioning" in each of the three areas. (See chapter 6 for a more detailed discussion of the implications of the tripartite model.)

The present discussion is based on our assessment not only of what ought to be, but of *what is* within the field of psychotherapy and its cultural and political milieu. It is our belief that failure to implement the above principles will mean a continued proliferation of scattered pieces of knowledge which cannot be integrated into an understanding of whether psychotherapy has any effects—either for good or ill—and how these effects are achieved. This chapter also calls attention to the fact that, while researchers must play an important role in evaluating therapy outcomes, they cannot answer the question of how a particular treatment result is to be judged, including how evaluations from the three domains are to be integrated. Such decisions go beyond empirical research and involve issues of human values and public policy.

Chapter 6

Summing Up

OVERVIEW

The discovery of any treatment for man's physical or emotional ills is understandably greeted with fanfare, although later it may develop that the initial claims fall short of realistic initial expectations. It thus comes as no surprise that the evolution of modern psychotherapy, beginning with Freud's seminal insights toward the end of the last century, was focused largely on its curative or ameliorative aspects. Although from the beginning Freud was keenly aware that psychoanalysis could not be regarded as a panacea—indeed, he was exceedingly cautious in restricting its major value to the so-called transference neuroses—the view gained prominence that psychotherapy (including psychoanalysis) was generally beneficial to a great many patients and that, at worst, it might have little or no positive impact. To be sure, problems of "suitability" or "analyzability" evoked a certain amount of discussion in the clinical literature, but these tended to be overshadowed by enthusiastic reports of radical therapeutic change. Freud's thinking on the limitations of therapy, expressed perhaps most clearly in "Analysis Terminable and Interminable" (1937) was interpreted as pessimistic, related to his advancing age and personal suffering from cancer. Deficiencies in the therapist were typically equated with transient and remediable "countertransference reactions" and were generally not seen as serious impediments to therapeutic progress; in any case, it was thought, the therapist's personal analysis would largely mitigate whatever personal difficulties or idiosyncracies might get in the way of his therapeutic effectiveness. In short, it was rarely acknowledged that psychotherapy could do harm as well as good, that inherent in any potent treatment is the potential of a negative outcome. More recently, however, it has become clear that the possibility of negative effects must be entertained unless one assumes that psychotherapy is not effective under any circumstances (a position that some of its severest critics have indeed taken).

Thus, only in recent years has serious attention been paid to the problem of negative effects in psychotherapy. Bergin's critical analyses of the empirical literature, clinical reports, increasing numbers of seminars and symposia, and the initiative of the National Institute of Mental Health (which led to our own exploration), attest to a growing awareness and concern that psychotherapy may be at times actively harmful to the patient.

Any form of psychotherapy clearly presents some intervention in a person's life. It may lay bare conflicts that have previously been denied by the patient or fended off in a variety of other ways. It may foster awareness of painful affects, traumas, and patterns of interaction that a patient finds difficult to face. It may create stress, deprivation, and struggle.

In short, therapy frequently increases the patient's suffering, at least for limited periods of time.

The sensitive therapist understands and empathizes with these struggles, and takes great pains not to wound the patient's narcissism unnecessarily. He realizes that the self-esteem of most patients is deficient. Accordingly, he seeks to strengthen the patient's self-respect and self-acceptance rather than undermine it. He is particularly mindful of the fact that any interpretation has the potential of hurting the patient, simply because it frequently exposes him to unpleasant aspects of himself, undesirable ways of dealing with others, as well as other painful truths.

Since psychotherapy, particularly therapy of the "investigative" variety, is intrusive, it carries with it some potential of aggravating the patient's difficulties rather than resolving them. As already indicated, the patient's emotional vulnerability to criticism and interpersonal distress adds to these hazards. Self-awareness, in itself, can be painful. But we must also take note of additional forces which in recent years have made salient the problem of negative effects in psychotherapy, and called forceful attention to its reality and implications.

1. For a variety of reasons, psychotherapy has become accessible to a greater number and a broader spectrum of persons than ever before. Community mental health centers, many of which engage in advertising and outreach programs, have increased the availability of therapy to the public. Since tax dollars and insurance programs are funding treatment for persons of lower social class and lower incomes, psychotherapy is no longer restricted to those members of society who are socially, educationally, and financially privileged. While still not as readily available as might be desirable, psychotherapy is being offered to a growing number of persons who differ widely in their conceptions and expectations of therapy—persons who are unprepared for the role they are asked to

assume as therapy patients, which is radically different from that of a medical patient who is passively ministered to. The implications of this trend for negative effects are twofold:

First, because of the relative absence of truly innovative approaches, therapeutic techniques designed for a select segment of the population are being applied to broader groups of patients, many of whom do not possess the requisite social and verbal skills to make optimal use of what is offered.

Second, many of these "new" clients expect immediate emotional relief or behavior change which typically is not provided by traditional insight therapies or any other form of psychotherapy. Thus, the patient's and the therapist's expectations may differ drastically, with the result that the therapist may perceive "normal" progress whereas the patient may identify the absence of spectacular change after a few sessions as dismal failure (a negative effect). It follows that there exists great need to educate the patient who holds erroneous or unrealistic conceptions, to appreciate what reasonably can be expected from psychotherapy.

2. Increasing numbers of patients are entering a vastly expanding arena of therapies and quasi-therapies. Many of these innovative approaches to human problems depart sharply from the better known traditional therapies. Indeed, many of these innovative approaches capitalize upon sensationalism, promising substantial results in brief periods of time. Significant change in these therapies is often predicated upon an intense emotionally-charged experience the patient is required to undergo. It is clear, of course, that any massive assault on a person's defenses, as occurs in weekend encounter groups, marathon groups, primal therapy, Erhard seminars training, and others, heightens the potential for uncontrolled arousal of powerful affects and the possibility of decompensation or other negative effects. Because of these increased hazards one might expect that close attention had

been paid by researchers and clinicians to the study of outcomes from these therapies. This, however, has not been the case, and the few reports that are available are frequently self-serving testimonials gathered by the proponents of a particular approach rather than objective and dispassionate investigations.

Even within the province of the more traditional therapeutic approaches, there is a movement toward brief, focused, and "product oriented" interventions. Correspondingly, evaluations of outcome are focused on a narrow range of outcome criteria or changes in "target complaints" which fail to provide a more complete assessment of the impact of these confrontative, short-term therapies on the totality of the patient's life and functioning.

3. The emerging consumer advocacy movement has begun to influence the mental health field, with the result that many patients scrutinize with greater care the process and outcome of their therapy experience. In addition, consumer guides for selecting therapies and therapists, the move toward therapist-patient contracts, and lawsuits based on allegations of therapist malpractice all reflect increased consumer consciousness and thus a concern with the problem of negative effects in psychotherapy.

4. As already mentioned, the influx of "third-party" funding for psychotherapy services has led to a "product" orientation toward psychotherapy, a trend that will gain in prominence if national health insurance becomes a reality. Accordingly, the "providers" of therapeutic services are being challenged to document precisely the nature of the services they "deliver," and terms like "cost-effectiveness," "accountability," and "risk-benefit ratio," adapted from the model of medical care, are being applied to the mental health field. While some voices, including some within the field of psychology, advocate that psychotherapy should not be

treated as analogous to medical treatment and thus should not qualify for health insurance reimbursement, it is more likely that the "medical model" of disease and its cure rather than the "growth model" will prevail in psychotherapy. In any event, the emerging shift in funding patterns has rendered the objective evaluation of treatment outcomes an absolute necessity. Whereas in the 1950s such studies were the province of a small cadre of investigators whose interest in the problem was primarily scientific, we are now entering an era in which the evaluation of therapy outcomes has become a matter of great *practical* concern—to the patient-consumer, insurance companies, and the federal government.

For the reasons mentioned, psychotherapy and its outcome is no longer exclusively the private concern of patients and their therapists. In bygone days, when a patient engaged the services of a psychoanalyst for a period of years, paying for these services out of his or her own (usually substantial) financial resources, the risks as well as the benefits were the patient's own. If progress seemed slow, if another year of therapy seemed indicated, if the patient became increasingly dependent upon the therapist and his daily sessions, there were no "third parties" who took an interest in the matter. As we have shown, this picture has drastically changed in recent years, and with this change has come an emphasis on closer scrutiny of the entire psychotherapeutic enterprise. Hard questions, previously asked only by skeptical researchers, have suddenly become a matter of public concern. For example:

Who can benefit from psychotherapy? What are the effects of the patient's social class, age, sex, motivation, education, etc., upon treatment outcomes? What is the nature of the problems for which psychotherapy is prescribed? What is the nature of the change that may be expected to result from five, ten, fifteen, or a hundred therapeutic sessions? How can we measure change? Is the cost of a particular therapeutic intervention worth the price? What constitutes a qualified therapist? How can such individuals be identified and accredited? Does therapeutic change last, and if so, how long? Is one form of therapy better than another? How can one document the superiority of one form over another? What are the risks in relation to the expectable benefits? At what point does psychological distress become a "health" problem? Who is qualified to judge whether therapy outcome is "positive" or "negative"? What criteria can be used to make such judgments objective and valid?

As we have shown in this volume, practicing psychotherapists, along with researchers and theoreticians, have become increasingly conscious of the ramifications and implications of the outcome problem in psychotherapy, including the issue of potential negative effects. Patients, therapists, and "third parties" (including the federal government) are all agreed that the issue can no longer be ignored, and that in the years to come concerted effort must be brought to bear upon its study and resolution. A significant part of the answer must come from scientific research. While stepped-up research efforts are absolutely indispensable, it is also clear that, in addition, important questions of social values and public policy must be confronted.

The tripartite model elaborated in this volume is our attempt to highlight the multiple values brought to bear on therapy evaluation and to identify and systematize the varied criteria by which negative effects may be identified. We consider the model valuable for illuminating the diverse perspectives and interests of society, the patient, and the therapist. At the same time, the model demonstrates the need for *simultaneous* evaluations of all three major aspects of an individual's functioning if one is interested in a truly comprehensive assessment of therapy outcome.

As presented, the three perspectives of the tripartite model are broad. Future development of the model must include descriptions of sub-categories within each perspective. In its present form, the model demonstrates that when we ask the question, "Are there negative effects of psychotherapy, and if so, how can we identify them?" the most appropriate response must be: "It depends." It depends on what we measure, what facets of the patient's functioning we emphasize, and how we—as members of society, as patients, and as mental health professionals—choose to define a negative effect. The apparent simplicity of this conclusion should not obscure its important implications.

The broadened definition of negative effects which we, together with many experts in the area, advocate necessarily implies attention to a greater variety of causative factors. In general terms, any therapy outcome is a function of the patient, the therapist, and their relationship. Nevertheless, while some clients deteriorate or improve despite anything the therapist may do, the therapist, as the expert and as the person exerting the major influence, is rightly expected to bear the preponderant responsibility for the outcome of therapy. It follows that therapist variables are the most common source of negative effects. Such variables may include inadequate training, noxious personality characteristics, and faulty technique.

Negative effects, as our analysis suggests, are often subtle, but nonetheless pervasive. They go far beyond such obvious indicators as suicide or psychotic break. Correspondingly, the causes of negative effects are exceedingly complex. For example, a therapist who assumes an air of omniscience or omnipotence, encourages the patient to pursue goals that lie beyond his or her capability, fails to identify the patient's core problem, or fosters undue dependency on the treatment may contribute as much to a deleterious outcome as one who violates the therapeutic contract in more blatant ways. The point to be made is that thus far, despite sporadic reports in the clinical literature, very little systematic attention has been paid to the multifarious ways in which psychotherapy may be conducive to unfortunate results.

IMPLICATIONS AND RECOMMENDATIONS

Identifying negative effects and possible causes is clearly the first step toward their ultimate elimination. In the long run, methodologically sophisticated research is required to pinpoint why and how some clinical practices contribute to negative effects. Toward this end, necessary improvements in therapy outcome research are discussed at the conclusion of this chapter. In the short run, our investigation suggests a number of practical measures that should be implemented without delay.

Implications for the selection and training of therapists. Perhaps one of the best ways to forestall negative effects is to select appropriate candidates for training. While psychoanalytic training institutes have long relied on fairly rigorous screening procedures (e.g., multiple clinical interviews by senior faculty members), graduate programs of psychology as well as psychiatry have typically relied on indices of academic rather than personal qualifications. College grades or standard tests (like the Graduate Record Examination) may predict academic performance, but they provide little information on whether a student has the potential of becoming a competent psychotherapist. Programs aimed at training practitioners are becoming increasingly aware of the need to assess variables directly relevant to clinical practice.

It has long been known, of course, that the therapist's personality makes an important contribution to the quality of the therapeutic relationships he creates as well as to their outcome. While a set of salient personality characteristics has been identified (e.g., Holt and Luborsky 1958), little progress has been made toward developing highly reliable and valid assessment procedures. Personality characteristics like sadism, exploitativeness, psychopathy, and pathological narcissism are universally regarded as serious contraindications for a career in psychotherapy. On the positive side, qualities like empathy, unconditional positive regard, and genuineness have been stressed by the client-centered school. Comprehensive personality assessment of candidates tapping these as well as other more complex factors must be achieved.

Even when suitable candidates are selected for training, there remains a need for continuing vigilance during the student's training and thereafter. It is insufficient to rely exclusively on the candidate's personal therapy to eliminate shortcomings he or she may initially exhibit. (Many clinical psychology training programs, as a matter of fact, do not require students to undergo personal therapy; nor do they at any time scrutinize the student's personality attributes. See, for example, the survey by Wampler and Strupp 1976.) Training programs must potentiate therapeutically productive personality traits trainees already possess. Although it is doubtful that students can be trained to be warm and empathic, they can learn to respect the patient as a person and they can become sensitive to the crucial importance of personal qualities of the therapist in conducting psychotherapy. Furthermore, students should be sensitized to the manner in which genuine warmth and understanding are best conveyed. Above all, students must gain in appreciation that the patient-therapist relationship is at least as important for a good therapy outcome as any technique.

Extensive and careful supervision is obviously the key to sound clinical training. Supervisors must pay particular attention to the manner in which the trainee's personality manifests itself in his therapeutic interactions. If supervisors become aware that a student's personal problems or personality exert a persistently negative influence upon his therapy, the training program should reserve the right to dismiss such students or counsel them to choose alternate careers.

In sum, our best hope for decreasing the likelihood of negative effects lies in selecting the most promising candidates for training and in eliminating those about whom serious questions are raised. Clearly, it is difficult to develop stringent screening procedures and to implement them. Nonetheless, enough is known at this time, particularly concerning potentially noxious personality characteristics, to institute screening procedures for prospective candidates even as we seek to improve our understanding of the relationship between therapist's personality characteristics and therapy outcomes.

Beyond the screening of applicants for therapeutic potential, training programs can further increase trainees' awareness of these outcomes and their causes. As part of their training, students should receive adequate instruction in psychological assessment procedures. Although intensive psychological testing of prospective patients has fallen out of favor in recent years, the importance of determining the patient's status prior to therapy cannot be overestimated (see chapter 4). Students must learn to identify danger signals and areas of vulnerability such as fragile ego organization and the attendant potential for decompensation.

Psychotherapy training itself must become broad, thorough and systematic. Orthodoxy, if it ever had a place in training programs, must give way to greater flexibility and breadth. It is no longer sufficient for students to be trained in only one treatment modality, whether it is psychoanalysis or some form of behavior therapy. Students must learn to tailor therapeutic techniques to the requirements of the patient and his problems rather than forcing patients to fit a particular technique. There is no single technique which can be applied indiscriminately; above all, students must realize that a technique which may be appropriate for one patient may be highly detrimental to another. We refer the reader to our discussion of this problem in chapter 4.

The time is rapidly approaching when the foregoing points will cease to be mere recommendations and will become *requirements* for therapy training. Bergin (1976), for example, has called for stricter screening of entering students as a criterion for accreditation of clinical training programs by the Education and Training Board of the American Psychological Association.

Implications for clinical practice. The best defense against negative effects in psychotherapy is a therapist who is aware and concerned. Therapists must acknowledge frankly that some patients deteriorate as a consequence of their therapy experience; therapists therefore must be willing to continually scrutinize themselves—their personalities and their techniques—to determine how they contribute to such negative outcomes.

A competent therapist, it goes without saying, must be capable of understanding the client's perspective. The time is past when one could conveniently blame the patient for lack of therapeutic progress or exacerbations of various kinds. The term "negative therapeutic reaction" has frequently been used as an umbrella to shift responsibility from the therapist to the client, and to exonerate the former from responsibility for possible negative outcomes. If a patient voices grievances against the therapist and his techniques, it may be more than "negative transference"; indeed, the patient may be right! In any case, the occurrence of persistent dissatisfactions in the patient must be regarded as a danger signal of basic flaws in the patient-therapist relationship.

Therapists must also be aware that changes in the patient's cognitions, feelings, and behavior brought about by the therapeutic experience have repercussions for his interpersonal relations outside of therapy and his functioning as a citizen in society. Frequently, a patient who gradually extricates himself from a neurotic relationship (e.g., in a marriage) causes a serious disequilibrium in his partner. A patient's relationships with job superiors, too, may suddenly undergo change, causing new struggles and conflicts.

Because their primary obligation is to the patient's well-being (Szasz 1965), many therapists downplay or ignore altogether the social aspects of therapy-induced change. This approach is short-sighted, however; sensitivity to the social context and concern for the individual patient are not necessarily antithetical. It is precisely because of their responsibility to the patient that we urge therapists to consider the reactions of significant others and of society in general to the patient. Feedback from these sources may have a profound impact on the progress and outcome of psychotherapy.

Particularly in our more complex and interdependent society, it is clear that we short-change patients with a "let the chips fall where they may" approach to social repercussions of therapy outcome. This is not to argue that therapists should encourage only socially sanctioned changes in their patients. Rather, therapists should increase their awareness of the social repercussions of the *changes sought by the patient*, and use such awareness to facilitate the patient's recognition of and preparation for the reactions of others.

In short, the patient does not live in a vacuum, but his psychological functioning is thoroughly intertwined with the fabric of his society. This has long been known, but there are probably still too many therapists who fail to pay sufficient attention to the interests of "multiple parties" in the therapeutic process, interests highlighted by our tripartite model. This problem becomes particularly pressing when the patient's own interests clash with those of society, including significant others in his life. To deal effectively with this problem is often a considerable challenge to the therapist's ingenuity and tact, especially when the therapist himself is placed in a state of conflict as a result of the patient's struggle. We must remind ourselves that, in addition to being the patient's agent, the therapist himself is a member of society and should be mindful of its concerns.

Sensitivity to the patient's and society's perspectives also has implications for the therapist's theoretical commitments. Whether the therapist has adopted the psychoanalytic framework or leans toward behavior therapy, he is increasingly being called upon to demonstrate the relevance of theory to measurable improvements in the patient's subjective well-being, as well as in his adaptive behavior. With reference, in particular, to the problem of negative therapeutic effects, therapists must acknowledge the possibility that judgments of outcome based on a structural model of personality functioning may be at variance with the patient's sense of well-being or his social performance. This implies that, to the extent that he is concerned with the totality of the patient's functioning, the therapist must look beyond his own theoretical notions.

To identify negative effects in psychotherapy is obviously valuable; even more desirable, however, is the *prevention* of negative outcomes. Therapists can do much to forestall their occurrence through continuous monitoring of their own personalities, their approach to therapy, and their relationships with patients.

Do some patients evoke strong feelings of dislike, disgust, or anger? Such emotions in a therapist may not be sufficient in themselves to produce negative reactions in the patient. The real issue is how the therapist deals with his feelings. If he is aware and capable of controlling his emotions, therapy may proceed to a satisfactory conclusion. If, however, he is unaware of the extent of his anger—or if his anger is expressed through hostile interpretations or frontal attacks on the patient's defenses—the likelihood of a negative outcome is great (see Strupp 1960).

The conscientious therapist must also evaluate the types of relationships he maintains with his patients. A therapist who gratifies his own needs by fostering dependence, by maintaining excessively close relationships, or by unduly prolonging therapy may do considerable harm to the patient. A therapist who encourages the patient to believe that he (the therapist) is omnipotent and who then capitalizes on that belief by manipulating and exploiting him financially, emotionally, or in any other manner is directly contributing to negative effects.

Unfortunately, some of the most noxious therapist personality traits—especially outright psychopathy—may in and of themselves prevent the rigorous self-scrutiny advocated here. It is precisely such instances which necessitate the careful screening of prospective therapists described earlier.

Therapists also need to initiate and maintain close scrutiny of their technique. Implicit assumptions of various kinds may be subtle but significant contributors to therapy outcome. For example, assumptions of omnipotence foster unrealistic therapy goals which in turn set the stage for disillusionment, guilt, and self-contempt in patients. Such emotions are rightly seen as negative effects attributable to therapy when they result from the patient's failure to reach excessive and overly demanding goals posited by the therapist.

The particulars of technique must also be examined. Foremost is the question of the appropriateness of a specific approach for a given patient. Therapists must be willing to scrutinize their technique for its suitability and to respond with flexibility—to adjust the technique or its intensity—when it is clear that a mismatch has occurred. The adjustment called for may require the therapist to adapt his procedures or modify his role slightly in some cases; in more extreme situations, the patient may best be served by referral to another therapist. In any case, the necessary adjustments should be carried out in a nondefensive manner, without making the patient feel guilty for not "fitting in."

Beyond evaluating the potential for negative effects in ongoing cases, the therapist may minimize the incidence of negative effects by more carefully evaluating patients before accepting them for therapy. As many of our experts have noted, some patients are incapable of handling the stresses of intensive insight oriented therapy. Fragile patients, especially borderline cases, should not be treated with such stress-producing techniques. To avoid decompensation in borderline patients, the therapist must expend greater energy on pretherapy assessment to determine whether the patient's ego is sufficiently strong to withstand the stress of therapy.

Careful pre-therapy assessment need not be limited to questions of accepting or rejecting a patient. The therapist should also determine precisely the *patient's goals*. Does he seek extensive personality reconstruction or symptom relief? Patients who are not psychologically sophisticated and who approach therapy seeking relief from some anxiety-producing symptoms may perceive the additional anxiety aroused by exploratory techniques as a negative change.

Of course, a therapist is under no obligation to accept a patient whose goals are irreconcilably at odds with his own. Pre-therapy assessment will go far toward eliminating incidents of negative effects associated with such mismatches. Conversely, when a therapist does accept a patient, he must recognize the patient's own goals and perceptions of therapy as valid data; by the same token, when the patient labors under misapprehensions or misperceptions concerning therapy, it becomes the therapist's responsibility—and indeed an important task—to correct them. These measures may go a considerable distance in assuring better patient-therapist matches and laying the groundwork for a trusting relationship leading to the patient's satisfaction with the eventual outcome of therapy.

While the foregoing discussion has focused on the one-to-one model of individual therapy along psychoanalytic lines, it is clear that very similar problems must be confronted in other forms of psychotherapy or behavior modification as well as in group therapy.

Implications for public policy. The fact that psychotherapy may occasionally be harmful to patients has clear implications for legislators and others concerned with public policy. Public officials have a direct responsibility to insure that psychotherapy funded by tax dollars (as in public mental health centers and governmentally-operated psychiatric hospitals) is maximally beneficial—or at the very least, not harmful. "Program evaluation" and "mental health services delivery evaluation" are thus an increasingly significant part of these officials' functions.

In carrying out these evaluative responsibilities, administrators must remain alert to the possibility of negative effects and particularly, to their varied manifestations. Administrators—to a far greater degree than mental health professionals or the individual patient—must be responsive to society's values. Negative effects are most often defined by public officials by such criteria as prolonged hospitalization, job absenteeism, and similar symptoms resulting in greater cost to taxpayers. We point this up not as a charge to be defended against, but as a fact based upon administrators' responsibilities to the public which must be openly acknowledged. At the same time, it is becoming increasingly apparent that a narrow conception of "mental health" comprising solely an assessment of an individual's work performance or the absence of gross infractions of society's rules fails to do justice to that individual's subjective sense of well-being and the totality of his interpersonal functioning. Administrators should pay greater heed to a truly comprehensive assessment of an individual's adaptation, as suggested by our tripartite model. This recommendation is not merely an academic nicety but has broad implications, for example, with respect to social indicators of the nation's mental and physical health.

Consider a situation in which the therapist encourages a patient to return to work sooner than he is prepared to do. Under these circumstances the therapist's interventions result in a short-run therapeutic "success," if success is narrowly defined as an expeditious return to employment. If, however, the individual remains fearful and anxious, feels guilty, depressed, resigns his position and begins to draw welfare checks, it is obvious that his therapy experience has had negative effects. To cite another example, a child who is referred to a therapist because of a behavior problem in the classroom may as a result of therapeutic interventions become less unruly and troublesome to the teacher. His changed social performance thus might be regarded as an improvement, but he may remain unhappy and troubled. Again, a restricted focus on the child's adaptation may be grossly misleading. Examples could be multiplied many times. The lesson to be learned is that public officials must learn to take a broader view of therapy and its outcomes. This is not merely a matter of theoretical desirability, but a pragmatic necessity for an adequate performance of their responsibilities.

Beyond their specific responsibility to exercise quality control over tax-sponsored therapy, public officials must seek to protect the public from incompetent or noxious therapists through certification and licensing. Most states provide some form of certification for therapists; in many cases, however, the applicant's grade on a written examination constitutes a major criterion for certification and only rarely, if at all, is in vivo observation of therapy a part of the examination process. As noted earlier, test scores are an inadequate index of therapeutic potential and competence. The need for improved certification procedures is clear. Furthermore, there is a need, as yet largely unmet, for improved recertification procedures for therapists beyond the mere payment of an annual fee.

Certification of therapists for the public's protection is particularly crucial as applied to therapists in private practice. While trainees and practicing therapists affiliated with institutions such as hospitals and mental health centers are subject to some scrutiny by supervisors and peers, no such surveillance exists for therapists in private practice. Programs of continuing education, while laudable in their intent to remedy this deficiency, have not progressed sufficiently to protect the public against lapses in the professional's competence due to increased age, lack of professional contact, or exposure to the pertinent literature.

The absence of clear-cut criteria for acceptable levels of competence further complicates the problem. Thus, while the highest standards of professional practice are crucially important in psychotherapy, we have as yet only imperfect techniques for guaranteeing their existence and maintenance. Legislators, judges, and other public officials responsible for the evaluation of mental health services, certification of therapists, and the like, are usually laymen who must rely on mental health professionals for the guidelines on which laws, court rulings, etc. will be based. What shall be included under the designation "therapy"? What is successful or unsuccessful therapy? Who are the beneficial and who are the noxious therapists? Since the drafting of pertinent legislation will be substantially influenced by input from mental health professionals, the ultimate responsibility for more enlightened laws and policies lies within the mental health field.

Implications for the patient. Psychotherapy patients are, of course, the ones most directly involved in the experience, and they are keenly—at times, painfully—aware of its impact. By the very nature of his involvement, objectivity for the patient is impossible. He cannot evaluate dispassionately what psychotherapy is doing to his social interactions, although he may be aware that as his difficulties are confronted in therapy, new or different problems arise in relationships with spouse, children, or superiors. The patient is even less in a position to gauge changes in his psychological make-up (which may be clearly evident to the therapist). Thus, patients typically—and rightfully—evaluate the outcome of their therapy in terms of their feeling-state and their sense of well-being. While it would be desirable for the patient, like others who evaluate therapy outcomes, to assume a broader view of the changes that have been affected, it is unlikely that social or clinical considerations ever override his personal feelings or that they should do so. It is noteworthy that in previous years little attention has been paid by therapists and researchers to these "consumer" judgments (for an exception, see Strupp, Fox, and Lessler 1969, which was one of the early attempts to focus attention on the patient's own experience).

It is difficult for a patient to evaluate whether feelings of anger, frustration, or hostility toward the therapist are displaced, "hold-over" emotions from the past or if they arise from genuine grievances with deficiencies in the therapist, therapeutic mismanagement, or any of the factors identified as possible sources of negative effects. What is transference? What is reality? Moreover, many patients, particularly those whose ego resources are weak, become profoundly dependent upon the therapist and largely incapable of evaluating whether their negative emotional reactions are transient, something to be endured as therapy progresses, or whether they are legitimate responses to a noxious therapist.

It must be recognized that even the most positive therapy experience is occasionally punctuated by anxiety and emotional stress for the patient. In our effort to sensitize patients to their role in reducing negative effects, we must also educate them to accept unavoidable stress which is not indicative of therapy-induced deterioration, but an inevitable and indeed intrinsic component of psychotherapy. A sensitive therapist, needless to say, can do much to place these stresses in perspective for the patient and help him deal with them.

Perhaps the best guidelines that can be offered patients are the following:

1. Do not enter therapy with unrealistic expectations; never view it as a cure-all. Realize that therapy means hard work (not an "ego trip"), that it requires experiencing occasional stress, and that it takes time to produce results.

2. In selecting a therapist, take advantage of any information available on therapists—consumer guides, recommendations by trustworthy people, etc. Select a therapist and a therapeutic approach that is consonant with your own goals, resources, and values. Avoid therapists who fail to show common courtesy in human interactions, who are overly zealous, who make extravagant claims, and who in general lack human qualities of warmth, concern, respect, understanding, and kindness. Beware of pompousness, hostility, harshness, lack of seriousness, seductiveness, inappropriate familiarity, and "phoniness" of all kinds. Above all, make sure the therapist impresses you as a decent human being whom you can trust.

3. Insist at the outset on clarifying with the therapist your goals in therapy and the chances that they may be accomplished.

4. If during the course of therapy, you find yourself experiencing sustained, intensely negative emotions, if these negative states appear to be exacerbated by therapy sessions,

and if talking about these feelings with the therapist does not lead to their diminution, consider that the therapy itself may be a causal factor—and exercise your right to make a change.

5. Don't be discouraged from trying again. The ultimate negative effect of an unsuccessful therapy experience is a patient's total rejection of therapy as a source of help. The problems that arise in a given patient-therapist interaction may well be unique to it. Try to determine the cause of the problems that occurred (including careful self-scrutiny) and exercise care in selecting a new therapist. With adequate precautions, the chances for a successful outcome may be markedly enhanced.

Implications for research.   In general terms, the problem of negative effects of psychotherapy in this volume indicates a clear and urgent need for better research. Furthermore, it is evident that the quality of research must be improved substantially if reliable and sound data are to be obtained.

The study of negative effects in psychotherapy, as we have shown, is an integral part of the study of outcome in general. Following are specific guidelines for needed improvements in research, some pertaining to outcome research in general, others to negative outcomes in particular. (We omit from this discussion the standards of methodology and design that any good psychotherapy study must meet as these have been well presented in Fiske et al. 1970, and Paul 1967b, among others.)

1. The most comprehensive and meaningful studies of psychotherapy outcomes are those which assess outcome from the three major perspectives described in the tripartite model—the patient, society, and the therapist. Negative effects in one are of an individual's functioning may not be obvious in other areas. Thus, a true picture of therapy outcome is provided only by comprehensive assessment of the patient before and after therapy.

Furthermore, the instruments employed in assessing therapy outcome must be capable of detecting negative effects. Many clinical rating instruments, perhaps reflecting the old view that "therapy can do no harm," make no allowance for scores or ratings of negative change; others fail to discriminate between negative change and no change. Serious study of negative effects requires the development of instruments which specify precisely the *kinds* of change measured and the *amount* of change, whether positive or negative.

2. Psychotherapy research designs should provide for therapy outcome to be assessed on at least two occasions— immediately following termination and again perhaps nine to twelve months later. It is essential that these short-term and long-term outcome assessments be applied to all outcome criteria in order that researchers can determine the implications of change in one area of functioning for change in other areas. Without such assessment, a true and comprehensive picture of psychotherapy outcome is impossible.

For example, therapy may give a patient strength to terminate a hopelessly unhappy marriage. In the short run, the patient's behavior and mood may indicate that therapy was a success. If, one year later, the patient continues to feel positive about his decision, if he has developed a satisfactory new life style, the initial judgment of positive outcome would be validated. If, on the other hand, the patient is found a year later to be lonely and depressed, if he has been unprepared for and unable to cope with the consequences of his decision, the initial judgment of a positive outcome would be questionable. Had therapy evaluations been restricted to short-term changes, a very distorted picture would have resulted.

The comprehensive, long-range outcome assessment described above has both theoretical and practical advantages. Theoretically, such an approach is particularly important for therapists and researchers who subscribe to a structural theory of psychodynamics. A broad assessment approach may provide an opportunity for judging the outcome in terms of such a theory.

Consider the patient described above. From a structural perspective, the divorce would be described as a positive outcome if it represented part of a resolution of a neurotic conflict, but as a negative outcome if it represented a continuation of an oedipal conflict. Such judgments of psychological structure and functioning are often misunderstood or dismissed by empiricists and lay persons. If, however, it can be shown that they are predictive of "real" variables such as subsequent behavior, then the value and necessity of structural judgments are clear—that is, the structural judgment of negative outcome is related to subsequent unhappiness and behavioral maladjustment for the patient.

From a practical point of view, taking a longer-range view of therapy outcome is essential for enabling researchers to provide data on the relative "cost-effectiveness" of various therapies in terms of the time, money, and effort they require. It may be true, for example, that certain therapies assist clients in achieving striking behavioral change in a relatively short time, but if the changes achieved by these approaches are not sustained or if the patient is not prepared to deal with the implications and consequences of the change, the apparent superiority of these methods may be specious.

Questions of cost-effectiveness will undoubtedly become more salient as the trend toward third-party payments gains momentum. A broad and long-term perspective on psychotherapy outcome is essential to provide the answers.

3. Concerted effort should be made to collect more systematic and valid data on negative effects. Such studies may take several forms. For example, patient-therapist dyads that resulted in negative effects in major process and outcome studies of psychotherapy should be subjected to close scrutiny

in order to learn more about factors that might have been responsible for the outcome. More complete data on negative outcomes might be obtained from practicing clinicians. For ethical reasons it is, of course, impossible to design studies in which negative outcomes are expected; and it is also true that negative effects produced by irresponsible practitioners are not likely to become available for study. Nonetheless, there are sufficient instances of negative effects in the practice of many practitioners who might, for the sake of scientific inquiry and with the proper assurance of anonymity, make their data available to researchers.

4. Finally, our analysis clearly suggests that researchers must take steps to adopt measuring instruments which can be uniformly applied in many research efforts—to a variety of patients and in a variety of therapies. This is obviously a difficult recommendation to implement. It will require considerable effort and time, not to mention willingness on the part of researchers to seek out common dimensions of assessment. A beginning in this direction is the compilation of instruments by Waskow and Parloff (1975). By contrast, the prevailing practice of individual researchers developing their own measurement devices provides no basis for comparisons among studies, or for conclusions concerning the relative effectiveness of different therapies. Is there a greater potential for negative effects associated with certain approaches to therapy? Are some therapists consistently noxious? Are some patients poor risks for therapy regardless of the form of therapy or the personality of the therapist? To answer these questions, common assessment criteria across research studies are essential.

Implementation of the recommendations set forth above should go far toward providing clear and unequivocal answers concerning the effects of psychotherapy and the process by which therapeutic change is brought about. We reiterate that in the final analysis, judgments of therapy outcome—positive or negative—are based on human values. Researchers can adduce information about these changes, whether behavioral, emotional, or structural. What researchers cannot do is determine the value placed on a given change.

Whether a particular therapy outcome is judged as positive or negative clearly depends on who is making the judgment— and the nature of the judge's perspective. Researchers can supply the data, but "interested parties"—the patient, society, and the mental health professional—must make the value judgments. Because they are made from various perspectives and because divergent values are involved, agreement on whether a given outcome is positive or negative is bound to be less than perfect; at times, judgments may indeed be diametrically opposed. Thus, as this volume demonstrates, there is ultimately no single answer to questions of outcome in psychotherapy. Many previous studies of psychotherapy outcomes, in addition to other failings, have unfortunately used extremely narrow assessments made at limited points in time which are then described as representative of psychotherapy's effectiveness "in general."

The best assessment of therapy outcome is that which is most *comprehensive*, tapping the three major areas of functioning *at both immediate and longer-term follow-up*. Such assessments provide the full data base from which knowledgeable judgments can be made.

References

Agras, W. S., Chapin, H. N., and Oliveau, D. C. (1972). The natural history of phobia: course and prognosis. *Archives of General Psychiatry* 26:315-317.

Aldrich, C. K. (1975). The long and short of psychotherapy. *Psychiatric Annals* 5:52-58.

Alexander, F., and French, T. (1946). *Psychoanalytic Therapy*. New York: Ronald Press.

Aronson, H., and Weintraub, W. (1968). Patient changes during classical psychoanalyses as a function of initial status and duration of treatment. *Psychiatry* 31:369-379.

Barron, F., and Leary, T. F. (1955). Changes in psychoneurotic patients with and without psychotherapy. *Journal of Consulting Psychology* 19:239-245.

Bergin, A. E. (1963). The effects of psychotherapy: negative results revisited. *Journal of Counseling Psychology* 10:244-250.

——— (1966). Some implications of psychotherapy research for therapeutic practice. *Journal of Abnormal Psychology* 71:235-246.

——— (1970). The deterioration effect: a reply to Braucht. *Journal of Abnormal Psychology* 75:300-302.

———— (1971). The evaluation of therapeutic outcomes. In *Handbook of Psychotherapy and Behavior Change*, ed. A. E. Bergin and S. L. Garfield, pp. 217-270. New York: John Wiley and Sons.

———— (1976). Identifying the pseudoshrink. In H. Strupp (chair), *Psychonoxious Therapy: Clinical, Theoretical, and Research Perspectives*. Symposium presented at the meeting of the American Psychological Association, Washington, D.C.

Bergin, A. E., and Garfield, S. L., eds. (1971). *Handbook of Psychotherapy and Behavior Change*. New York: John Wiley and Sons.

Bergin, A. E., and Strupp, H. H. (1972). *Changing Frontiers in the Science of Psychotherapy*. Chicago: Aldine-Atherton.

Berleman, W. C., and Steinburn, T. W. (1967). The execution and evaluation of a delinquency prevention program. *Social Problems* 14:413-423.

Blackwood, G. L., Jr. (1975). Accurate empathy: critique of a construct. Unpublished manuscript, Vanderbilt University.

Braucht, G. N. (1970). The deterioration effect: a reply to Bergin. *Journal of Abnormal Psychology* 75:293-299.

Breuer, J., and Freud, S. (1893-1895). Studies on hysteria. *Standard Edition* 2.

Bruch, H. (1974). Perils of behavior modification in treatment of anorexia nervosa. *Journal of the American Medical Association* 230:1419-1422.

Butler, J. M., and Haigh, G. V. (1954). Changes in the relation between self-conceptions and ideal concepts consequent upon client-centered counseling. In *Psychotherapy and Personality Change*, ed. C. R. Rogers and R. F. Dymond, pp. 55-75. Chicago: University of Chicago Press.

Carkhuff, R. R., and Truax, C. B. (1965). Lay mental health counseling. *Journal of Consulting Psychology* 29:426-431.

Cartwright, D. S. (1956). Note on "Changes in psychoneurotic patients with and without psychotherapy." *Journal of Consulting Psychology* 20:403-404.

Cartwright, D. S., Kirtner, W. L., and Fiske, D. W. (1963). Method factors in changes associated with psychotherapy. *Journal of Abnormal and Social Psychology* 66:164-175.

Cartwright, R. D., and Vogel, J. L. (1960). A comparison of changes in psychoneurotic patients during matched periods of therapy and no therapy. *Journal of Consulting Psychology* 24:121-127.

Chinsky, J. M., and Rappaport, J. (1970). Brief critique of the meaning and reliability of "accurate empathy" ratings. *Psychological Bulletin* 73:379-380.

Cooper, C. L. (1975). How psychologically dangerous are T-groups and encounter groups? *Human Relations* 28:249-260.

Davison, G. C. (1969). Appraisal of behavior modification techniques with adults in institutional settings. In *Behavior Therapy: Appraisal and Status*, ed. C. N. Frank, pp. 220-278. New York: McGraw-Hill.

Dewald, P. A. (1964). *Psychotherapy: A Dynamic Approach*. New York: Basic Books.

DiLoreto, A. O. (1971). *Comparative Psychotherapy: An Experimental Analysis*. Chicago: Aldine-Atherton.

Endicott, N. A., and Endicott, J. (1963). "Improvement" in untreated psychiatric patients. *Archives of General Psychiatry* 9:575-585.

Fairweather, G. W., Simon, R., Gebhard, M. E., Weingarten, E., Holland, J. L., Sanders, R., Stone, G. B., and Reahl, J. E. (1960). Relative effectiveness of psychotherapeutic programs: a multi-criteria comparison of four programs for three different patient groups. *Psychology Monograph* 74(5), Whole no. 492.

Feifel, H., and Eells, J. (1963). Patients and therapists assess the same psychotherapy. *Journal of Consulting Psychology* 27:310-318.

Feifel, H., and Schwartz, A. D. (1953). Group psychotherapy with acutely disturbed psychotic patients. *Journal of Consulting Psychology* 17:113-121.

Feighner, J. P., Brown, S. L., and Olivier, J. E. (1973). Electrosleep therapy: a controlled double blind study. *Journal of Nervous and Mental Diseases* 157:121-128.

Fiske, D. W., Hunt, H. F., Luborsky, L., Orne, M. T., Parloff, M. B., Reiser, M. F., and Tuma, A. H. (1970). Planning of research on effectiveness of psychotherapy. *Archives of General Psychiatry* 22:22-32.

Frank, J. D. (1967). Does psychotherapy work? *International Journal of Psychiatry* 3:153-155.

—— (1973). *Persuasion and Healing*. Baltimore: Johns Hopkins Press.

—— (1974). Therapeutic components of psychotherapy. *Journal of Nervous and Mental Diseases* 159:325-342.

Frank, J. D., Gliedman, L. H., Imber, S. D., Stone, A. R., and Nash, E. H. (1959). Patient's expectations and relearning as factors determining improvement in psychotherapy. *American Journal of Psychiatry* 115:961-968.

Freud, S. (1910). The future prospects of psycho-analytic therapy. *Standard Edition* 11.

—— (1916-1917). Introductory lectures on psycho-analysis. *Standard Edition* 16.

—— (1933). New introductory lectures on psycho-analysis. *Standard Edition* 22.

—— (1937). Analysis terminable and interminable. *Standard Edition* 23, pp. 209-253.

Fromme, D. K., Jones, W. H., and Davis, J. O. (1974). Experiential group training with conservative populations: a potential for negative effects. *Journal of Clinical Psychology* 39:290-295.

Garfield, S. L., and Bergin, A. E. (1971). Therapeutic conditions and outcome. *Journal of Abnormal Psychology* 77:108-114.

Garfield, S. L., Bergin, A. E., and Prager, R. A. (1971). Evaluation of outcome in psychotherapy. *Journal of Consulting and Clinical Psychology* 37:307-313.

Giel, R., Knox, R. S., and Carstairs, G. M. (1964). A five-year follow-up of 100 neurotic outpatients. *British Medical Journal* 2:160-163.

Gottman, J. M. (1973). N-of-one and N-of-two research in psychotherapy. *Psychological Bulletin* 80:93-105.

Gottschalk, L. A., Mayerson, P., and Gottlieb, A. (1967). Prediction and evaluation of outcome in an emergency brief psychotherapy clinic. *Journal of Nervous and Mental Diseases* 144:77-96.

Greenson, R. R. (1967). *The Technique and Practice of Psychoanalysis*. Vol. 1. New York: International Universities Press.

Guttman, H. A. (1973). A contraindication for family therapy: the prepsychotic or postpsychotic young adult and his parents. *Archives of General Psychiatry* 29:352-355.

Harper, R. A. (1975). *The New Psychotherapies.* New Jersey: Prentice-Hall.

Hartley, D., Roback, H. B., and Abramowitz, S. I. (1976). Deterioration effects in encounter groups. *American Psychologist* 31:247-255.

Henry, W. E. (1947). The thematic apperception technique in the study of culture-personality relations. *Genetic Psychology Monographs* 35:3-135.

Henry, W. E., and Shlien, J. M. (1958). Affective complexity and psychotherapy: some comparisons of time-limited and unlimited treatment. *Journal of Projective Techniques* 22:153-162.

Hoch, P. H. (1947). *Failures in Psychiatric Treatment.* The proceedings of the 37th annual meeting of the American Psychopathological Association.

Holt, R. R., and Luborsky, L. (1958). *Personality Patterns of Psychiatrists: A Study in Selection Techniques.* Vol. 1. New York: Basic Books.

Horwitz, L. (1974). *Clinical Prediction in Psychotherapy.* New York: Jason Aronson.

Imber, S. D., Nash, E. H., Stone, A. R., Hoehn-Saric, R., and Frank, J. D. (1968). A ten-year follow-up study of treated psychiatric patients. In *An Evaluation of the Results of the Psychotherapies*, ed. S. Lesse, pp. 70-81. Springfield, Charles C Thomas.

Jahoda, M. (1958). *Current Concepts of Positive Mental Health.* New York: Basic Books.

Jonckheere, P. (1965). Considerations sur la psychotherapie. *Acta Neurologica et Psychiatrica Belgica* 65:667-684.

Jurjevich, R. M. (1968). Changes in psychiatric symptoms without psychotherapy. In *An Evaluation of the Results of the Psychotherapies*, ed. S. Lesse, pp. 190-200. Springfield: Charles C Thomas.

Kernberg, O. F., Burnstein, E. D., Coyne, L., Appelbaum, A., Horwitz, L., and Voth, H. (1972). Psychotherapy and psychoanalysis: final report of the Menninger foundation's psychotherapy research project. *Bulletin of the Menninger Clinic* 36:1-276.

Kittrie, N. N. (1971). *The Right to Be Different: Deviance and Enforced Therapy.* Baltimore: Johns Hopkins Press.

Koegler, R., and Brill, N. Q. (1967). *Treatment of Psychiatric Outpatients.* New York: Appleton-Century-Crofts.

Kringlen, E. (1965). Obsessional neurosis: a long-term follow-up. *British Journal of Psychiatry* 111:709-722.

Lambert, M. J., Bergin, A. E., and Collins, J. L. (1977). Therapist-induced deterioration in psychotherapy. In *The Therapist's Contributions to Effective Treatment: An Empirical Assessment*, ed. A. S. Gurman and A. M. Razin. New York: Pergamon.

Langfeldt, G. (1969). Schizophrenia diagnosis and prognosis. *Behavioral Science* 14:173-182.

Lieberman, M. A., Yalom, I. D., and Miles, M. B. (1973). *Encounter Groups: First Facts.* New York: Basic Books.

Ling, T. M., Purser, J. A., and Rees, E. W. (1950). Incidence and treatment of neurosis in industry. *British Medical Journal* 2:159-161.

Ling, T. M., Zausmer, D. M., and Hope, M. (1952). Occupational rehabilitation of psychiatric cases: a follow-up study of 115 cases. *American Journal of Psychiatry* 109:172-176.

Little, M. (1951). Counter-transference and the patient's response to it. *International Journal of Psycho-Analysis* 32:32-40.

Lowry, F. H. (1970). The abuse of abreaction: an unhappy legacy of Freud's cathartic method. *Canadian Psychological Association Journal* 15:557-565.

Luborsky, L., Singer, B., and Luborsky, L. (1975). Comparative studies of psychotherapies: is it true that "everybody has won and all must have prizes?" *Archives of General Psychiatry* 32:995-1008.

Ludwig, A. M., Marx, A. J., Hill, P. A., and Browning, R. M. (1969). The control of violent behavior through faradic shock. *Journal of Nervous and Mental Diseases* 148:624-637.

Malan, D. H., Bacal, H. A., Heath, E. S., and Balfour, E. H. G. (1968). A study of psychodynamic changes in untreated patients. *British Journal of Psychiatry* 114:525-551.

Marin, P. (1975). The new narcissism. *Harper's*, October, pp. 45-56.

Masserman, J. H., and Carmichael, H. T. (1938). Diagnosis and prognosis in psychiatry: with a follow-up study of the results of short-term and general hospital therapy of psychiatric cases. *Journal of Mental Science* 84:893-896.

Matarazzo, J. D. (1967). Some psychotherapists make patients worse! *International Journal of Psychiatry* 3:156-157.

May, P. R. A. (1968). *Treatment of Schizophrenia: A Comparative Study of Five Treatment Methods*. New York: Jason Aronson.

——— (1971). For better or for worse? Psychotherapy and variance change: a critical review of the literature. *Journal of Nervous and Mental Diseases* 152:184-192.

Meltzoff, J., and Kornreich, M. (1970). *Research in Psychotherapy*. New York: Atherton Press.

Mink, O. G., and Isaksen, H. L. (1959). A comparison of effectiveness of nondirective therapy and clinical counseling in the junior high school. *School Counselor* 6:12-14.

Mittelman, B. (1947). Failures in psychosomatic case treatments. In *Failures in Psychiatric Treatment*, ed. P. H. Hoch. Proceedings of the 37th annual meeting of the American Psychopathological Association, New York.

Nunnally, J. C. (1967). *Psychometric Theory*. New York: McGraw-Hill.

Orr, D. (1954). Transference and countertransference: a historical survey. *Journal of the American Psychoanalytic Association* 2:621-670.

Parloff, M. B., Kelman, H. C., and Frank, J. D. (1954). Comfort, effectiveness, and self-awareness as criteria of improvement in psychotherapy. *American Journal of Psychiatry*, November, 3:343-351.

Paul, G. L. (1966). *Insight Versus Desensitization in Psychotherapy: An Experiment in Anxiety Reduction*. Stanford: Stanford University Press.

——— (1967a). Insight versus desensitization in psychotherapy two years after termination. *Journal of Consulting Psychology* 31:333-348.

———— (1967b). Strategy in outcome research in psychotherapy. *Journal of Consulting Psychology* 31:109-118.

———— (1968). Two-year follow-up of systematic desensitization in therapy groups. *Journal of Abnormal Psychology* 73:119-130.

Powers, E., and Witmer, H. (1951). *An Experiment in the Prevention of Delinquency*. New York: Columbia University Press.

Quality psychiatric care vs. political realities. *Behavior Today* 7, no. 26 (June 1976).

Rapaport, D. (1960). The structure of psychoanalytic theory: a systematizing attempt. *Psychological Issues* 2, no. 2 (Monograph 6).

Rappaport, J., and Chinsky, J. M. (1972). Accurate empathy: confusion of a construct. *Psychological Bulletin* 77:400-404.

Ricks, D. F. (1974). Supershrink: methods of a therapist judged successful on the basis of adult outcomes of adolescent patients. In *Life History Research in Psychopathology*, Vol. 3, ed. D. Ricks, M. Roff, and A. Thomas, pp. 275-297. Minneapolis: University of Minnesota Press.

Rogers, C. R. (1951). *Client-Centered Therapy*. Cambridge, Massachusetts: Houghton Mifflin.

Rogers, C., and Dymond, R. F. (1954). *Psychotherapy and Personality Change*. Chicago: University of Chicago Press.

Rogers, C., Gendlin, E. T., Kiesler, D., and Truax, C. B. (1967). *The Therapeutic Relationship and Its Impact: A Study of Psychotherapy with Schizophrenics*. Madison: University of Wisconsin Press.

Rosenbaum, M., Friedlander, J., and Kaplan, S. M. (1956). Evaluation of results of psychotherapy. *Psychosomatic Medicine* 18:113-132.

Rosenthal, D. (1955). Changes in moral values following psychotherapy. *Journal of Consulting Psychology* 19:431-436.

Sacks, J. M., and Berger, S. (1954). Group therapy techniques with hospitalized chronic schizophrenic patients. *Journal of Consulting Psychology* 18:297-302.

Sager, C. J., Riess, B. F., and Gundlach, R. (1964). Follow-up study of the results of extramural analytic psychotherapy. *American Journal of Psychotherapy* 18:161-173.

Saslow, G., and Peters, A. (1956). Follow-up of 'untreated' patients with behavior disorders. *Psychiatric Quarterly* 30:283-302.

Schofield, W. (1964). *Psychotherapy: The Purchase of Friendship*. New Jersey: Prentice-Hall.

Sloane, R. B., Staples, F. R., Cristol, A. H., Yorkston, N. J., and Whipple, K. (1975a). *Psychotherapy Versus Behavior Therapy*. Cambridge: Harvard University Press.

———— (1975b). Short-term analytically oriented psychotherapy versus behavior therapy. *American Journal of Psychiatry* 132:373-377.

Stone, L. (1954). The widening scope of indications for psychoanalysis. *Journal of the American Psychoanalytic Association* 2:567-594.

Strupp, H. H. (1960). *Psychotherapists in Action*. New York: Grune and Stratton.

———— (1973). *Psychotherapy: Clinical, Research, and Theoretical •Issues*. New York: Jason Aronson.

Strupp, H. H., and Bergin, A. E. (1969). Some empirical and conceptual bases for coordinated research in psychotherapy. *International Journal of Psychiatry* 7:18-90.

Strupp, H. H., Fox, R. E., and Lessler, K. (1969). *Patients View Their Psychotherapy*. Baltimore: Johns Hopkins Press.

Strupp, H. H., Wallach, M. S., and Wogan, M. (1964). Psychotherapy experience in retrospect: questionnaire survey of former patients and their therapists. *Psychology Monographs* 78(11), Whole no. 588.

Stuart, R. B., and Lott, L. A. (1972). Behavioral contracting with delinquents: a cautionary note. *Journal of Behavior Therapy and Experimental Psychiatry* 3:161-169.

Subotnik, L. (1972). "Spontaneous remission" of deviant MMPI profiles among college students. *Journal of Consulting and Clinical Psychology* 38:191-201.

Szasz, T. S. (1961). *The Myth of Mental Illness: Foundations of a Theory of Personal Conduct*. New York: Hoeber-Harper.

———— (1965). *The Ethics of Psychoanalysis: The Theory and Method of Autonomous Psychotherapy*. New York: Basic Books.

————(1970). *The Manufacture of Madness: A Comparative Study of the Inquisition and the Mental Health Movement*. New York: Harper and Row.

Tinsley, H. E. A., and Weiss, D. J. (1975). Interrater reliability and agreement of subjective judgments. *Journal of Counseling Psychology* 22:358-376.

Truax, C. B. (1963). Effective ingredients in psychotherapy. *Journal of Consulting Psychology* 10:256-263.

———— (1967). Research findings: translations and premature translation into practice. *International Journal of Psychiatry* 3:158-160.

Truax, C. B., Wargo, D. G., Frank, J. D., Imber, S. D., Battle, C. C. Hoehn-Saric, R., Nash, E. H., and Stone, A. R. (1966). Therapist empathy, genuineness, and warmth and patient outcome. *Journal of Consulting Psychology* 30:395-401.

Uhlenhuth, E. H., and Duncan, D. B. (1968). Subjective change in psychoneurotic outpatients with medical students: I. The kind, amount, and course of change. Unpublished manuscript, Johns Hopkins University.

Varble, D. L., and Landfield, A. W. (1969). Validity of the self-ideal discrepancy as a criterion measure for success in psychotherapy—a replication. *Journal of Counseling Psychology* 16:150-156.

Volsky, T., Jr., Magoon, T. M., Norman, W. T., and Hoyt, D. P. (1965). *The Outcomes of Counseling and Psychotherapy*. Minneapolis: University of Minnesota Press.

Wampler, L. D., and Strupp, H. H. (1976). Personal therapy for students in clinical psychology: a matter of faith? *Professional Psychology* (May):195-201.

Warne, M. M., Canter, A. H., and Wiznia, B. (1953). Analysis and follow-up of patients with psychiatric disorders. *American Journal of Psychotherapy* 7:278-288.

Waskow, I. E., and Parloff, M. B., eds. (1975). *Psychotherapy Change Measures*. Rockville, Maryland: National Institute of Mental Health.

Weber, J. J., Elinson, J., and Moss, L. M. (1965). The application of ego-strength scales to psychoanalytic clinic records. In *Developments in Psychoanalysis at Columbia University. Proceedings of the 20th Anniversary Conference*, ed. G. S. Goldman and D. Shapiro, pp. 215-273. New York: Columbia Psychology Clinic for Training and Research.

Wispé, L. G., and Parloff, M. B. (1965). Impact of psychotherapy on the productivity of psychologists. *Journal of Abnormal Psychology* 70:188-193.

Appendix A
Studies Cited
as Evidence of Negative Effects

Aronson and Weintraub, 1968

Description of sample:
Nonrandomly selected analysands, 69 character disorders, 42 neurotic, 15 borderline psychotic
Experimental group: 126
No control group

Therapists:
28 psychoanalysts (members of the American Psychoanalytic Association or candidates in psychoanalytic training), experience not stated

Type of Therapy:
Psychoanalysis of analytically oriented therapy (not clearly stated for borderlines)

Duration of therapy:
28: less than 1 year
48: 1-2 years
32: 3-4 years
17: 5 or more years

Negative effects

Frequency	Criteria
1% (1 of 126)	Vocational worsening rating
2% (2 of 126)	Symptomatic worsening rating
3% (4 of 126)	Object relations worsening rating
1% (1 of 126)	Pleasure capacity worsening rating

Negative effects attributed to:
Data indicated greatest incidence of negative change among borderline patients, particularly those who terminated prematurely

Shortcomings in the research:
1. No control group
2. Questionable reliability of outcome criteria

Barron and Leary, 1955
(reinterpreted in Cartwright, 1956)

Description of sample:
  Neurotic outpatients
  Experimental group: 127
  Control group: 23

Therapists:
  Unstated number of psychiatrists, social workers, and psychologists, all with 3 or more years postdoctoral experience

Type of therapy:
  Experimental group: brief, ego-oriented therapy, 42 individual, 85 group
  Control group: none, on waiting list for above

Duration of therapy:
  Experimental group: 1 session per week, minimum 3 months, average 8 months
  Control group: waiting list, average 7 months

Frequency of negative effects:
  Greater change score variance for individual therapy group than for controls

Criteria of negative effects:
  MMPI scales F, Hs, D, Pt, Sc, and Es

Negative effects attributed to:
  Not discussed

Shortcomings in the research:
  1. Inadequate information on therapists
  2. Inaccuracy of "greater variance" interpretation

Berleman and Steinburn, 1967

Description of sample:
Seventh grade black male children with evidence of acting out behavior
Experimental group: 21
Control group: 26

Therapists:
3 social workers, "more experienced" than other social workers at the agency

Type of therapy:
Experimental group: group meetings, family social services
Control group: untreated

Duration of therapy:
One 2½-hour group meeting per week for 5 months, 75 hours median length of social service to the boy and his family

Frequency of negative effects:
At 4-month follow-up: treated were "worse" than controls
At 6-month follow-up: treated were "worse" than controls

Criteria of negative effects:
1. School disciplinary record
2. Percentage with school disciplinary record
3. Average score per boy with disciplinary record

Negative effects attributed to:
Not discussed

Shortcomings in the research:
1. Treatment could not be considered psychotherapy
2. Inappropriate control group
3. Relapsed and deteriorated cannot be distinguished

Carkhuff and Truax, 1965

Description of sample:
Older (average 50 years) chronic schizophrenic hospitalized patients not expected to be discharged within 3 months
Experimental group: 74
Control group: 70

Therapists:
5 lay volunteers given 100 hours of training in "therapeutic conditions," no experience

Type of therapy:
Experimental group: client-centered group therapy
Control group: milieu treatment

Duration of therapy:
Experimental group: twice a week, 24 sessions over a 3-month period

Negative effects

Frequency		Criteria
(experimental)	(control)	(ward staff ratings of deterioration in:)
1% (1 of 74)	17% (12 of 70)	Overall functioning
26% (19 of 74)	10% (5 of 50)	Psychological disturbances
19% (14 of 74)	4% (2 of 50)	Interpersonal concerns
22% (16 of 74)	8% (4 of 50)	Intrapersonal concerns

Negative effects attributed to:
Not discussed

Shortcomings in the research:
1. Inexperienced therapists
2. Psychotic patients
3. Bias in the patient sample
4. Probably confounded treatment
5. Questionable reliability of outcome criteria

Cartwright and Vogel, 1960

Description of the sample:
Applicants to university counseling center, average age 27
Experimental group: 22
Control group: 22 (patients served as their own controls)

Therapists:
10 "experienced" psychologists, 6 or more previous cases, mean of 26
9 "inexperienced" psychologists, less than 6 cases, mean of 1

Type of therapy:
Client-centered psychotherapy

Duration of therapy:
Experimental group: mean of 33.4 hours, range of 6-97 hours
Control group: waiting list, mean waiting time 8 weeks, range of waiting time 3-24 weeks

Negative effects

Frequency	Criteria
Experienced: 50% (6 of 12) Inexperienced: 30% (3 of 10)	Q-score: no change or worse
Experienced: 33% (4 of 12) Inexperienced: 90% (9 of 10)	TAT score: no change or worse

Negative effects attributed to:
Authors suggested inexperienced therapists may have deleterious effect

Shortcomings in the research:
1. Bias in the patient sample
2. Unchanged and worse categories not differentiated
3. Questionable reliability of outcome criteria

DiLoreto, 1971

Description of sample:
600 volunteers from an introductory psychology class: 196 meeting criteria for inclusion, 100 randomly selected from among these
Experimental group: 60
Control group: 40

Therapists:
6 psychologists, advanced graduate students in final stages of doctoral program

Type of therapy:
Experimental group: (1) 20 systematic desensitization—SD, (2) 20 rational emotive—RE, (3) 20 client-centered—CC
Control group: (1) 20 placebo group controls—NPC, (2) 20 no-contact controls—NCC

Duration of therapy:
Experimental group: 10 weeks, one 1-hour group meeting per week

Negative effects

Frequency (experimental)	(control)	Criteria (small mean negative changes, not necessarily significant, on:)
	NCC	Multivariate assessment of interpersonal anxiety
	NCC	Trait anxiety
RE, CC	NCC	Self-report of defensiveness

Negative effects attributed to:
Not discussed

Shortcomings in the research:
1. Inexperienced therapists
2. Subjects were not genuine patients

Fairweather, Simon, Gebhard et al., 1960

Description of sample:
  32 nonpsychotics, 32 short-term psychotics, 32 long-term psychotics (equal distribution by diagnosis among conditions)
  Experimental: 72
  Control: 24

Therapists:
  7 psychologists with 2-5 years experience
  1 psychiatrist with 6 years experience
  8 residents and psychology interns

Type of therapy:
  Experimental: analytically oriented, some drugs in all treatment types; (1) individual, (2) group (3) group living and group therapy
  Control: work assignment in hospital and planning for post-hospitalization living

Duration of therapy:
  114-day mean treatment for all patients
  (1) 2-4 sessions per week, (2) two 1½-hour sessions per week
  (3) two 1½-hour sessions per week

Negative effects

Frequency	*Criteria*
Greater criteria variability within experimental group	MMPI, ward behavior ratings, vocational interest inventory, TAT, Q-sort
11% (11 of 96)	Treatment team's judgment of no progress or decrement in general adjustment after 6 months of treatment

Negative effects attributed to:
  Authors suggested long-term psychotics may get worse when subjected to intense interpersonal situations

Shortcomings in the research:
  1. Confounded treatment
  2. Results from trainees and experienced therapists combined
  3. Psychotic patients
  4. Bias in the patient sample
  5. Questionable validity of outcome criterion (Q-sort)
  6. Inaccuracy of greater variance interpretation

Feifel and Eells, 1963

Description of sample:
　Veterans at a VA hospital in a 4-year follow-up study
　Experimental group: 63
　No control group

Therapists:
　12 psychologists
　12 psychiatrists
　 4 social workers

　One third residents or interns, two thirds staff members with at
　　least 4 years experience

Type of therapy:
　Individual therapy, predominantly analytically oriented

Duration of therapy:
　Range, 10–324 sessions

Frequency of negative effects:
　8%

Criterion of negative effects:
　Therapist's global rating: unchanged or worse

Negative effects attributed to:
　In general, patients reported therapists' feelings of anger,
　　irritation, and boredom and frequent changes of therapist were
　　"nonhelpful" or "set them back"

Shortcomings in the research:
　　1. Results from trainees and experienced therapists combined
　　2. Bias in the patient sample
　　3. No control group
　　4. Unchanged and worse categories not differentiated

Feighner, Brown and Olivier, 1973

Description of sample:
 Chronically ill patients with primary symptoms of anxiety, insomnia, and/or depression of more than 2 years' duration
 Experimental group: 23
 Control group: 23 (patients served as their own controls)

Therapists:
 Unstated number of staff psychiatrists, experience unspecified

Type of therapy:
 Experimental group: electrosleep therapy, concurrent psycho-tropic drug therapy
 Control group: "sham treatment"

Duration of therapy:
 Experimental group: 10 sessions
 Control group: 10 sessions

Negative effects

Frequency	Criteria
17% (4 of 23)	Researchers' judgment of "massive worsening" of depressive symptoms

(at 1-month follow-up)

88% (7 of 8)	Relapse of "improved patients" on global rating of improvement

Negative effects attributed to:
 Authors suggested that technique was inappropriate for patients with a diagnosis of primary depression

Shortcomings in the research:
 1. Treatment could not be considered psychotherapy
 2. Questionable reliability of outcome criteria

Garfield and Bergin, 1971
(also reported in Garfield, Prager, and Bergin, 1971a, b)

Description of sample:
  Neurotic patients applying to outpatient clinic
  Experimental group: 38 seen, data analyzed for 31
  No control group

Therapists:
  21 psychologists, advanced graduate students with an average of
    434 hours of individual therapy experience

Type of therapy:
  Therapist self-report:
    10 eclectic
    7 eclectic-analytic
    2 eclectic, client-centered
    2 no response

Duration of therapy:
  Mean of 18 sessions

Negative effects

Frequency	*Criteria*
6% (2 of 35)	Patient self-rating: "somewhat worse"
3% (1 of 38)	Therapist rating: "somewhat worse"
3% (1 of 38)	Supervisor rating: "somewhat worse"

Negative effects attributed to:
  Not discussed—however, contrary to hypothesis, warmth,
    empathy, and genuineness were not related to outcome

Shortcomings in the research:
  1. Inexperienced therapists
  2. No control group

Gottschalk, Mayerson, and Gottlieb, 1967

Description of sample:
Emergency clinic outpatients with acute and severe symptoms,
higher proportion of psychotics than in usual clinic population
Experimental group: 36
Control group: 17

Therapists:
3 psychiatric residents

Type of therapy:
Experimental group: brief crisis intervention, some drugs
Control group: untreated (drop-outs)

Duration of therapy:
6 sessions 25-50 minutes long, 1 per week

Negative effects

Frequency		*Criteria*
(experimental)	(control)	

pretherapy to termination — Changes in negative direction
6% (2 of 34)   29% (4 of 14) — on Psychiatric Morbidity
Scale, a multifaceted
pretherapy to follow-up — rating of outcome
3% (1 of 31)   20% (2 of 10)

termination to follow-up
26% (8 of 31)   20% (2 of 10)

Negative effects attributed to:
Data indicated high initial malfunctioning was best predictor of
poor therapeutic outcome

Shortcomings in the research:
1. Very brief therapy
2. Inexperienced therapists
3. Heterogeneous patient population
4. Inappropriate control group
5. Confounded treatments

Henry and Shlien, 1958

Description of sample:
  Applicants to university counseling center
  Experimental group: 40
  No control group

Therapists:
  No information reported

| Therapy | | Frequency of |
Type	Duration	negative effects
26 time unlimited	Mean of 37 sessions	0%
14 time limited	Twice-weekly sessions, maximum 20 sessions, mean of 18	80%

Criterion of negative effects:
  TAT ratings of affective complexity, decreases in complexity at
  follow-up relative to pretreatment or termination ratings

Negative effects attributed to:
  Authors suggested time limited therapy does not allow "re-
  emergence of affect and increased utilization of unblocked
  inner feelings"

Shortcomings in the research:
  1. Inadequate information on therapists
  2. Questionable reliability and validity of outcome criteria
  3. Relapsed and deteriorated cannot be distinguished

Horwitz, 1974
(see also Kernberg, Burstein, Coyne et al., 1972)

Description of sample:
Selected patients at Menninger, mixed neurotic and borderline psychotic
Experimental: 42
No control group

Therapists:
Unstated number of psychoanalysts, experience unspecified

Type of therapy:
Psychoanalysis, "expressive" and "supportive" psychotherapy

Duration of therapy:
Not stated

Negative effects

Frequency	*Criteria*
45% (10 of 22)	"Unanalyzable" (not necessarily evidencing negative changes)
14% (6 of 42)	Global ratings of absolute change: "worse"

Negative effects attributed to:
Mechanisms said to account for "unanalyzability":
1. Borderline personality organization
2. "Oral conflicts"
3. Passive dependency
4. Countertransference error bringing about failure to resolve a "core conflict"
5. Inability of treatment to arrest illness in course
6. Influence of variables outside the treatment situation

Shortcomings in the research:
1. Inadequate information on therapists
2. No control group
3. Sole reliance on a global outcome criterion

Imber, Nash, Hoehn-Saric et al., 1968

Description of sample:
  White outpatient neurotics—a 10-year follow-up, this is 64% of
    those initially studied
  Experimental group: 34
  No control group

Therapists:
  3 second-year psychiatric residents

Therapy

Type	*Duration*
Individual	1 hour per week
Group	1-1/2 hours per week
Minimal contact	1/2 hour every two weeks
	(minimum 1 month, most more than four months)

Frequency of negative effects:
  41% (14 of 34)

Criterion of negative effects:
  Patient's global self-rating: "same or worse"

Negative effects attributed to:
  Authors suggested unimproved patients were unable to
    introspect and communicate effectively in therapy

Shortcomings in the research:
  1. Inexperienced therapists
  2. Bias in the patient sample
  3. Unchanged and worse categories not differentiated
  4. Relapsed and deteriorated cannot be distinguished

Jonckheere, 1965

Description of sample:
Neurotics, trait disturbance patients, some psychotics
Experimental group: 72
No control group

Therapists:
Unstated number of analytically oriented therapists, experience unspecified

Type of therapy:
Individual, eclectic with emphasis on Freudian theory, also drugs

Duration of therapy:
For most, 4-12 sessions

Frequency of negative effects:
9%

Criterion of negative effects:
Global judgments (probably therapists') of change in negative direction, pre- to post therapy

Negative effects attributed to:
Negative changes more frequent among phobic-obsessionals, anxiety-neurotics, and character disorders than among depressed, hysterical, or psychosomatic patients

Shortcomings in the research:
1. Inadequate information on therapists
2. No control group
3. Confounded treatment
4. Sole reliance on global outcome criterion

Koegler and Brill, 1967
(brief therapy)

Description of sample:
Outpatient adults, 23% psychotic
Experimental group: 162
No control group

Therapists:
Unstated number of psychiatric residents

Type of therapy:
Brief contact therapy, substantial use of drugs

Duration of therapy:
60% had fewer than 10 sessions, usually weekly, 15-60 minutes in length

Frequency of negative effects:
3% (5 of 162)

Criterion of negative effects:
Therapists' global ratings: "worse"

Negative effects attributed to:
Not discussed

Shortcomings in the research:
   1. Inexperienced therapists
   2. Inadequate information on therapists
   3. Heterogeneous patient population
   4. No control group
   5. Confounded treatment
   6. Sole reliance on global outcome criterion

Koegler and Brill, 1967
(long-term)

Description of sample:
Female patients, no psychotics or severely depressed
Experimental group: 27 psychotherapy, 86 drug-treated
Control group: 17 waiting list, 30 placebo drug

Therapists:
29-37 psychiatric residents

Therapy		Frequency	
Type	*Duration*	*Experimental*	*Control*
Individual psychotherapy	1 session per week, average 7-12 months	3%	
Drug interviews	1-4 times per month, 15-30 minutes, average 5.5 months	12-21%	
Control placebo drug			24%
Control waiting list			unstated

Criterion of negative effects:
Patients' self-reports that they had not been helped by treatment

Negative effects attributed to:
Not discussed

Shortcomings in the research:
1. Inexperienced therapists
2. Inadequate information on therapists
3. Unchanged and worse categories not differentiated

Kringlen, 1965

Description of sample:
A 13-20 year follow-up of 122 hospitalized Norwegians (psychotic, phobic, and obsessional)
Experimental group: 91
No control group

Therapists:
No information reported

Type of therapy:
60 of 91 received ECT and sometimes "supportive psychotherapy"; during follow-up 7 of 91 received psychotherapy

Duration of therapy:
2.1 months hospitalization

Frequency of negative effects:
At discharge: 5% (5 of 91)
At follow-up: 7% (6 of 91)

Criterion of negative effects:
Clinician's rating "worse state of adaptation"

Negative effects attributed to:
Author suggested "obsessive premorbid personality and severe clinical picture" at admission give less favorable prognosis

Shortcomings in the research:
1. Confounded treatments
2. Inadequate information on therapists
3. Bias in the patient sample
4. No control group
5. Sole reliance on a global outcome criterion

Lieberman, Yalom, and Miles, 1973

Description of sample:
  Students at Stanford University recruited by mail and public announcement to participate in encounter groups for academic credit
  Experimental group: 210
  Control group: 38 could not be scheduled for groups, 31 were nominated by friends as likely candidates for groups

Therapists:
  16, primarily psychologists and psychiatrists representing "widely used" group techniques, all "highly experienced" and peer-nominated

Type of therapy:

1. NTL	6. Synanon
2. Gestalt	7. Psychodrama
3. TA	8. Marathon
4. Esalen	9. Psychodynamically oriented
5. Personal growth	10. Leaderless tape groups

Duration of therapy
  Maximum 30 hours in varied format

Negative effects

Frequency		Criteria
(experimental)	(control)	
8% (16 of 206)		Casualties: "as a direct result of . . . experience in the encounter group became more psychologically distressed and/or employed more maladaptive mechanisms of defense"
8% (17 of 206)	23% (16 of 69)	Negative changers: "experienced downward shifts on three or more signs on the change indicators" not necessarily attributable to the group experience

Negative effects attributed to:
Authors suggested that these variables contributed to the development of casualties:
1. "Attack" (10 of 16)
2. Rejection (6 of 16)
3. Failure to achieve unrealistic goals (4 of 16)
4. Coercive expectations (2 of 16)
5. Input overload, "value shuffle" (3 of 16, all three experienced psychotic episodes)

Shortcomings in the research:
1. Treatment could not be considered psychotherapy
2. Subjects were not genuine patients
3. Inappropriate control group

Ling, Zausmer, and Hope, 1950, 1952

Description of the sample:
Inpatient neurotics with serious occupational problems but "who appear to have fundamentally good personalities"
Experimental group: 100
No control group

Therapists:
No information reported

Type of therapy:
"Purposefully superficial" eclectic therapy, some ECT, some insulin shock, some sedatives

Duration of therapy:
6-8 weeks during hospitalization

Frequency of negative effects:
18% (18 of 100)

Criterion of negative effects:
Global judgment of "worse health" made 2 years after treatment

Negative effects attributed to:
Not discussed

Shortcomings in the research:
1. Confounded treatment
2. Relapsed and deteriorated cannot be distinguished
3. Questionable reliability and validity of outcome criterion
4. Sole reliance on global outcome criterion
5. Inadequate information on therapists

Masserman and Carmichael, 1938

Description of sample:
Heterogeneous inpatient population, 54% psychotic
Experimental group: 114
No control group

Therapists:
No information reported

Type of therapy:
Variety of treatments, including narcosis, hypnosis, hydrotherapy, medical and surgical procedures, "superficial psychotherapy," and "rest cure"

Duration of treatment:
Average 25 inpatient days, range 1-244 days

Negative effects

Frequency	Criteria
4% (5 of 114)	Exacerbation of somatic or mental symptoms
(at 1-year follow-up)	
2% (2 of 100)	Suicided in the interval following treatment; both had refused further treatment
14% (14 of 100)	"Worse" somatic symptoms
17% (17 of 100)	"Worse" mental symptoms
12% (12 of 100)	"Worse general status"
7% (6 of 85)	Developed further delusions or somatic symptoms as a result of attempts at therapy

Negative effects attributed to:
Not discussed

Shortcomings in the research:
1. Confounded treatment
2. Inadequate information on therapists
3. Psychotic patients
4. No control group
5. Sole reliance on global outcome criteria

Mink and Isaksen, 1959

Description of sample:
Junior high school students who reported concerns about making mistakes on Mooney Problem Checklist (students "sent for" counseling, not self-referred)
Experimental group: 48
Control group: 48

Therapists:
1 graduate student, 1 school counselor, experience of neither stated

Type of therapy:
Experimental group: 24 nondirective counseling, 24 "clinical" counseling
Control group: untreated

Duration of therapy:
4 months, number of sessions unknown

Frequency of negative effects:
Greater change score variance for clinical counseling group than for control group

Criterion of negative effects:
California Test of Personality

Negative effects attributed to:
Authors suggested short-term counseling may agitate the problems of some students, causing temporary regression in social adjustment

Shortcomings in the research:
1. Treatment inadequately specified
2. Inadequate information on therapists
3. Subjects were not genuine psychotherapy patients
4. Inaccuracy of greater variance interpretation

Paul, 1967
(individual)

Description of sample:
Motivated volunteers in a public speaking class at college
Experimental group: 30
Control group: 15 attention placebo, 44 matched untreated

Therapists:
5 clinical and counseling psychologists with 6-18 years experience

Type of therapy:
Experimental group: 15 insight therapy, 15 desensitization therapy
Control group: attention placebo controls given placebo tranquilizer and supposedly anxiety-producing task which in reality was sleep-inducing; silent controls untreated

Duration of therapy:
Experimental group: five 50-minute sessions over 6-week period

Frequency of negative effects:
Insight therapy: 4%
Attention placebo controls: 5%
Silent controls: 8%

Criterion of negative effects:
Patient report of no benefit from therapy

Negative effects attributed to:
Patient's uncertainty about therapist's feelings, lack of therapist warmth, and believing that the therapist did not understand the patient's feelings—all were negatively related to therapeutic change as reported by the patient

Shortcomings in the research:
1. Very brief therapy
2. Subjects were not genuine patients
3. Relapsed and deteriorated cannot be distinguished

Paul, 1968
(group)

Description of sample:
Student volunteers with long-standing (2-20 years) performance anxiety
Experimental group: 30
Control group: 10 attention placebo, 32 matched untreated

Therapists:
2 "experienced" psychologists, 5 "experienced" client-centered and neofreudian psychologists

Therapy

Type	Duration
experimental:	
10 group desensitization	9 sessions over 9 weeks
10 individual desensitization	5 sessions over 6 weeks
10 individual insight therapy	5 hours over 6 weeks
control:	
Attention placebo controls given placebo tranquilizer and supposedly anxiety-producing task which in reality was sleep-inducing; silent controls untreated	

Negative effects

Frequency		Criteria
(experimental)	(control)	
Group desensiti-zation 4%	Attention placebo 8%	Significant negative change, pretherapy to follow up, on any
Insight ther-apy 2%	Silent controls 7%	of 6 scales tapping emotionali-ty, anxiety, and extroversion
Insight ther-apy 13%	Attention placebo 10%	SR exam of speech anxiety

Negative effects attributed to:
Not discussed

Shortcomings in the research:
1. Very brief therapy (individual)
2. Subjects were not genuine patients
3. Relapsed and deteriorated cannot be distinguished

Powers and Witmer, 1951

Description of sample:
    Predelinquent boys, age 6-12, median age 10-1/2
    Experimental group: 254
    Control group: 254
    Matched sets of patients available at termination: 148; at follow-up: 91

Therapists:
    8 professional social workers
    6 with some social work training
    2 psychologists
    1 nurse
    2 "experienced boys' workers"

Type of therapy:
    Experimental group: friendship and supportive social services, social casework
    Control group: untreated, tested at points during program

Duration of therapy:
    Up to 6 years, but variable duration and frequency of contact, average of about 30 "contacts" per year per client

Negative effects

Frequency	*Criteria*
Greater criterion variability within experimental group	Researchers' ratings of adjustment
9% (24 of 254)	Worse adjustment
3% (8 of 254)	Researchers' judgment of "harmed by treatment"

Negative effects attributed to:
    Authors suggested "harm" may have been caused by breaking off contact after a close relationship had been established and by using the relationship in a way that was psychologically unsound (e.g., overindulgence of acting-out behavior)

Shortcomings in the research:
1. Treatment could not be considered psychotherapy
2. Inexperienced therapists
3. Bias in the patient sample
4. Questionable reliability of outcome criteria
5. Inaccuracy of greater variance interpretation

Ricks, 1974

Description of sample:
   From the files of a major child guidance center, the childhood records of 196 adult schizophrenics and a demographically matched sample of 196 nonschizophrenics was drawn; subsamples of patients seen by therapists A and B were extracted from the larger group of 392
   Experimental group: 15 seen by A, 13 seen by B
   No control group

Therapists:
   2 therapists, training unspecified, both with a large number of patients, more than other therapists at the center

Type of therapy:
   Dynamically oriented therapy

Duration of therapy:
   Therapist A: average of 25 hours
   Therapist B: average of 16 hours

Negative effects

Frequency	*Criteria*
	(adult outcomes, derived from hospital records and telephone follow-up)
Therapist A 0% (0 of 15) Therapist B 23% (3 of 13)	Chronic schizophrenia
Therapist A 27% (4 of 15) Therapist B 62% (8 of 13)	One or more episodes of schizophrenia, followed by release from hospital

Negative effects attributed to:
Authors suggested that the following therapist variables contributed to poor adult outcomes:
1. Misallocation of effort to the less ill
2. Overloading tenuous therapeutic relationships with depressive and anxiety-laden material
3. Failure to utilize resources outside the immediate therapy situation, e.g., foster homes, summer camps
4. Failure to coordinate or direct parental response to change in child
5. Failure to unlock parent-child symbiotic impasses
6. Failure to anchor therapy in reality situations, failure to focus therapy hours on real-life problems, overindulgence in intrapsychic pathology
7. Failure to promote mastery and competence of the child in real-life situations, failure to resolve role and identity confusions with adolescents

Shortcomings in the research:
1. Bias in the patient sample
2. No control group

Rogers and Dymond, 1954
(includes Butler and Haigh, 1954)

Description of sample:
  Experimental group: 29 applicants to a university counseling center, mostly mildly neurotic, 16 students, 13 from surrounding community
  Control group: approximately half the experimental subjects served also as "wait list" controls prior to receiving therapy; an additional group of 23, termed "equivalent controls," were demographically similar "normal" volunteers

Therapists:
  Psychologists, all with a minimum of 1 year's experience or 341 interviews, 7 with more than 4 years' experience, 5 "inexperienced"

Type of therapy:
  Experimental group: client-centered
  Control group: waiting list "own controls," untreated "equivalent controls"

Duration of therapy:
  Experimental group: 6-108 interviews, mean of 31
  Control group: approximately 60 days

Negative effects

Frequency	*Criteria*
pretherapy to posttherapy 8% (2 of 25)	
pretherapy to follow-up (experimental) (control) 24% (6 of 25) 44% (7 of 16)	Decrease in Q-sort self-ideal correlation
(subset of 8 "own controls") prewait to therapy 75% (6 of 8)	
pretherapy to follow-up 13% (1 of 8) posttherapy to follow-up 63% (5 of 8)	Negative changes in Q-sort adjustment scores

Negative effects attributed to:
  Not discussed

Shortcomings in the research:
  1. Results from trainees and experienced therapists combined
  2. Bias in the patient sample
  3. Inappropriate control group

Rogers, Gendlin, Kiesler et al., 1967

Description of sample:
Hospitalized schizophrenics, acute (less than 8 months hospitalization) and chronic (more than 8 months)
Experimental group: 24
Control group: 24

Therapists:
8 primarily client-centered, experienced primarily with outpatients

Type of therapy:
Experimental group: milieu treatment plus client-centered individual therapy, some drugs
Control group: usual milieu treatment

Duration of therapy:
Experimental group: 4 months to 2-1/2 years, sessions twice weekly

Negative effects

Frequency		Criteria
(experimental)	(control)	
42% (5 of 12)	70% (7 of 10)	Clinical ratings based on MMPI: no change or negative change
8% (1 of 12)	36% (4 of 11)	TAT ratings: negative changes
	("normal" controls) 70% (7 of 10)	

Negative effects attributed to:
Not discussed

Shortcomings in the research:
1. Psychotic patients
2. Unchanged and worse categories not differentiated
3. Questionable reliability of outcome criteria

Rosenbaum, Friedlander, and Kaplan, 1956

Description of sample:
13% psychotics
48% character disorders
39% neurotics
Experimental group: 210 from 4 clinics
No control group

Therapists:
Unstated number of first, second, and third year psychiatric residents with dynamic training

Type of therapy:
Individual therapy ("suppressive" to "uncovering"), some ECT, some drug therapy

Duration of therapy:
Once a week, number of weeks not stated

Frequency of negative effects:
1% (2 of 210)

Criterion of negative effects:
Therapist rating of global improvement: "worse"

Negative effects attributed to:
Patients with worse interpersonal relations at outset of therapy were more likely to do poorly (authors did not discuss deteriorated cases)

Shortcomings in the research:
1. Inexperienced therapists
2. Inadequate information on therapists
3. Heterogeneous patient population
4. No control group
5. Confounded treatment
6. Sole reliance on a global outcome criterion

Rosenthal, 1955

Description of sample:
Clinic patients (9 inpatients, 3 outpatients), not psychotic, not having had ECT, who agreed to testing
Experimental group: 12
No control group

Therapists:
Unstated number of psychiatric residents

Type of therapy:
Individual

Duration of therapy:
3 weeks to 1 year, mean of 5 months, number of sessions unspecified

Frequency of negative effects:
25% (3 of 12)

Criterion of negative effects:
Judges' global ratings of clinician's report of patient's perception of changes attributable to therapy

Negative effects attributed to:
Authors suggested that patients judged unimproved or worse tended to "move away" from the therapist's value system

Shortcomings in the research:
1. Inexperienced therapists
2. Inadequate information on therapists
3. Bias in the patient sample
4. Sole reliance on a global outcome criterion
5. No control group
6. Questionable reliability of outcome criterion

Sager, Riess, and Gundlach, 1964

Description of sample:
Randomly selected outpatients having had more than 1 year of therapy and having terminated at least 2 years prior to the study (70% neurotic, 15% schizophrenic, 10% schizoid)
Experimental group: 201 subjects sampled, data analyzed for 103
No control group

Therapists:
Unstated number of analytically oriented therapists: experience unspecified

Type of therapy:
Individual analytically oriented, with supportive and drug therapy in certain cases

Duration of therapy:
Most under 2 years, 200 or fewer sessions, range of 31-400+ sessions

Negative effects

Frequency	Criteria
2% (2 of 103)	Therapist's global judgment at termination: same or worse
2% (2 of 103)	Patient's evaluation 2+ years after termination: same or worse
14% (14 of 103)	Researchers' evaluation based on symptoms, interpersonal relations, social, sexual, occupational functioning, patient's feelings about therapist: same or worse

Negative effects attributed to:
Authors did not discuss negative effects, percentages of negative effects varied with diagnosis and perspective of judge

Shortcomings in the research:
1. Inadequate information on therapists
2. Bias in the patient sample
3. No control group
4. Unchanged and worse categories not differentiated

Sloane, Staples, Cristol et al., 1975a, b

Description of sample:
Adult neurotic outpatients applying for help at a major U.S. clinic, not psychotic, not requiring medication, two thirds psychoneurotic, one third personality disorders, equal distribution between treatments by sex and severity
Experimental group: 61
Control group: 33

Therapists:
1 psychologist, 5 psychiatrists, all formally trained in psychotherapy or behavior therapy, all with more than 6 years' experience (2 with more than 20)

Type of therapy:
Experimental group:
30 in brief intensive psychotherapy (PT)
31 in behavior therapy (BT)
From posttherapy to follow-up, 15 BT and 9 PT patients received some further (usually insight-oriented) therapy
Control group: telephone contact with waiting list patients

Duration of therapy:
4 months, 1 session per week, average of 13-14 sessions

Negative effects

Frequency		*Criteria*
(experimental)	(control)	
	(at 4 months)	
3% (1 of 31BT)	3% (1 of 33)	Assessor rating: symptomatic anxiety worsening
6% (2 of 30PT)		
3% (1 of 30PT)	3% (1 of 33)	Assessor rating: overall worsening
	6% (2 of 33)	Patient rating: symptomatic worsening
3% (1 of 30PT)	6% (2 of 33)	Patient rating: overall worsening
	(at one year)	
3% (1 of 30PT)	3% (1 of 33)	Assessor rating: overall worsening

Negative effects attributed to:
Not discussed

Shortcomings in the research:
None

Strupp, Wallach, and Wogan, 1964

Description of sample:
Outpatient adults, mostly well-educated, upper SES, selected by
their therapists to receive questionnaires an average of 32
months after treatment termination
Experimental group: 44
No control group

Therapists:
10 psychiatrists, 1 psychologist, all with 200-900 hours of personal
therapy, 10 years average experience

Type of therapy:
Individual, generally analytically oriented

Duration of therapy:
Average of 166 sessions (2 years, 4 months)

Frequency of negative effects:
2% (1 of 44)

Criterion of negative effects:
Patient report of no benefit from therapy

Negative effects attributed to:
Patient's uncertainty about therapist's feelings, lack of therapist
warmth, and believing that the therapist did not understand the
patient's feelings—all were negatively related to therapeutic
change as reported by the patient

Shortcomings in the research:
1. Bias in the patient sample
2. No control group

Stuart and Lott, 1972

Description of sample:
Junior high school predelinquent and delinquent boys referred for intervention
Experimental group: 79
Control group: 15

Therapists:
5 social work students, no experience
1 medical student, no experience
4 social workers, 1-6 years experience

Type of therapy:
Experimental group: behavioral contingency contracting in a social casework framework
Control group: no therapy, families refused to participate

Duration of therapy:
15, 45, or 90 day treatment

Frequency of negative effects:
Number and percentage of patients showing decrements on the criteria not stated; instead, average decrement of a particular therapist's patients is reported; no data relevant to deterioration reported for controls

Criteria of negative effects:
6 criteria (e.g., attendance at school, tardiness, grades), unclear if these are the objects of the contract

Negative effects attributed to:
Therapist skill interacted with different clients and modes of intervention (note missing data artifacts); the one therapist with the most negative indicators (4 of 6 criteria) also had the most missing data (5 of 6 criteria)

Shortcomings in the research:
1. Results from trainees and experienced therapists combined
2. Bias in the patient sample
3. Inappropriate control group
4. No data relevant to deterioration reported for controls

Truax, 1963

Description of sample:
1. 4 deteriorated and 4 improved schizophrenic inpatients
2. 14 hospitalized schizophrenic patients, 14 counseling clients, 14 controls
3. 24 patients on a continuing treatment ward

Therapists:
Varying number of client-centered therapists, experience unspecified

Type of therapy:
Experimental group: client-centered
Control group: untreated

Duration of therapy:
6 months to 3-1/2 years

Frequency of negative effects:
4 patients were selected from a larger sample of unknown size on the basis of showing clear evidence of deterioration

Criteria of negative effects:
Global outcome rating based on symptoms, patient self-report, and projective test results; other data cited are MMPI, Wittenborn Psychiatric Rating Scale, WAIS, F (authoritarianism) Scale, and Q-sort

Negative effects attributed to:
Data indicated that lack of therapist warmth, empathy, and genuineness resulted in deterioration

Shortcomings in the research:
1. Inadequate information on therapists
2. Psychotic patients
3. Probably confounded treatment
4. Questionable reliability of outcome criteria
5. No control group (samples 1 and 3)

Truax, Wargo, Frank et al., 1966

Description of sample:
Neurotics, no alcoholic brain-damaged, retarded, or patients with previous therapy
Experimental group: 40
No control group

Therapists:
4 psychiatric residents

Type of therapy:
Brief individual

Duration of therapy:
1 hour per week, maximum 4 months, minimum 4 appointments

Negative effects

Frequency	Criteria
25% (10 of 40)	Patient self-report of discomfort: deterioration
30% (12 of 40)	Therapist ratings of global improvement: no change or deterioration
26% (9 of 34)	Patient ratings of global improvement: no change or deterioration

Negative effects attributed to:
Therapists' empathy and genuineness directly related to sucessful outcome, warmth inversely related

Shortcomings in the research:
1. Inexperienced therapists
2. No control group
3. Unchanged and worse categories not differentiated
4. Questionable reliability of ratings

Uhlenhuth and Duncan, 1968

Description of sample:
  Outpatients, no organics or sociopaths
  Experimental group: 128
  No control group

Therapists:
  128 medical students on a clerkship of 9-10 weeks, no experience

Type of therapy:
  Individual

Duration of therapy:
  1-10 sessions, mean of 6

Frequency of negative effects:
  26% (33 of 126)

Criterion of negative effects:
  Increase in subjective distress as measured by patient's self-report of number and intensity of symptoms

Negative effects attributed to:
  Not discussed

Shortcomings in the research:
  1. Very brief therapy
  2. Inexperienced therapists
  3. No control group

Varble and Landfield, 1969

Description of sample:
Clients at a university "mental hygiene" clinic, none suicidal, homicidal, or psychotic; controls were "normal" students of similar age, class level
Experimental group: 36
Control group: 35

Therapists:
6 psychologists with at least 1 year full-time experience

Type of therapy:
Experimental group: "Developmental learning approach," de-emphasizing illness
Control group: untreated "normal" persons

Duration of therapy:
Average of 8 weekly sessions

Frequency of negative effects:
Experimental group (subgroups constituted on independent judges' ratings of typescripts):
Improved group: 33% (9 of 27)
Minimal or no improvement group: 22% (2 of 9)
Control group: not stated

Criterion of negative effects:
Increase in self-ideal discrepancy as measured by Kelly Role Construct Repertory Test

Negative effects attributed to:
Authors suggested clients with the greatest self-ideal discrepancy at outset were too disturbed to benefit from short-term therapy (note, however, that a higher percentage of the Improved Group had decreased self-ideal discrepancies than did the Minimal or No Improvement Group)

Shortcomings in the research:
1. No data relevant to deterioration reported for controls
2. Inappropriate control group
3. Questionable validity of outcome criterion

Volsky, Magoon, Norman et al., 1965
(includes data from Jewell, 1958)

Description of sample:
Male university counseling center clients with personal, nonvocational problems
Experimental group: 80
Control group: 20

Therapists:
8 unspecified therapists, probably counseling center staff, experience unspecified

Type of therapy:
Experimental group: brief "counseling"
Control group: waiting list

Duration of therapy:
Mean of 3 sessions, range of 1-13 sessions

Negative effects

Frequency	Criteria
Experimentals show greater variance than controls	MMPI scale of manifest anxiety

(judges' ratings for a subset of 20 experimentals: Jewell, 1958)

10%	Worse problem solving
28%	Worse defensiveness
20%	Worse anxiety

Negative effects attributed to:
Not discussed

Shortcomings in the research:
1. Very brief therapy
2. Inadequate information on therapists
3. Questionable reliability of outcome criteria
4. Inaccuracy of greater variance interpretation

Warne, Canter, and Wiznia, 1953

Description of sample:
  Veterans with service connected neuroses
  Experimental group: 60
  Control group: 30

	Therapy	
Therapists	*Type* (experimental)	*Duration*
Unstated number of VA therapists, not further specified	30: VA clinic, insight-oriented	Mean of 8.9 months (27 hours)
5 private practice therapists (3 psychiatrists, 2 M.D.'s without psychiatric training), experience not stated	30: private therapists offering both psychological and somatic treatment	Mean of 33 months (125 hours)
	(control)	
	Untreated	

Frequency of negative effects:
  VA clinic experimentals: 7%
  Private practice experimentals: 70%
  Controls: 66%

Criteria of negative effects:
  Clinician's ratings of work, social, marital adjustment symptoms, insight, and overall adjustment from case records: "significantly" or "slightly" worse

Negative effects attributed to:
  Authors suggested that private practice patients may have received primarily somatic treatment, with the result that psychological issues "remained hidden" and became " more impregnable"

Shortcomings in the research:
  1. Treatment components inadequately specified
  2. Confounded treatments
  3. Questionable reliability and validity of outcome criteria

Weber, Elinson, and Moss, 1965

Description of sample:
  All outpatients treated at Columbia clinic over 18-year period, psychoneurotic, psychosomatic, and psychotic or borderline psychotic
  Experimental group: 1296
  No control group:

Therapists:
  Unstated number of psychoanalysts or candidates in training, experience unspecified

| Therapy | |
Type	Duration
564: analysis	Average 3 years
732: analytically oriented therapy	Average 9 months
	(Range for both, 3 months to over 3 years)

Frequency of negative effects:
  Analysis: 4-6%
  Psychotherapy: 4-6%
  Psychotic or borderline psychotic: 4-20%
  Neurotic personality disorder: 2-6%
  Psychoneurotic: 3-6%

Criteria of negative effects:
  "Worse" on 9 scales of ego functioning, as rated from case records and auxillary data by nine independent clinicians: dependency, pleasure, sex, affect, defense, emergency emotions, guilt, pathology, and social functioning

Negative effects attributed to:
  Deterioration varied with diagnostic category, length of treatment, and severity at onset; psychotics had very high negative effects, up to 44% in psychoanalysis

Shortcomings in the research:
  1. Inadequate information on therapists
  2. No control group
  3. Questionable reliability of outcome criteria

Wispé and Parloff, 1965

Description of sample:
Experimentals were male psychologists reporting more than 60 hours of psychotherapy (controls were matched on age or date of Ph.D., type of professional activity, area of specialization, and earlier productivity)
Experimental group: 55
Control group: 55

Therapists:
Unstated number of psychiatrists and psychologists, experience unspecified

Type of therapy:
Experimental group:
69% analytically oriented
16% eclectic orientation
Control group: untreated

Duration of therapy:
60 hours minimum, 41% saw more than 1 therapist

Frequency of negative effects:
Increased variability in the experimental group relative to the control group

Criterion of negative effects:
Productivity (quantity of professional publications): decrease from pretherapy to posttherapy

Negative effects attributed to:
Authors suggested a negative relationship between length of therapy and posttherapy activity

Shortcomings in the research:
1. Inadequate information on therapists
2. Inappropriate control group
3. Questionable validity of outcome criterion

The following six studies deal with the natural course of mental or emotional disturbances in the absence of specific psychotherapeutic interventions. Thus all patients are considered controls.

Agras, Chapin, and Oliveau, 1972

Description of sample:
    30 phobic individuals identified via an epidemiological survey

Duration of no-treatment period:
    5-year follow-up

Frequency of negative effects:
    Persons older than 20 years: 37%
    Persons younger than 20 years: 0%
    Overall: 24%

Criterion of negative effects:
    Respondent self-report yielding an "intensity" rating of phobia

Negative effects attributed to:
    Data showed individuals with high fearfulness and generalized
    phobias less likely to improve: age an intervening variable

Shortcomings in the research:
    1. Subjects never sought treatment

Endicott and Endicott, 1972

Description of sample:
40 neurotic, borderline, personality disorder, psychophysiologic
reaction, and schizophrenic reaction wait list patients

Duration of no-treatment period:
6-month no-treatment waiting period

Negative effects

Frequency	Criteria
14% (5 of 35)	Hospitalized during waiting period
60% (24 of 40)	Unimproved or worse on global rating

Negative effects attributed to:
Not stated, although the natural course of the illness was implied;
data showed only 9% of the borderline or schizophrenic
patients were rated "improved" vs. 52% of all other patients

Shortcomings in the research:
1. Unchanged and worse categories not differentiated
2. Questionable reliability of outcome criteria

Giel, Knox, and Carstairs, 1964

Description of sample:
Retrospective random subsample (100) of patients who presented 5 years earlier for psychiatric consultation, suicide attempters excluded

Duration of no-treatment period:
5-year follow-up (one half of patients had received "a modicum" of outpatient care, 20 were temporarily admitted to hospital)

Frequency of negative effects:
4% (4 of 93) includes two suicides

Criterion of negative effects:
Clinician judgment of overall change (includes 2 suicides)

Negative effects attributed to:
Not stated, although the natural course of the illness was implied

Shortcomings in the research:
1. Reasons why the subjects were untreated were unclear
2. Sole reliance on a global outcome criterion

Jurjevich, 1968

Description of sample:
Applicants at a military mental health clinic
62 long-term follow-up
50 short-term follow-up

Duration of no-treatment period:
Long-term: 30 weeks
Short-term: 10 days

Frequency of negative effects:
Long-term: 29%
Short-term: 28%

Criterion of negative effects:
Patient self-rating of increase in number of symptoms

Negative effects attributed to:
Not discussed

Shortcomings in the research:
1. Reasons why the subjects were untreated were unclear

Saslow and Peters, 1956

Description of sample:
First 100 patients at an outpatient clinic diagnosed as having a behavior disorder (neurotic, psychotic, psychosomatic)

Duration of no-treatment period:
1.3-6.6 year follow-up

Negative effects

Frequency	*Criteria*
20% (17 of 82)	Patient self-report of more symptoms
5% (4 of 83)	Hospitalized in mental hospital
12% (10 of 82)	Report health as worse, 3 due to specific medical illness
12% (10 of 82)	Clinician rating of worse

Negative effects attributed to:
Not discussed

Shortcomings in the research:
1. Bias in the patient sample
2. Reasons why the subjects were untreated were unclear
3. Questionable reliability and validity of outcome criteria

Subotnik, 1972

Description of sample:
  A 422-subject sample of college students identified as "probably disturbed" based on the MMPI

Duration of no-treatment period:
  9-33 month follow-up

Negative effects

Frequency	*Criteria*
21% (34 of 166) to 37% (61 of 166), depending on judge	Judgments based on MMPI of worse functioning of students initially considered "disturbed"
21% (71 of 332) to 22% (54 of 243), depending on judge	Judgments based on MMPI of evidence of disturbance in students initially considered "normal"

Negative effects attributed to:
  Not discussed

Shortcomings in the research:
  1. Subjects never sought therapy
  2. Questionable reliability of outcome criteria

Appendix B
Survey Respondents

D. Wilfred Abse, M.D.
Professor of Psychiatry
University of Virginia Medical School
Charlottesville, Virginia

Ann Appelbaum, M.D.
The Menninger Foundation
Topeka, Kansas

John M. Atthowe, Jr., Ph.D.
Professor of Psychiatry
Rutgers Medical School
Piscataway, New Jersey

Aaron T. Beck, M.D.
Professor of Psychiatry
Department of Psychiatry
University of Pennsylvania
Philadelphia, Pennsylvania

Leopold Bellak, M.D.
22 Rockwood Drive
Larchmont, New York

Irving N. Berlin, M.D.
Professor of Psychiatry and Pediatrics
University of California, Davis
Sacramento Medical Center
Sacramento, California

Barbara J. Betz, M.D.
906 Iliff Street
Pacific Palisades, California

Irving Bieber, M.D., P.C.
132 East 72nd Street
New York, New York

Edward S. Bordin, Ph.D.
Professor of Psychology
Director, Counseling Center
University of Michigan
Ann Arbor, Michigan

Pietro Castelnuovo-Tedesco, M.D.
Blakemore Professor of Psychiatry
Department of Psychiatry
Vanderbilt University
Nashville, Tennessee

Jacob Cohen, Ph.D.
Professor of Psychology
Department of Psychology
New York University
New York, New York

Gerald C. Davison, Ph.D.
Professor of Psychology and Psychiatry
Department of Psychology
State University of New York
    at Stony Brook
Stony Brook, New York

John Dollard, Ph.D.
305 Crown
New Haven, Connecticut

Jarl E. Dyrud, M.D.
Professor and Associate Chairman
Department of Psychiatry
The University of Chicago
Chicago, Illinois

Albert Ellis, Ph.D.
Executive Director
Institute for Advanced Study
    in Rational Psychotherapy
New York, New York

Jean Endicott, Ph.D.
Director, Evaluation Section
Biometrics Research Unit
New York State Psychiatric Institute
New York, New York

George L. Engel, M.D.
Professor of Medicine and Psychiatry
Department of Psychiatry
The University of Rochester
Rochester, New York

O. Spurgeon English, M.D.
449 Righters Mill Road
Penn Valley
Narberth, Pennsylvania

Norman L. Farberow, Ph.D.
Principal Investigator
Veterans Administration
Wadsworth Hospital Center
Los Angeles, California

C. B. Ferster, Ph.D.
Professor of Psychology
Department of Psychology
American University
Washington, D.C.

Reuben Fine, Ph.D., P.C.
225 West 86th Street
New York, New York

Donald W. Fiske, Ph.D.
Professor of Psychology
Department of Behavioral Sciences
The University of Chicago
Chicago, Illinois

Donald H. Ford, Ph.D.
Dean, College of Human Development
The Pennsylvania State University
University Park, Pennsylvania

Daniel X. Freedman, M.D.
Professor and Chairman
Department of Psychiatry
University of Chicago
Chicago, Illinois

Lawrence Friedman, M.D.
50 East 72nd Street
New York, New York

Sol L. Garfield, Ph.D.
Professor and Director
Clinical Psychology Program
Department of Psychology
Washington University
St. Louis, Missouri

Robert W. Goldberg, Ph.D.
Psychology Service
Cleveland Veterans
    Administration Hospital
Brecksville, Ohio

Israel Goldiamond, Ph.D.
Professor of Psychiatry
    and Behavioral Sciences
University of Chicago
Chicago, Illinois

Louis A. Gottschalk, M.D.
Professor and Chairman
Department of Psychiatry and
    Human Behavior
University of California
Irvine, California

Ralph R. Greenson, M.D., P.C.
1800 Fairburn Avenue
Los Angeles, California

Alan S. Gurman, Ph.D.
Assistant Professor of Psychiatry
Department of Psychiatry
Center for Health Sciences
University of Wisconsin-Madison
Madison, Wisconsin

Michel Hersen, Ph.D.
Professor of Psychology
Western Psychiatric Institute
    and Clinic
University of Pittsburgh
Pittsburgh, Pennsylvania

Marc H. Hollender, M.D.
Professor and Chairman
Department of Psychiatry
Vanderbilt University
Nashville, Tennessee

Donald J. Holmes, M.D.
2140 East Third Street
Tucson, Arizona

Frederick H. Kanfer, Ph.D.
Professor of Psychology
Children's Research Center
University of Illinois at
    Urbana-Champaign
Champaign, Illinois

Otto F. Kernberg, M.D.
Professor of Clinical Psychiatry
Department of Psychiatry
College of Physicians and Surgeons
 of Columbia University
New York, New York

Jane W. Kessler, Ph.D.
Leffingwell Professor of Psychology
Director of Mental Development Center
Case Western Reserve University
Cleveland, Ohio

Donald J. Kiesler, Ph.D.
Professor of Psychology
Psychology Department
Academic Center of Virginia
Commonwealth University
Richmond, Virginia

Peter H. Knapp, M.D.
Professor and Associate Chairman
Division of Psychiatry
Boston University
Boston, Massachusetts

Heinz Kohut, M.D.
180 North Michigan Avenue
Chicago, Illinois

Leonard Krasner, Ph.D.
Professor of Psychology
State University of New York
 at Stony Brook
Stony Brook, New York

Robert J. Langs, M.D.
Editor-in-Chief
*International Journal of
 Psychoanalytic Psychotherapy*
New York, New York

Arnold A. Lazarus, Ph.D.
Professor of Psychology
Graduate School of Applied
 and Professional Psychology
Rutgers University
Brunswick, New Jersey

Robert P. Liberman, M.D.
Research Professor of Psychiatry
Institute of Psychiatry
De Crespigny Park
London, England

Morton A. Lieberman, Ph.D.
Professor of Human Development
Department of Behavioral
 Sciences and Psychiatry
University of Chicago
Chicago, Illinois

Lester Luborsky, Ph.D.
Professor of Psychology
 in Psychiatry
Department of Psychiatry
University of Pennsylvania
Philadelphia, Pennsylvania

Michael J. Mahoney, Ph.D.
Department of Psychology
The Pennsylvania State University
University Park, Pennsylvania

David Malan, M.D.
The Tavistock Clinic
Adult Department
Tavistock Centre
London, England

Isaac Marks, M.D.
The Maudsley Hospital
Denmark Hill
London, England

Judd Marmor, M.D.
School of Medicine
University of Southern California
Los Angeles, California

Joseph D. Matarazzo, Ph.D.
Chairman, Department of Medical
 Psychology
University of Oregon
Health Sciences Center
Portland, Oregon

Philip R. A. May, M.D.
Professor of Psychiatry
University of California
Neuro-Psychiatric Institute
The Center for the Health Sciences
Los Angeles, California

Paul E. Meehl, Ph.D.
Regents' Professor of Psychology
Department of Psychiatry,
    Research Unit
University of Minnesota
Minneapolis, Minnesota

Neal E. Miller, Ph.D.
Professor of Psychology
Psychology Department
The Rockefeller University
New York, New York

John C. Nemiah, M.D.
Psychiatrist-in-Chief
Beth Israel Hospital, and
Professor of Psychiatry
Harvard Medical School
Boston, Massachusetts

Martin T. Orne, M.D., Ph.D.
Director, Unit for Experimental
    Psychiatry
Department of Psychiatry
University of Pennsylvania
Philadelphia, Pennsylvania

James O. Palmer, Ph.D.
Associate Professor of
    Medical Psychology
University of California
Los Angeles, California

Gordon L. Paul, Ph.D.
Professor of Psychology
Psychological Clinic
Children's Research Center
University of Illinois at
    Urbana-Champaign
Champaign, Illinois

George H. Pollock, M.D.
Director, Institute for Psychoanalysis
Chicago, Illinois

Arthur J. Prange, Jr., M.D.
Professor of Psychiatry
Department of Psychiatry
The University of North Carolina
Chapel Hill, North Carolina

S. Rachman, Ph.D.
Psychology Department
Institute of Psychiatry
De Crespigny Park
Denmark Hill
London, England

John M. Rhoads, M.D.
Professor of Psychiatry
Director of Residency Training
Department of Psychiatry
Duke University Medical Center
Durham, North Carolina

Howard B. Roback, Ph.D.
Associate Professor of Psychiatry
Department of Psychiatry
Vanderbilt University
Nashville, Tennessee

Leon Salzman, M.D.
110 Riverside Drive
New York, New York

Robert L. Spitzer, M.D.
Chief of Psychiatric Research
Biometrics Research Unit
New York State Psychiatric Institute
New York, New York

Hans H. Strupp, Ph.D.
Distinguished Professor of Psychology
Department of Psychology
Vanderbilt University
Nashville, Tennessee

Leonard P. Ullmann, Ph.D.
Professor of Psychology
Department of Psychology
University of Hawaii at Manoa
Honolulu, Hawaii

Robert S. Wallerstein, M.D.
Professor and Chairman
Department of Psychiatry
University of California
Langley Porter Neuropsychiatric
   Institute
San Francisco, California

Irving B. Weiner, Ph.D.
Professor and Chairman
Department of Psychology
Case Western Reserve University
Cleveland, Ohio

Walter Weintraub, M.D.
Professor of Psychiatry
Department of Psychiatry
University of Maryland
Baltimore, Maryland

Otto Allen Will, Jr., M.D.
Medical Director
Austen Riggs Center, Inc.
Stockbridge, Massachusetts

Lewis R. Wolberg, M.D.
Casa Midalimi, Apartado 35
La Penita de Jaltemba
Municipio de Compostella
Nayarit, Mexico

Joseph Wolpe, M.D.
Professor of Psychiatry
Director, Behavior Therapy Unit
Department of Psychiatry
Temple University
Philadelphia, Pennsylvania

Benjamin Wolstein, Ph.D.
Clinical Professor
Institute of Advanced
   Psychological Studies
Adelphi University
Garden City, New York

Irvin D. Yalom, M.D.
Professor of Psychiatry
Department of Psychiatry and
   Behavioral Sciences
Stanford University Medical Center
Stanford, California

Clifford Yorke, M.D.
Medical Director
The Hampstead Child-Therapy
   Clinic
London, England

Joseph Zubin, Ph.D.
Professor Emeritus of Psychology and
   Special Lecturer in Psychiatry
Department of Psychiatry
College of Physicians and Surgeons
   of Columbia University
New York, New York

Appendix C
Letters from Survey Respondents

Text of the letter sent to psychotherapy experts listed in Appendix B. Following are replies from those granting permission to publish.

As part of a project my research group is currently pursuing (with encouragement and support from the National Institute of Mental Health), we are exploring the problem of negative effects in psychotherapy and related forms of therapy. Specifically, we are addressing the following questions:

1. Is there a problem of negative effects, i.e., can we legitimately speak of a patient getting worse as a result of psychotherapy or related interventions?

2. If so, what would constitute a negative effect? What are the indicators of a negative effect? By what criteria would one judge a patient as having become worse as a result of therapy?

3. While any therapy outcome is obviously a function of many factors, which factors would you prominently associate with, or consider responsible for, a negative effect?

We would greatly appreciate your thoughts on these questions. Be as brief or as elaborate as you wish. While we have done a fair amount of thinking on the problem already, it would be most helpful at this time to have the ideas and suggestions of a small group of expert clinicians, theoreticians, and researchers who are specialists in a particular area. Eventually, we may want to invite more comprehensive contributions that might be included in a book, but for the time being any comments, however brief, may prove exceedingly helpful.

If you are interested, we would be glad to share with you our own ideas (and those of persons like yourself) as the work progresses. In the meantime, please accept my sincere thanks for your time and effort.

Hans H. Strupp

From D. Wilfred Abse, M.D.:

Of course there is a problem of negative effects. Sometimes this is very complex. For example, I had in prolonged intensive analytically oriented psychotherapy a young man who had been on the ward diagnosed (accurately) as a florid paranoid schizophrenic—he was delusional, and had tried to commit suicide before admission. Over about three-and-a-half years as an outpatient in four-times-a-week sessions, he became symptom free and changed considerably, becoming a very aggressive, often hostile character, married a masochistic young woman, and though well-adjusted, making progress in his work, worried me considerably because of his sadistic (and impaired) "object relationships." He gave up the work with me as he was satisfied with himself and his ambitious way of life, and by usual worldly standards he was successful. I could not keep him in further therapy. His former passive-masochistic core was everted and the manifest result was not only ego syntonic but in useful adaptation to general materialistic aspects of the American scene he inhabited. Since a number of people in the university from time to time congratulated me on a remarkable therapeutic triumph, I leave you to imagine my feelings! This illustrates that in some cases of overt paranoid schizophrenia (similarly in some cases of severe obsessional neurosis) the identifiable psychiatric syndrome following intensive analytic work may be succeeded by personality malfunctioning vis-a-vis other people, though adapted to "sick" aspects of our present society. On the other hand, I also know of cases of apparent and severe symptom neurosis which cleared up following prolonged psychoanalysis, with later evident paranoid trends characterologically. What I am discussing here is the problem of keeping some analytic work going with some very sick patients after disability in the clinically crude sense is obviated. "Negative effects" are then visited upon the patient's entourage or on others in general, in ways which may be far from punishable in our society. My own experience, directly and indirectly with these negative effects, is predominantly concerned with men who are domineering, subjugating and basically hostile to women, and who are yet sexually potent, and with women who reorganize themselves (and their depressive difficulties) in a paranoid way, both groups relinquishing analytic treatment prematurely. The women are usually partially or altogether frigid. We are not left with the result of a very loving creature in such an instance of premature termination of analytic work. To put this problem into a general formula which comprises both the analyst's and the analysand's major contributions (sometimes it is only the analysand's contribution which is decisive): Analyst's narcissistic defense + analysand's unacknowledged, unworked-through negative transference → unacknowledged "negative effects."

While I think we should try to be as critical as possible about our own analytic work, this does not mean that we should be uncritical of other kinds of psychotherapy. I've discussed some aspects of encounter group-type negative effects in my book on Group Analytic Psychotherapy. Here, to be brief, I might mention that behavior modification and therapy have so many possibilities of negative effects, not the least being that some people best treated analytically are seduced along the lines of their resistance to change by behavior therapy—and this is not mere armchair theory. I have seen some patients, for example, who some months or years after behavior therapy—which relieved their then current symptom (especially phobic difficulties) became depressed and suitably entered into analytic work. Of course, they had swelled the statistics of behavioral-type therapy success.

This "negative effects" problem thus also raises the question of what is ideal for a particular patient and the discrepancy with what is available, or advised by the psychiatrist he or she consults.

[December 3, 1975]

From Ann Appelbaum, M.D.:

In answer to your letter, I shall try to respond to your questions about the negative effects of psychotherapy.

1. Your research group asks whether there is a problem of negative effect. I think there certainly is a problem, and that patients can and do get worse as a result of psychotherapy. For example, intense transference feelings mobilized in a patient with poor ego strength and poor impulse control can result in impulsive and sometimes fatal action, as in the case of an alcoholic young man who committed suicide shortly after learning that his psychotherapist was pregnant. People who supervise psychiatric residents often have the opportunity, I believe, to observe hospitalized schizophrenic patients who respond with marked improvement to the intense and well-intentioned psychotherapeutic efforts of young physicians, only to regress into an even more florid and stubborn psychotic state upon the therapist's being transferred to another service. The effect of psychotherapy has been to arouse hopes for love and nurture, and to channel intense and primitive needs for a symbiotic relationship toward the person of the therapist, without the concomitant strengthening of the ego so as to enable the person to tolerate these hopes and expectations being disappointed. I have seen instances of efforts at a "deep" expressive psychotherapy with a patient with poor ego strength leading to a steady loosening of the person's thought processes, eventuating in a psychosis which was not detectable clinically or on psychological testing at the beginning of psychotherapy. Then there are instances in which a patient with a poorly integrated, "borderline" personality, in the grip of intense wishes to please the therapist, takes on excessively difficult tasks (marriage, parenthood, graduate studies, for example) which place an excessive strain upon the person's psychological resources, and eventuate in experiences of failure, increased anxiety and pain, so that on balance one

could say that the patient is worse rather than better even though a certain amount of "good" psychotherapeutic work had been done.

2. You asked what would constitute a negative effect, and I have touched upon that in the previous paragraph. Certainly I would consider suicide a negative effect. The development of severe or fatal psychosomatic reactions to excessively intense transference feelings or to an excessively deep and terrifying awareness of the person's primitive longings and/or of the actual discrepancies between legitimate instinctual needs and their likelihood of satisfaction in reality would, I think, constitute a negative effect.

Your next question about the criteria by which one would judge a patient as having become worse as a result of therapy is a difficult one. For example, a chronic schizophrenic patient, incapacitated and hospitalized for years, who becomes considerably better in psychotherapy, in the sense that he thinks more clearly, is aware of his feelings and of their internal and external sources, who is capable of tolerating sexual and aggressive feelings toward the therapist, but who now realistically faces the fact that he is now fifty years old and will have to do a tremendous amount of psychological work to make even a minimally satisfactory life for himself at this point becomes depressed and commits suicide: Is this a negative effect? Would the person have been better off if left alone to live out his life as a chronic hospital patient? Psychological testing before the suicide might show the person to be remarkably "better" as compared to testing prior to therapy: but now he kills himself. His suicide might be looked at as a sensible, mature and "positive" action based upon a realistic assessment of the pros and cons of continuing to live. In such a case I would be hard put to decide whether this suicide was a "positive" or a "negative" effect of excellent psychotherapeutic work. I feel I am here getting into very delicate issues. A person who has lived for some years as a conventionally good wife and mother at the price of suppressing her hatred for an unloving, emotionally limited and intellectually inferior husband, and who as the result of psychotherapy becomes aware of her own needs for love and stimulation, enters into an affair and eventually divorces her husband—is she "worse" or "better"? Would her children have been better off had she lived out the marriage at least until they grew up so as to provide them a stable home? I think the answer to this would depend on the kind of life the woman would be able to create for herself and her children after the divorce, and the extent to which her awareness and acceptance of her own emotional needs went hand in hand with a growing capacity for concern and a growing capacity to take into account the needs of others as well as of herself.

Another negative effect of psychotherapy may be that the therapeutic work begins to assume priority over other tasks and goals of the person's life, with the person remaining primarily committed to his therapy or analysis for a period of many years, postponing important life decisions on the grounds that he is not psychologically ready to take them yet, foregoes opportunities for travel, adventure, the taking of a more interesting or lucrative job, etc. because being a good patient has come to assume priority higher than that of living life to the fullest.

3. You asked about factors I would consider prominently associated with or responsible for negative effects: First among these I would list inadequate diagnostic study prior to undertaking psychotherapy. If the patient's ego strength, impulse control, intelligence, motivation to change, and the life circumstances that may limit his capacity to exploit whatever changes do occur are not adequately understood before beginning psychotherapy, the likelihood of negative effects is greatly enhanced. With inadequate preliminary diagnosis, the therapist is more prone either to probe more

deeply than the patient is capable of tolerating, and hence to provoke untoward regressions, or else to not work intensively enough, and thus cheat the patient of the possibility of experiencing as much change for the better as he is capable of. Incidentally, this raises another "negative" effect, which would be not that the patient is worse at the end of therapy, but that he is not nearly as much better as he might have been with more expert therapeutic work. Inadequate initial diagnosis may lead a therapist to undertake outpatient psychotherapy with a patient who absolutely cannot be treated adequately without the support of concomitant hospitalization. This error is responsible, I believe, for many negative results in patients with "borderline" personality organization who commit suicide or leave therapy worse than they were to begin with because of being unable to tolerate psychotherapy when this is undertaken outside a hospital.

Another factor responsible for negative results is lack of skill on the part of the therapist. I already alluded to the enthusiastic resident who works intensively with the schizophrenic patient without taking into account the fact that he can work only for six months, while the patient needs the commitment of a therapist over a period of many years, and who hence leaves the patient in much worse condition than he found him. Lack of skill leads to inadequate recognition of transference manifestations, as in the case of the pregnant therapist who failed to sense the depths of her patient's envy of the fetus, his rage at the "unfaithfulness" of the therapist, and his despair at being abandoned. Similarly lack of skill is evident in the therapists who uncover unconscious conflicts too rapidly without providing concomitant support to the patient's ego in the course of therapy.

Along with lack of skill I would count the psychopathology of the therapist as among the factors responsible for negative effects. The cold, obsessive, uninvolved therapist who sits for years with a patient in analysis, quite content to let the patient's life pass by as long as "analyzing" is happening, is inflicting his own limited capacity to enjoy life upon the patient. The therapist who is seductive to the patient without being aware of it mobilizes transference reactions which the therapist is then incapable of dealing with adequately. The therapist whose voyeuristic impulses are poorly controlled, and perhaps disguised under the heading of being a researcher or an investigator may again be one who uncovers unconscious material without being able adequately to deal with it. The therapist who has an excessive need to "make" people change, and who resorts to drugs, shock treatment, or other ancillary interventions that may not be necessary, can produce negative effects as a result of his therapeutic furor. And of course we shouldn't neglect stupidity as one of the factors in a therapist that leads to negative effects.

I certainly would be interested in having you share your ideas with me, and I appreciate being included in this study.

[January 19, 1976]

From Stephen Appelbaum, Ph.D.:

I am not sure that "getting worse" gets at the issues which I assume you are trying to ascertain. Getting worse in various ways, along with better in various ways, might be closer to it. There might then be something like an algebraic sum on which to base a better or worse judgment.

One way patients may get worse is when the therapy enables them to get into situations which are traditionally taken as evidence of improvement but which they cannot master successfully, e.g., education, occupation, marriage, children. I think that therapists, therapies, and patients suffer from social values attached to these things, with all parties overlooking the fact that all things are not available to all people, that objectives and goals need to be tailored to the person's capacities. It is not writ in stone that all people should conform to American middle-class values, and many patients would be well-advised to stay out of them. This point is related to—

Patients and therapists suffer from feeling they have to achieve an ideal, usually an unachievable ideal, an abstraction—generative personality, genital functioning, normality, adjustment, etc. The patient feels guilty when he does not achieve such idealistic goals, and this kind of guilt becomes added to the infantile sources of guilt. Now, he is a worse failure than ever, having had the advantages of psychotherapy, and paid so much for it, without achieving these lofty aims. This guilt may make it appear that he is "worse," when in fact he is "better."

Finally, the therapy can become a substitute for action, reinforcing a kind of passivity, confirming elements of the personality in some patients which allow them to substitute having completed a job of developing insight for the sweaty activity of making dreams come true.

I hope this has been of some help in what, if I know you, will turn out to be a provocative, interesting, and timely contribution.

[December 24, 1976]

From John M. Atthowe, Jr., Ph.D.:

Your project is coming at a critical time. I believe the stress on accountability will point out that there are more negative effects than we suppose. Many of my colleagues would say that we should expect no improvement or negative effects until the person is "ripe" for change. I believe a dynamic approach to therapy would promote this latter view while a more behavioral orientation would stress continuous positive change. The orientation of the therapist, the population chosen to be evaluated and the evaluation instruments are all variables which might be looked at individually. Anyway, I would be quite interested with what conclusions or ideas your group arrives at.

Questions:

1. There is no doubt in my mind that patients do get worse. I think of the early work on the process of therapy by Carl Rogers as one example. But, of even greater importance, is the negative outcome rather than "ups" and "downs" in the therapy process. Can the therapist ethically or professionally stop seeing someone when they have worsened without referring them to some other treatment facility and following up on that referral? For that matter, if someone has worsened and maintains that status or never improves, is it ethical to continue to see them? I suspect the emergence of "time-limited" treatment plans or contracts will bring this issue to a head—lawyers and third party payers will have a field day in this area.

2. Some examples: I have seen some chronic schizophrenics worsen. One diagnosed catatonic schizophrenic refused to eat and did nothing when put in an ongoing ward token program. Another patient stopped communicating (became mute) when he was pushed too fast. I have seen individuals whose progress I was not pleased with say they were getting help and vice versa. One patient (diagnosed manic-depressive psychosis) who was rapidly improving, left the hospital, was working and was seeing (in love with) a married woman. The woman stopped seeing him, and he committed suicide. Another person, paroled by the courts to therapy, who was into "hard" drugs, was improving in family and individual therapy, but he became involved on one occasion with his old buddies in the drug culture, was "busted" and sent to prison. Another parolee, "a sexual psychopath," over a period of two years was working and contributing to the community. He had no police record and his performance was quite adequate; however, he

continued to draw detailed pictures of young boys with mutilated genitalia.

Are all these instances negative effects? A person may be improving in his own estimation as well as in that of the therapist, yet one social-community problem, especially with the law, could end treatment with a decided negative effect. Suicides are another example. Most individuals on a chronic ward showed marked improvement in their activity level and responsibility, as well as decreasing their symptomatic behavior; yet, most of them were rated by staff as non-improved. We have evidence that patients who leave a State Institution and return every so often for a few days or months are functioning better (working, socially more effective and more self-sufficient) than those who leave the institution and never return. Recidivism, as far as mental institutions go and possibly mental health centers, is not a very good indicator of negative change per se.

My impression is that a negative effect could be seen as occurring in the process of undergoing treatment or as a result of receiving treatment (an outcome measure). Outcome measures might be classified as short-term and long-term. Short-term goals of treatment could be rated by patients, therapists or significant others in a goal attainment model or in a problem or symptom check list model. (Success being moving toward a defined goal and a reduction in the problem; negative effects would be the polar opposite). However, improvement in the reduction of symptoms or goal attainment may not be associated with changes in performance. Long-term goals, such as amount of time working, effective community functioning (survival skills) and social effectiveness, are most critical to the ultimate outcome of treatment but may not be correlated with short-term measures of outcome. We have evidence that cost-effectiveness may not be directly related to any of the latter measures of outcomes. High costs are associated with patients who stay in institutions. Low costs were found with those who left the hospital and never returned and intermediate costs with the "in-and-outers." However the "in-and-outers" were the most effective functioning group. Measurements must be multi-dimensional. The problem-oriented record will probably have goal attainment and problem reduction scales built into the treatment record. Patient satisfaction should become more important for accountability. What is needed, however, are better short-term and long-term measures of performance (social and community effectiveness or survival skills). The effort expended by others toward the client is one cost-related measure that might be utilized across all populations.

3. I think the factors most often associated with negative effect are:

a. poor therapist-client rapport in non-chronic, better populations—we have some suggestions that too much or too little rapport is not as good as an intermediate amount.
b. lack of respect for the person as a human being.
c. failure to involve the patient's environment in his treatment (especially in long-term treatment).
d. the inability of therapists to shift their mode of treatment (a rigid and uncompromising psychoanalyst or behavior therapist will lose some patients).
e. the inability to be comprehensive—not to treat the relevant social-community systems, not to treat the symptoms, not to treat the host in which the problem occurs (e.g., development of self-control, better nutrition and physical well-being and more experiences of success and confidence).

In reading over this paper, I feel there is an awful lot of speculation in our field. We need to explore rigorously a number of our speculations, the platforms from which we operate, before we move too far astray.

Thank you for jingling my senses. Good luck. Please keep me informed.

[February 5, 1976]

From Aaron T. Beck, M.D.:

1. In regards to the problem of negative effects, I do believe on the basis of my early psychotherapy experience that some of my own patients did get worse as a result of psychotherapy. I believe that I learned a great deal from these "deterioration effects" and attribute many of the major revisions in my approach to psychotherapy to these negative effects.

2. Obviously, in determining whether a patient's deterioration is due to the therapy or external factors, it is essential to have as much hard data as possible regarding the patient's reactions to both these sets of circumstances. On an intuitive basis, I have generally taken the patient's word for it when he says that he is feeling worse as a result of an adverse reaction to a specific therapeutic session or whether it is the result of some other (external) event. Also, patients seem to be aware when they are doing badly as the cumulative result of sessions over a long period of time. I no longer hold to the view that a patient has to "get worse before he gets better." Consequently, if the patient has any presenting complaint such as depression or a psychosomatic disorder, any worsening of this condition is an indicator of an adverse effect (either of therapy or of other factors). If the patient develops symptoms in therapy that exceed his base rate of appearance of symptoms (for example, anxiety attacks, depression, psychosomatic disorders), I would consider this a negative effect.

3. In my opinion, the major reason for a negative effect is that the therapist is so theory-bound that he actually misses the patient's problem. In addition to having to grapple with his own crazy view of the world, the patient is forced to

incorporate the therapist's theories. This not only weakens the patient's structure of reality, but the various interpretations by the therapist often undermine his customary coping strategies and adaptive mechanisms. I have found, for instance, that "attacking the patient's defenses" generally erodes what ego strengths he has.

4. Certain personality characteristics of the therapist obviously are antitherapeutic but these are so well known, I don't think I need to list them.

I believe that I could document the above remarks on the basis of my own experiences, and also the experiences of colleagues, and also students whose work I have supervised. I would say that my greatest personal learning experience was finding that "getting the patient to express hostility" was the single most counterproductive therapeutic maneuver I have engaged in and probably accounts for my reluctance to incorporate inverted hostility into my psychological models.

[March 29, 1976]

From Leopold Bellak, M.D.:

In response to your query re negative effects of psychotherapy, some tentative thoughts.

If psychotherapy is effective, it would—using the medical model—be virtually the only therapeutic modality which could not do harm, if it is potent enough to do good. (The curious notion of the homeopath—similia similibus curentur—holds true for amazingly many drugs: notably, digitalis given to a healthy person will produce the symptoms it usually affects beneficially.)

Conceptually, isn't the null hypothesis involved in your question?

At any rate, I believe a patient may get worse as a result of inappropriate psychotherapeutic intervention, to wit:

A negative therapeutic reaction is well recognized as part of a masochistic character structure: whether some such effects are temporary or some permanent (e.g., if a patient breaks off treatment) is another question.

"Analyzing" in the presence of insufficient synthetic functions sometimes leads to dissociation and obsessive "analytic" ruminations.

It is not clear from your question whether you mean temporarily worse or worse for a long period of time which could theoretically approach "forever"—the time factor needs to be separately stated, but does not enter in principle.

Other than analytic therapies do harm by excessive awareness (encounter groups—see published reports of suicide and psychotic episodes), excessive repression by stupid value judgments, substitution of symptoms in behavior therapy, etc.

I would suggest that any worsening of my twelve ego functions could occur as the result of unsuccessful or unskilled or inappropriate therapy, just as they can be used for indicating progress. As I am biased in that direction, I think it would be a good theme. (One of my published cases showed a decrease in adaptive regression in the service of the ego. Two, as a matter of fact, one a borderline, the other a schizophrenic.)

[December 8, 1975]

From Irving N. Berlin, M.D.:

In the volume that I edited with Dr. Szurek on *Clinical Aspects of Childhood Psychoses*, I described several negative effects of psychotherapy and the interventions of a children's psychiatric ward in working with severely psychotic children. In brief, these negative effects were related to countertransference problems of the therapist in dealing with the severely disturbed children of very disturbed parents whose children also were difficult to deal with psychotherapeutically. This, therefore, added to the burdens of the therapist and his tendency to blame parents for their children's condition, which seriously interfered with their therapeutic work with the parents. Similarly, I identified in that book some issues of the milieu team in dealing with parents and the children who were very difficult, and again related the issue of parental blame to some of the problems of working and collaborating with parents, as well as some of the issues in dealing with the child.

In a long chapter in which I describe failure after ten years of work with a psychotic child, I described the number of factors which militated against successful psychotherapeutic intervention with a very seriously disturbed child. In part, these had to do with the failure to recognize some of the ego gains that were made and to capitalize on these. It also had to do with the countertransference issues related to the parents, which also affected work with the child. Further, it was related to the problem of dealing therapeutically with the violent behavior of such seriously disturbed children.

In another part of that same volume, I described some of the difficulties which may lead to failure in dealing with seriously disturbed children, especially young children, when one does not understand their nonverbal communications and, therefore, relates to them in an inappropriate way, which shuts off all communication.

In a chapter which I am currently writing for a book on communication in psychotherapy, I have described work with silent young children from very primitive families where talking is not the mode of interaction and expression of feelings, beliefs and ideas. In the context of work with the "overintellectualized child," the little adult who is not amenable to the usual play therapy techniques, and work with the young adolescent, who finds it very difficult to talk about his problems, I describe the issues which lead to failure if one does not utilize nonverbal means of communicating and engaging the child in therapy. The continued effort to use talking techniques with these youngsters inevitably leads to psychotherapeutic failure.

The criteria that we would use to judge failure as a result of therapy is: (1) no remission of symptoms or the symptoms become worse and requiring hospitalization or institutionalization; (2) with parents, a breakdown of their current defenses which allow them to function at least in the home or on their jobs. This leads to decompensation and greater difficulty in functioning in these areas.

As I have mentioned above, the factors which I have considered to be associated with the negative effects in work with seriously disturbed children are parental blame; the difficulty of working with very seriously disturbed, aggressive, hostile and destructive children without a clear sense of what it takes to deal therapeutically with these issues; the problems of working with nonverbal children of various ages and from various socioeconomic classes; and the problems of working with the typically nonverbal young adolescent and using means of communicating with them other than speech.

In the chapter which I am just now finishing, I have described the use of competitive games, especially checkers, as a way of involving these youngsters in a collaborative effort and using that modality as the beginning effort to obtain communication and eventually some talking over the game as a way of getting at some problems.

[January 21, 1976]

From Barbara J. Betz, M.D.:

The questions you pose are not so easy to respond to. They seem most pertinent, and I mull them over.

The thoughts they have aroused must be aroused quite generally, and really don't satisfy me at other than superficial levels. A few of them are as follows. Basically, I feel that positive effects in therapeutic interventions, whatever they are descriptively, are indicators of a shift from a more dependent to a more self-sufficient personality organization (better defined self-other boundaries, better capacities for mutuality, reciprocity, etc.). Therefore, interventions and conditions which set the compass point of movement in the opposite direction (negative effect) would constitute deleterious factors.

In the same vein, aims that seek "fusion" with others or the universe, or involve directives from others however pleasing, while producing some immediate gratification and "improvement," may in the longer run be, in fact, negative in their effect.

Obviously, neglect, pessimism, sadism, seductiveness, impatience and an absence of genuineness in intervention providers are negative effect factors. Likewise, more subtle derogatory attitudes toward patient status (even addressing patients as "dear"). Derogation of the human personality by impersonal dispensation of drugs, I believe has long-range negative effects, and denies probable potentials in patients which may then atrophy over time.

I'd like to hear some of your thoughts and ideas, as the work progresses. I will contribute more specifically if I am able.

[February 4, 1976]

From Irving Bieber, M.D., P.C.:

I am sorry I cannot answer your questions in greater detail than the following:

I do not think one can speak of negative effects. One does, of course, have to differentiate between the natural course of a condition which may be one of progressive deterioration and the iatrogenic influences which lead to the negative effects.

I must say that in my experience negative effects are infrequent and generally not dramatic. I have seen many patients in consultation whom I interviewed after their treatment with other therapists. The therapeutic errors I noted could be classified into those of omission and those of commission. Under the former, I would include that of keeping a patient in treatment for years when nothing much has happened to change the patient's symptoms or adaptation. Apart from the therapy constituting a loss of time and money to the patient, fruitless treatment may create a sense of futility an the idea that psychotherapy cannot help.

Under errors of commission, I would include therapeutic activity that disturbs the patient's relationship with the therapist. This would consist of interpretations and/or behavior that shakes the patient's confidence in the therapist's competence, or shakes the patient's confidence in the therapist's genuine and constructive interest in him. I would also include such disturbances in communication as the therapist's inability to communicate ideas clearly and the inability to determine whether the patient is comprehending what he, the therapist, is saying; also, the failure to remain in relevant communication, that is, to stay "on the line" of the patient's theme.

I have received anecdotal reports on the negative effects of the newer confrontational and tactile techniques. Apparently, when already very disturbed individuals enter into such groups and are not prepared for the assault on their rather fragile personalities, some, I have been told, rapidly decompensate. What the incidence of such negative effects is, I am not in a position to say.

I hope my remarks will be of some help to you. My best wishes on the success of your project.

[January 25, 1976]

From Edward S. Bordin, Ph.D.:

Your letter raises some interesting questions and stimulates new ways of looking at old ideas. Rather than procrastinate, I am jotting down some relatively undigested thoughts.

Included in concern with negative effects should be the distinction between temporary vs. enduring ones. My experience leads me to believe that with certain kinds of persons and certain kinds of methods, temporary negative effects are to be expected. I can be more specific in describing the methods than the persons. The conditions of therapy that induce the patient to depart radically from his established modes of filtering his awareness of his actions and feelings and his modes of translating them into actions, e.g., time, physical posture, direct therapeutic interventions aimed at these modes, are likely to bring on temporary states of increased discomfort and potentials for more erratic actions. With regard to individual differences, the severity of pathology dimension is surely an important one. Whether it is possible to specify further factors, e.g., degree of quality of integration of cognition and affect, quality of object relations and self-differentiation or self-other boundaries, is, as you well know, problematical, but surely should be pursued.

Though I do not think all psychotherapy is marked by temporary negative effects, I would be astonished to find instances of enduring negative effects which were not initially manifested during the course of psychotherapy. What then could account for the differences in outcome between a temporary and an enduring negative effect? I think there will be both patient and therapist factors. There may be a critical level in the above mentioned patient factors where a point of no return is reached for the course of therapy. The patient lacks sufficient resources to snap back. With regard to the therapist, assume the difference in outcome resides in a complex of expertness/ignorance (by the field)/inappropriate personality (includes but not confined to countertransference).

Finally in suggesting that the difference will reside in the strength and quality of the working alliance, I seek not to escalate our level of ignorance, but to forecast where our search for further knowledge will take us.

[December 19, 1975]

From Pietro Castelnuovo-Tedesco, M.D.:

Probably the most common negative outcome (not necessarily an effect of psychotherapy) is patient disappointment. Yet this disappointment should not be attributed simply to inadequacy of the therapist or to ineffectiveness of the method. Neurotics are people who are unusually prone to disappointment and they have a special talent for seeking it (and finding it) even as they yearn for deliverance from it. Even very skilled psychotherapists have disappointed patients, although probably not as often as the less skillful ones. This point, I believe, has major implications for "public policy." I think it is well to remember that in this area there will always be unhappy "consumers," regardless of how stringent are the consumer protection policies that may be enacted.

I hope these comments are helpful. I'll be happy to talk more about any of this, if you would like.

[June 15, 1976]

From Jacob Cohen, Ph.D.:

I found the questions in your letter somewhat puzzling, but that is probably because I'm not in the swim of current psychotherapy research. For what they may be worth, I'll try some short answers:

1. We had better be able to legitimately speak of a patient getting worse. If for whatever reason it is argued that we cannot, it would follow that we cannot speak of him getting better, either. Similarly, whether it is the result of psychotherapy constitutes a single problem

2. Again, I find the issue symmetrical. "Better" is defined as a change along some dimensions in a given direction. "Worse" is then a change on these same dimensions in the opposite direction.

3. Perhaps my puzzlement is that I read the first two questions as posing methodological issues when your intention was that they be substantive. The third is clearly substantive, and not being a psychotherapist, I wouldn't know how to begin to answer it.

[February 10, 1976]

From Gerald C. Davison, Ph.D.:

Your first question relates to negative effects, and I certainly believe that people can get worse as a result of psychotherapy or related interventions. Although I have not kept up with that part of the psychotherapy research literature, I think of course of Allen Bergin's classic study of negative effects, but beyond that, my own teaching and clinical experience has unfortunately apprised me of frequent instances of people getting hurt.

To be more specific, I can try to respond to your second question, namely what would constitute such an effect and how one would judge a patient becoming worse. It is commonplace that many people enter therapy because they are confused, in addition to suffering from more specific debilitating conditions. As people like Halleck have argued (and as I have suggested also in my paper on the ethics of treating homosexuals for change of sexual preference), the therapist is in an undeniably powerful position with respect to the client when it comes to conceptualizing what has to be changed, in addition to what we usually talk about, namely how to change it. Therapists teach patients what they should want. Although this is an extreme statement, as made by Halleck, I believe it is at least as defensible as the "liberal" position that the principal task of the therapist is to help people decide what they want. That may be a legitimate goal, but I seriously have to question its practicality. And so, it would seem to me that therapists can hurt, and do occasionally hurt, patients by helping them focus on goals in treatment that may not be to their best interest. (Of course, how to define "best interest" is a tale in itself.)

How can we know when we are having a negative effect? A most obvious indicator would be that the patient is getting more unhappy rather than less so, or more confused rather than less so, or more debilitated rather than becoming strong. It used to be thought, for example, that desensitization required the therapist to terminate an anxiety image as soon as it became troublesome to the relaxed client. Although I believe there is little reason to worry about this, and although I have myself changed my way of doing desensitization so that extended exposure does occur, nonetheless, it may be that certain people, for reasons that we know little of thus far, can be hurt and have been hurt by being kept in troublesome situations (not just in desensitization, of course) longer than they should have been. People can be pushed into facing challenges that they are not ready for. It would seem to me that it would be relatively easy to specify observable criteria for such negative effects.

While I am rambling (I am dictating this letter rather than typing it out, as I typically do with my correspondence), there would seem to be other factors associated with negative effects. There are some therapists who think that their status not only permits them to play god but that indeed they are god. I believe the literature on encounter group casualties confirms that suggestion, that especially charismatic group leaders run a greater risk of hurting people than those who are less forceful and magnetic. I think particularly in a group setting the danger is high that the therapist will not assess properly all the controlling variables for all the patients in the group, and may push certain people too hard, or perhaps certain people not hard enough.

It seems to me also that people can be hurt by therapists promising more than they can deliver. There is a literature on negative placebo effect in drug therapy whereby people actually can get worse from a placebo rather than remain unchanged, apparently because they conclude that, since "the drug" did not help me, I must really be in bad shape. I believe Rickels and his colleagues have documented this. Perhaps this has been done in the psychotherapy research literature as well, but at any rate I offer the clinical observation that people are occasionally harmed by having their hopes and expectations raised by therapists, perhaps even unethically so, only to be sorely disappointed at the very least when the good outcomes promised or implied are not forthcoming. By the way, I believe that those behavior therapists who have concentrated heavily on aversion therapy with so called sexual deviations may be committing this error because, as I am coming to believe, such "problems" as homosexuality may indeed be impervious to being altered in the way that is promised by aversion therapy. Furthermore, if as some of my gay activist friends and colleagues suggest, homosexuals go to aversion therapists because they want to be punished, one has to wonder what in fact is being learned by these unfortunate patients when they are shocked or nauseated when exposed to instances of people they love.

[January 10, 1976]

From John Dollard, Ph.D.:

1. Yes, they can get worse. If they come with hope of cure of alcoholism, for instance, and cannot be cured, they can end up in deeper despair.

2. Yes, if problem is identified and therapist does not have time or skill to work out, patient may be worse off. Could be sexual, aggressive or characterological...

3. (a) Revelations of a problem which increases patient's difficulty in his ordinary life; (b) Disillusion with therapist—that he shows self to be less admirable than had seemed; (c) If therapist does not respond so as to show he is really listening, patient gets worried.

[November 24, 1975]

From Jarl E. Dyrud, M.D.:

I am pleased that you are plugging along with this elusive topic of psychotherapy effects.

What are "related forms of therapy" that are not psychotherapy?

Question 1. Yes.

Question 2. This immediately becomes more complex. Can we accept transient or enduring increases in discomfort and decreases in functioning during treatment as evidence of the process working, and then use these same criteria for negative effects if they persist following termination?

Question 3. A negative effect in my opinion must be linked to therapist error. Either inappropriate technique or misapplication.

Suicide in a suicide-prone patient is not necessarily a negative effect, but rather a calculated risk in many instances.

Let me know how it goes.

[January 28, 1976]

From Albert Ellis, Ph.D.:

1. Yes, I think that psychotherapy can easily lead to negative effects, and that clients can get worse as a result of it or related interventions.

2. The usual main negative effects would be increases in anxiety, depression, hostility, or self-downing, instead of decreases in these feelings. Other symptoms, such as procrastination, inhibition, shirking of responsibilities, and other behavioral deficiencies could also occur. In my own terms, negative effects would also be shown by an increase in irrational ideas: such as the ideas that the individual utterly needs love; must do very well in achievements; cannot change his or her emotional reactions; is a rotten person for doing poor performances; must have immediate gratification rather than future gains; etc.

3. The main factors responsible for a negative effect would include: (1) ignorance and stupidity of the therapist— particularly one who follows classical kinds of psychoanalysis, primal therapy, rolfing, bioenergetics, religiosity, transpersonal therapy, and other forms of therapy which are often iatrogenic; (2) incompetence of the therapist; (3) need of the therapist to depend on clients emotionally or exploit them in other ways; other emotional disturbances of the therapist; (4) misleading and idiotic theories of psychotherapy, such as some of those listed above; (5) refusal to refer clients to other forms of therapy when the one used is obviously not working for a long period of time.

I shall be glad to get reports on your study of the problem of negative effects in psychotherapy as it progresses.

[January 12, 1976]

From Jean Endicott, Ph.D.:

Clinically, I have seen a number of patients whom I felt had a definite "negative" effect from psychotherapy (broadly defined). However, in thinking about your questions, I find it difficult to think of a good research strategy to document such effects or to adequately describe them. The most common negative effect I have seen is a tendency to use psychological jargon as an "alibi" for certain actions or lack of action, a tendency to focus on "explanations" based upon assumed past experiences rather than upon the need for current change. Another negative effect I have observed in patients is an increased tendency of some to adopt a negative self image which seems to have little positive effect on their current functioning ("I found out I am a latent homosexual . . . or very hostile . . . or very dependent . . . etc."). With borderline patients or schizophrenics, too much focus on fantasy life, dreams, "unconscious" desires, etc. seems to produce disorganization and flooding of affect which is difficult for them to handle.

I think a very common "cause" of negative effect is the inappropriate use of interpretations by inexperienced therapists who "know" a particular theoretical approach and attempt to apply it to almost all patients.

Another source of negative effect in my experience has been from interaction with hostile or grandiose therapists.

I would be interested in receiving copies of any reports or studies you conduct in this area. I hope your other respondents were more helpful.

[March 15, 1976]

From George L. Engel, M.D.:

The question you pose is an important one and certainly defies any simple answer. Certainly symptoms may get worse and functioning may deteriorate during psychotherapy but that is not necessarily a bad effect, even among patients who leave psychotherapy on that account. Further, the terms "psychotherapy or related interventions" cover such a multitude of activities that I would be at a loss to know where to begin. Then one has to address oneself to the issue of the competence of the therapist. Certainly "negative effects" of therapy conducted by an ill-trained or incompetent person or one who abuses his position as a therapist is quite a different matter from "negative effects" encountered in the course of well conducted therapy. And one can still have therapy well conducted by a skillful therapist but inappropriate for that particular patient, with a negative outcome. I am sure these are matters you have already thought of. I can see how this would make a fascinating subject for an ongoing seminar extended over many months but do not feel comfortable about addressing myself to such a question in a letter.

[December 8, 1975]

From O. Spurgeon English, M.D.:

My first reaction on receiving your letter was to reply that I had not seen negative effects from psychotherapy. However, upon closer reflection, I think there are some and as examples, I would give the statement of an inexperienced psychotherapist to the patient that he felt the patient's wife's negativity was such that a successful treatment outcome would not be possible without a dissolution of the marriage. Knowing both patient and wife in this situation, my opinion would be that this was a premature and unfortunate statement to make because it undermined the patient's confidence and increased his anxiety unnecessarily. If it were true that the marriage was going to dissolve as the patient recovered, then in my opinion it would have been better to have left this unsaid and deal with the marriage difficulty later when the patient was stronger.

I think I have seen negative effects also from a therapist who had too little experience with somatic symptomatology and as a result of his own anxiety deferred too much to the patient's desire for repeated examinations and overconcentration on his body's symptomatology whereas the real pathology lay in the psyche.

I do not have any other specific examples to comment upon at present. I think your letter would cause me to watch more closely and make a note of cases in which I thought a negative therapeutic effect had occurred and what I deemed to be its cause.

In replying to your third question, I would say that a negative therapeutic outcome would be most likely to occur when the therapist's integrity, competence or degree of experience were such as to impair the patient's trust and positive therapeutic alliance with the physician.

[December 1, 1975]

From Norman L. Farberow, Ph.D.:

Your question is important and the topic fascinating. I will answer briefly at this point and more or less off the top of my head in order not to delay a response any longer. There are in my experience some very important negative effects of therapy and therapists which occur in suicide prevention and crisis intervention work. The most important single factor in helping depressed, self-destructive people is evidence of continuing interest and concern. This isn't too difficult to provide in crisis work generally because the contact is short and it is possible to invest one's self heavily, knowing that the investment will not be required over too long a period. However, when the case becomes chronic and the suicidal person continues to call and to demand service, we tend to get a "burned out" syndrome in our personnel. I know that this kind of feeling becomes communicated to the patient with sometimes tragic results.

We attempt to forestall this feeling in our workers by providing the whole agency for the chronic caller rather than any individual person. This shares the responsibility and lightens the load. However, many psychotherapists in private practice are not aware of the importance of their response to the depressed, continually suicidal patient. Also, they are either too proud to seek consultation or too resentful to obtain help. Not infrequently, we have patients calling our services when they feel they no longer can turn to their individual therapist. Our task at that point is to reestablish the relationship and to offer help to the beleaguered therapist.

Another negative effect of therapy for suicidal patients may be the feeling a patient has on discharge from the hospital after treatment for a suicidal episode. If he has been difficult on the ward and staff reactions to him have been negative, he may feel the hospital is no longer available to him and he has no place to return to when suicidal impulses recur (as they invariably do).

[no date]

From Reuben Fine, Ph.D., P.C.:

1. It is legitimate to speak of a patient getting worse as a result of psychotherapy (or any other intervention, or non-intervention).

2. To establish such an effect, norms would have to be available about the probable life history of any individual. Unfortunately, the available norms are extremely crude, and scarcely usable for scientific work.

3. Assuming, for the sake of argument, that properly conducted psychotherapy leads to improvement, a negative effect could be demonstrated to result from (a) improper technique; (b) poor training of the therapist; and/or (c) unpredictable factors in the personality structure.

My own feeling is that at the present time negative effects are associated primarily with (a) excessive rigidity on the part of the therapist, where the patient is forced to submit to a preestablished procedure; (b) excessive unconscious hostility on the part of the therapist, often disguised by diagnosing the patient as "borderline" or "schizophrenic."

[December 26, 1975]

From Donald W. Fiske, Ph.D.:

I am pleased to be included in your "small group" of respondents. However, I don't claim detailed knowledge of the substance of psychotherapy research.

1. Yes, there is a problem of negative effects, a problem for society, for the practice of psychotherapy, and for the researcher. Intuitively, it seems almost certain that the net effects of some interactions between therapist and patient will be negative. Empirically, there are data indicating negative gains, and these cannot be dismissed as measurement errors.

2. Negative effect can refer either to some overall judgment about the total set of effects of treatment or it can refer to an unfavorable change on some component score. I take a multiple criterion approach to assessing mental health and illness and believe that a variety of different methods involving persons in different roles and relationships to the patient must be used. Strictly speaking, any negative change observed by one measuring procedure is an indicator of a negative effect.

To determine criteria for judging a patient as having become worse, I would start by deciding how to judge that a patient had improved. Given multiple criterion measures, there are many rationales and ways to integrate the set of scores. One is by a clinician operating without instruction or asked to integrate the evidence in a particular way. I would prefer a more overt process for making the decision. I would set a cutting score between gain and no-gain on each criterion measure. Then one overall index would be the number of measures indicating gain minus the number indicating no gain or loss. Alternatively, each post-treatment measure could be converted into a standard score based on the pre-treatment distribution for that measure. The algebraic difference between that score and the patient's pre-treatment standard score on that measure could be obtained and averaged over all available measures, with a positive average indicating gain.

Of course, any assessment of change in an individual by means of differences scores introduces fundamental psychometric problems. There is no consensus on how to handle difference or change scores, and some people (like Cronbach and Furby) tell us not to use such scores.

Two substantive problems: if one criterion (based upon an observer in a particular role or on some one component of mental health) shows very appreciable gain, should it be given extra weight? Again, if treatment goals have been set, providing a focus for the treatment, should change toward or away from these goals (e.g., change on presenting complaints) be emphasized? Yes.

Once the rationale for measuring improvement has been developed, a mirror-image rationale for measuring negative effect can readily be worked out. There are two advantages in starting with a rationale for positive gain: first, we are more familiar with the matter of positive gain; second, the rationale for judging negative effect should be identical in form with that for positive effect. Of course, I assume that, overall or on any one component score, one will ordinarily have a middle zone for no appreciable movement up or down.

3. With what factors should negative effects be associated? Any overall negative effect is due to the fallibility of the therapist. Ideally, he should be able to tell when the treatment is harming the patient, at which point he should change the treatment, even changing the therapist if necessary. More charitably, negative effects are due to our limited knowledge about treating persons. They occur when the therapist is unable to determine the appropriate treatment for the particular patient.

I would be interested in learning about your ideas and those of your other respondents.

Good luck on your project! It is on an important topic which should throw light on how to make treatment more effective for more patients.

[December 15, 1975]

From Donald N. Ford, Ph.D.:

I was interested in your letter and the focus of your research group on exploring the problems of negative effects in psychotherapy and related forms of therapy. Not only is it an important direction from which to approach some issues, but it also sounds like fun. I find myself somewhat envious of the efforts.

Of course, there is the potential of negative effects from any procedures which intervene in a living process. Since psychotherapy and related interventions are indeed interventions in the living process, negative effects are possible.

How does one define an effect as "negative"? It would appear at base to be a value judgment, and whether or not an effect is considered negative probably depends upon the value reference base of the person or persons making the judgment. For example, an effect may be negative if it produces a result which the individual undergoing psychotherapy evaluates as undesirable. It can be considered negative if it produces a result that the individual providing the psychotherapy consideres negative. Obviously, these two judgments might not necessarily be the same. It could be considered negative if it produced effects other than those toward which the therapeutic effort were aimed. Such an unintended effect might in some other value framework be judged as desirable even though inadvertent. And so on. It would follow then that the early stages of the effort to examine the problem of negative effects might conceptually canvass and try to explicate the value frameworks within which such judgments might be made and to elaborate the alternatives. Empirically, the initial steps probably ought to focus on some category of potential negative effects rather than using it as a global concept such as "improvement" in psychotherapy. It seems to me dealing in a sophisticated conceptual way with this issue initially is absolutely essential if the more empirical efforts that would follow are to be useful and solid.

One dimension on which one can break down the issue of negative effects into subcategories could be in response process domains analogous to those around which psychological literature is organized in psych abstracts. For example, a psychotherapeutic approach aimed at producing some change in the way a person thinks about himself, about others, about social contexts, etc. (i.e., is focused upon cognitive processes) may be a catalyst for producing change in an individual's social interaction patterns (a different response domain). If the therapy was not focused upon this second kind of effect, then it should be considered fortuitous. That could be defined as a negative effect. On the other hand, if the change in the behavior is judged to be desirable by the therapist, that might be identified as a positive effect or perhaps, if it is identified as an undesirable result by the client, it might be considered a negative effect. Similarly, conditioning therapies aimed at changing eating behavior may have as a corollary increased fear responses (an emotional or motivational response domain) in the context of certain stimulus configurations. A change in eating behavior, being the target of the therapeutic intervention, might be construed as desirable, and the increase in fear responses as necessary though perhaps undesirable if it could be avoided. And so on.

In summary, the value frame of the observer (e.g., client, therapist, the client's family, the employer, "society") may produce a different judgment about whether an effect is positive or negative depending upon the value frame from which the judgment is made and value frames are correlated with different observers. It would be possible for investigatory purposes to adopt a value frame and treat it as absolute (e.g., life is good, therefore anything which prolongs life is good and anything which shortens it is bad), but that might obscure as many issues as it would reveal. In addition, psychotherapeutic interventions with a particular client characteristically have certain definable targets, targets identified by the client, by the therapist or by concurrence by both (or sometimes by others such as family member or an employer). In any event, it is seldom that the entire response domain of the person and all of his or her interactions are the target of the intervention. The primary target may be to change certain patterns of social interaction, may be to change certain patterns of self-evaluative thoughts, and so forth. Intervention strategy may be aimed at a mediating response as a means of altering the primary target responses. Therefore, it would seem that a second way of subdividing the issue would be to examine the issue in relationship to particular response domains and their interrelationships. These two dimensions alone then provide a kind of two-by-two matrix as a starting point.

There is also the issue of establishing whether an effect is indeed a product of or an event independent of a therapeutic intervention. One aspect of this involves a time dimension. In what time frame in relationship to the intervention is an effect to be considered connected to the intervention? For example, osteoporosis in women around the age of fifty appears to be the consequence of about thirty years of minute progressive withdrawals of calcium from the body's calcium bank. Historically there has been a tendency to associate osteoporosis with menopausal syndromes because they occurred together in time.

Another example is the development of cancer after several years of usage of a drug. Is it possible there are analogs to this in psychotherapy? Is it possible the therapeutic interventions which produce an immediate effect characterized as positive (analogous to preventing pregnancy in intercourse) but have longer-term effects which are deleterious (analogous to circulatory problems or uterine cancer problems or breast cancer problems growing from the use of birth control pills)?

I guess it's clear from these comments that it would be my view that if you were going to tackle this problem, and I believe it to be a very important one, I would hope you would avoid the mistake that has been made with regard to "research on psychotherapeutic outcomes." I would hope you would be able to start with much greater analytic precision in breaking the big problem down into subsets so that the results would be more fruitful.

I'd be interested in being informed about your work. Good luck with it.

[January 22, 1976]

From Lawrence Friedman, M.D.:

I was very pleased to receive your invitation to set down my thoughts on negative effects of therapy. By the nature of my practice I am not in a position to have seen a large number of therapy outcomes, and my opinions are therefore of little value. But for what they are worth, here they are.

1. In general, it seems to me that a relationship always has the possibility of being destructive, and so must the relationship between the therapist and patient.

The worst consequence I have personally seen was in a man with a process-type schizophrenia, who had seriously and continuously loosened associations, and very great difficulty keeping track of the elementary procedures of daily life. His expressed interest in becoming a physician was enthusiastically welcomed by a group psychotherapist who was culturally and ideologically sold on upward mobility, and who encouraged his group to challenge the patient to implement his ambition, and simultaneously strip away his rationalizations and ways of maintaining his self-esteem. He decompensated, became catatonic and required hospitalization.

2. I would list negative effects on a spectrum. At one end would be the precipitation of an overt psychosis, or the transformation from ambulatory to hospital status. Next might be, the intensification of a symbiotic-type struggle, or the explosion of a psychotic transference, eventuating in suicide, and next to that a chronic struggle that does not cost a life. (I place this second because the margin between ultimate success and total failure in this kind of situation is probably very slender.) Next I think of recurrent exacerbation of anxiety and disorganization brought on by psychotherapy sessions. Over at the other end of the spectrum, I would place the subtle blunting of a person's ability to deal directly with his feelings, and with the people in his life, by the intervention of an artificial, esoteric terminology and ideology, as might take place when therapy becomes a patient's career. (I recall a professional in training who, after several years of analysis, declared that she no longer found anything in common with people who weren't analyzed, or any pleasure in their company. I would regard this as a negative influence of therapy, even though the patient did not complain of it.) I don't know how one should rate the establishment of a

permanent dependency on the therapist. Is it a worsening or a meliorative substitution? I suppose that would have to be judged on the individual circumstances. A bad experience in therapy that precludes further necessary therapy would have to be counted as a negative effect.

Thus I consider as indicators and criteria: suicide, loss of contact with reality, loss of ability to handle life problems, the production of gross psychotic symptoms, constant intensification of anxiety or depression correlated with sessions, estrangement from extratherapeutic life experiences, and decreased self-reliance.

The responsibility of therapy for these effects would have to be established on the basis of temporal sequence, and also on the details of the patient's pathology and the therapist's procedure. Only rarely, I suppose, could one assess the responsibility of therapy for negative effects by simply judging the patient's state on starting, and comparing it with his state on outcome. But maybe we should be more hard-nosed, and regard those cases where a patient reports that he feels worse about himself because of therapy, as ipso facto instances of a negative effect of therapy, without necessarily attaching any blame to the therapist.

3. Since people pretty much get from other people what they want, and leave when they can't get anything, the factor responsible for the most severe and blatant negative effects is probably the patient's fragility, or, stated otherwise, the magnitude of the therapeutic problem he presents to the therapist. I think other factors are: therapist's insensitivity to the patient's situation; therapist's unrealistic offering of more than he is really prepared to give to the patient, with consequent betrayal, perhaps in an angry or distancing fashion; therapist's reluctance to encourage direct expression of anger and resentment toward himself; therapist's frustrated repetition of an unfruitful characterization of the patient; therapist's enjoyment of patient's dependency; occasional

unwise interference in patient's outside life; the offering of psychiatric jargon as a tool for handling relationships; therapist's one-sided interest in some particular aspect of the patient, e.g., his dreams, his career, his status in society, some fascinating aspect of his early life and development; therapist's one-sided encouragement of a standard behavior, such as free expression of anger, guilt-free selfishness or bluntness, aggressiveness or extroversion, all the result of a covert ideology masquerading as a technical definition of health. And, of course, any exploitiveness on the part of the therapist, securing sexual or other services from the patient.

It is my impression that some abrupt terminations are destructive. Some patients carry a lasting scar from a contemptuous dismissal. I also know of one therapist who actually ordered a patient out of his office during the first session, declaring that he disliked him intensely for reasons which he would not explain. This therapist had a Zen orientation, and doubtless described the action to himself as an honorable and therapeutic authenticity.

It seems to me that some patients become more symptomatic in investigative psychotherapy no matter how it is handled. I am not sure why, but one gets the distinct impression that life is much better for them after they have discontinued, and precisely because they have discontinued. (They are people one would usually call borderline.) I have wondered whether this might be because all examination inevitably appears to them as fault-finding, and their own discoveries always as self-condemnation. I have also wondered whether in therapy they find themselves continually undertaking a task that they are not suited for, and it amounts to a constant exercise in defeat. Some other patients, who are not necessarily borderline, seem to experience any deep feeling always only hopelessly and helplessly, and as a continual reminder of an insoluble agony, and I don't know whether proper technical means can actually overcome this. Obviously that kind of thing is worked on fruitfully with most patients, but it seems to me that there are some patients who put up with a fruitless self-torment simply in exchange for the unrelated friendship with the therapist. Then there are also patients who experience therapy as a continuous tease: a never fulfilled promise that the bewilderments that are stirred up will eventually be resolved. And there are other patients who seem so locked into a masochistic pattern of experiencing the helping situation as a humiliation, and the therapist's distance as an insult, that no approach seems tolerable, and they just seem to function everywhere better than in therapy.

The therapist's fault in these cases could be (1) not to have discovered other, perhaps less orthodox ways of being with the patient, and (2) a reluctance to "allow" termination when the patient begins to perceive its wisdom. Holding on to a patient can be harmful. (But so can getting rid of him because he doesn't fit into a prejudged pattern of the good patient.)

I doubt that these rambling, common-place free-associations of mine can be much use to your project, but I did want to respond to your interesting question, and I will be extremely interested in the outcome of your deliberations.

[March 15, 1976]

From Sol L. Garfield, Ph.D.:

I do believe that a patient can get worse as a result of psychotherapy. I believe, on the basis of my experience and reading, that negative effects are most possible when the therapist attempts to uncover repressed material which is very threatening to the individual, and which he is not capable of assimilating. This is most likely to occur with an individual who is not well integrated. A similar kind of effect may be produced when the individual in any way is pushed to reveal himself, or is concerned with critical evaluations. This appears as one possibility, for example, in encounter groups.

Indicators of a negative effect can vary. Tests may reveal this, but behavioral observations, reports of others, hospitalization, etc., all are possible indicators.

P.S.: You might be interested in this reference: Lehrman, N.S. (1961). *Journal of Clinical and Experimental Psychopathology* 22:106-111.

[January 6, 1976]

From Robert W. Goldberg, Ph.D.:

1. *Is there a problem of negative effects?* Yes, some patients definitely get worse as a result of therapy. Many patients get temporarily worse, though ultimately better.

2. *What constitutes a negative effect?* In general, whether a patient is psychotic, neurotic, or characterological, I believe that the following general guidelines are applicable to deciding what a "negative" effect of therapy would entail:

(1) *Poorer adaptation to outer reality:* (In comparison with pre-therapy adaptation): worse reality testing, adaptationally poorer decision making, selection of a less intimate living situation, decrease in status and perhaps pay vocationally, increasing social withdrawal. These general factors could be more objectively appraised by ratings by self and others, objective facts about the patient (e.g., what job, where living), and perhaps adjustment inventories as well. Incidence of antisocial acting out might be appropriate for some patients.

(2) *Poorer adaptation to inner reality:* less control of primary process ideation, less sophisticated defenses, less capacity for delay and control of impulses, less secure sense of self and identity, lower self-esteem, greater anxiety and depression, and the like. These general factors could be more objectively appraised by self report, various traditional

psychological tests (or specialized scales based thereupon, e.g., Holt's), categorization of patient material by expert judges early vs. late in therapy, the patient being assigned after therapy to a more pathological DSM II classification, and MMPI.

3. Which factors do you prominently associate with a negative effect? These include the following:

(1) *Poor initial assessment.* With diagnostics being less popular, I feel incidence of misdiagnosis is going up. Emphasis on behavioral approaches in training fractionates the patient, socialization in assessment methods emphasizes debunking of the importance and validity of assessment. Consequently, when the so-called "eclectic" attempts to do something like "add some therapy tools" and "do some therapy" he has little expertise or experience in appraising the nature of the whole person before him. I have seen students and professionals doing uncovering work with pseudoneurotic schizophrenics and borderline syndromes with no awareness of the fragility of the patient's ego structure. Treating hysteriform and overly ideational borderline schizophrenics as high ego strength neurotics seems to me the biggest mistake. In general, too much therapy proceeds today without diagnostic appraisal, be it by the first few interviews or through psychological testing. If Columbus had had a map, he certainly would have traveled west along a more certain course!

(2) *Inexplicit treatment contract.* The patient and therapist fail to establish goals. While these may be general in nature (rather than discrete behaviors), some sense of direction is necessary. The patient's realistic hopes need to be distinguished from his fantasies (of course, many of the fantasies only emerge in treatment and then need definitely to be resolved then, to prevent the patient from undermining the treatment unconsciously because they are not being served). The idea that this will be work, rather than fun, groovy, or a

chance to make a pal, needs to be approached and dealt with (esp. with college students and the lonely).

(3) *Low or absent patient motivation.* Inpatients, court referrals, and adolescents brought by parents frequently perceived that they have been "sentenced to treatment" and I believe make effective therapy virtually impossible. Attempts to force treatment upon these types of people seem to result in their getting worse more often than evidencing sudden flight into health. On the other hand, a variety of hostile transferences can be dealt with if the patient is at least ambivalent to the process rather than completely against it from the outset.

(4) *Hostile countertransference.* I believe this to be more destructive to the treatment process per se than sexual countertransference which (if it does not involve sexual acting out) tends rather to bog down or hinder the work rather than destroying it. Hostile countertransference takes many forms. At the outset, it prevents the establishment of a "real relationship" or "working alliance." It is sometimes manifest as a lack of respect for the patient's pain, sometimes as impatience, sometimes as a failure to allow the patient to experience choice in the material he discusses, sometimes as an aggressive assault on defenses (as opposed to an aim-inhibited confrontation), and sometimes as a rejecting or disappointed attitude toward the patient as a person and towards his progress. Of course there are countless other manifestations but these I believe to be the ones that contribute most to "negative effects," since these do not permit the patient to put trust in the therapist or to establish him as a "good object" with whom to identify. The therapist needs also to recognize real gains when the patient makes them, even if there are subsequent discussions of the defensive aspects of these gains. The more severe the psychopathology of the patient, the more devastating the effect of hostile countertransference in any form of intervention.

More general than any of these, yet possibly more influential, is the relatively inadequate training, supervision, and practice in psychotherapy which many mental health professionals continue to receive, thus making recognition of these other more specific factors much more difficult to recognize.

I would be willing to elaborate on these ideas if you wish. I would indeed be interested, in any event, in learning how you are progressing along these lines.

[February 3, 1976]

From Louis A. Gottschalk, M.D.:

I have your letter and your inquiries on the problem of negative effects in psychotherapy. I am responding to your questions off the top of my head, and so I cannot promise that my ideas will add much to what you and your research group have already considered.

1. I believe that we can, indeed, legitimately speak of a patient getting worse as a result of psychotherapy or related interventions. Much as with pharmacotherapy, there are patients whose symptoms or signs are definitely exacerbated by the administration of psychoactive drugs. Or, if their original symptoms and other manifestations are not made worse, the adverse side effects of the pharmacological agent contribute to make the patient worse off than he was without the drug. The more obvious examples of adverse effects from a type of psychotherapy are, perhaps, those psychopathological or psychophysiological complications of sensitivity or t-groups which I and others have described.

2. Negative effects of psychotherapy might include a worsening of the presenting symptoms or pathological behavior or the development of some new type of psychopathological manifestations or, even, physical or psychosomatic dysfunctions that did not previously exist. Or the negative effect might be manifest in drug or alcohol abuse or criminal behavior that was not previously a problem. The negative effects that would be most clear-cut would be those that appear immediately in temporal relationship with the psychotherapy. There could, in addition, be delayed adverse effects appearing weeks or many months after the termination of the psychotherapy. The latter would, obviously be more difficult to establish as being related to the psychotherapy, and supportive evidence for such might have to be obtained from the patient. Whether to label "a negative effect" those adverse psychological reactions that ex-patients often develop long after termination of psychotherapy and when the therapist temporarily or permanently leaves town is a moot question.

3. There could be a number of factors accounting for negative effects. Therapists variables would, I think, predominate. But the wrong kind of psychotherapy, although the therapist was okay, could also produce negative effects. Another factor associated with negative effects constitutes the patient or the client; certain types of masochistic patients do not feel comfortable when functioning well or if they are succeeding too much. I believe that special psychotherapeutic techniques, including recognition of this aspect of their personality problems, can limit this kind of result from psychotherapy.

I would be interested in hearing more about your own ideas as your research in this area progresses.

[December 4, 1975]

From Ralph R. Greenson, M.D.:

I am very interested in the research project concerning the problem of negative effects in psychotherapy.

(1) I believe every experienced psychotherapist has his share of negative effects, as long as he is openminded and not a fanatic. I would go so far as to say that the longer you practice, the more qualms you have about any particular form of therapy and, in addition, you can see the long term results of your therapy and others you respect. It can be quite shocking, mostly in terms of "others you respect."

(2) I would consider a negative effect: suicide in a patient who was not overtly suicidal. All decompensations in patients who had some equilibrium. Worsening of symptoms or making latent symptoms manifest without being able to be helpful. Therapy which dehumanizes patients, i.e. drug therapy with children, too much shock therapy, lobotomies, and any therapy which makes the patient an addict to the therapy and therapist. Can often be seen with a change of therapist and/or therapy.

(3) Mismatching the patient and his illness with the therapy and the therapist. Psychotherapists who love their theory and/or their mentor more than their patients. Closemindedness, greed and narcissism in the therapist. Also, the lack of real dedication to their work, as well as a dearth of vigorous self-scrutiny.

I am interested in sharing your ideas as the work progresses.

[December 2, 1975]

From Alan S. Gurman, Ph.D.:

Your letter canvassing people about the negative effects of therapy, is intriguing. I have been interested in this issue in the context of marital-family therapy for a couple of years and, I believe, was the first (in my 1973 *Family Process* article) to make it a public issue in this area. I am now beginning to prepare a chapter entitled, "Research in Marital and Family Therapy: An Empirical and Conceptual Analysis," with David Kniskern, for the revised edition of Allen and Sol's *Handbook*. In that chapter we will discuss the deterioration issue. Also, Dave and I have submitted a paper for SPR in San Diego this year on "Deterioration in Marital and Family Therapy." Dave and I are, to our knowledge, the only researchers actively thinking about and trying to develop a *comprehensive* model for the assessment of negative (and positive) change in marital and family therapy. We believe (we're both active clinicians, as well as researchers) that there are a variety of theoretical and clinical issues that make the deterioration issue far more complex in marital-family therapy than in individual therapy and, therefore, in fact even more exciting, in that attempts to operationalize change (positive or negative) in these forms of therapy must, as we see it, pay a great deal more attention to the theory of therapeutic change than is required in studies of individual therapy.

I hope you may have some interest in the negative change issue beyond one-to-one therapy and I would be very excited about continuing to be a part of your project, from the marital-family therapy perspective. Please do keep me up-to-date on your group's ideas and work.

[January 19, 1976]

From Michel Hersen, Ph.D.:

Thank you for your letter asking me to comment on the problem of negative effects in psychotherapy. I am most interested in this issue as it pertains to the single case experiment, and we have dealt with some of the issues at hand in a book that should appear this spring (Hersen, M., and Barlow, D. H., (1976). *Single Case Experimental Designs: Strategies for Studying Behavior Change*. New York: Pergamon Press).

Therefore, in light of the above, I would like to respond to the specific questions by concentrating on the single case strategy in psychotherapy research. As dictated by single case strategies, each patient must first be evaluated during baseline until a stable pattern (graphically) of the target behavior(s) appear. Target behaviors, of course, involve individually or in combination, self-report, motoric or physiological measures. Under these circumstances, a negative effect would be detected during the treatment phase by deterioration in any one, combination, or all of the targets under consideration. In both baseline and treatment phases repeated measurements are to be taken. This is of considerable import inasmuch as a deteriorating trend begun in baseline and then continued during treatment could erroneously be attributed to the introduction of the treatment, which indeed may have *no effect* (positive or negative). Only by having a sufficient number of observations made in baseline and treatment and then by completing the experimental analysis would this be accurately determined. Unfortunately, in the group outcome study, where only pre- and post-measures are taken, such trends would not be detected.

A second way to assess deterioration is to evaluate concurrent behaviors that are not targeted for modification. It is quite possible that treatment may result in positive change in targeted measures but may lead to deterioration in non-targeted measures. Thus, unless a wide array of measures were to be taken during the course of a given experimental analysis, such negative "side effects" (as in the case of pharmacotherapy) would not be ascertained. (See Sajwaj, Twardosz, and Burke 1972.)

Finally, in evaluating negative effects, I believe a distinction needs to be made among drop-outs, treatment failures, and relapse. Drop-out refers to the patient who does not complete treatment for any particular reason; treatment failure refers to no change or deterioration as a function of the treatment's application (i.e., a demonstration of the functional relationship); relapse refers to a return to pre-treatment level or worse after completion of a presumed "effective" treatment. Each of these three classifications, although not usually conceptualized as such, has implications in terms of negative effects.

With respect to your third question concerning factors associated with "negative effects," only the functional analysis can lead to conclusions relating to causal factors (i.e., the experimental analysis of behavior).

Reference

Sajwaj, T., Twardosz, S., and Burke, R. (1972). Side effects of extinction procedures in a remedial preschool. *Journal of Applied Behavior Analysis* 5:163-175.

P.S.: I would greatly appreciate your apprising me how your work on this particular problem progresses. Also, if at some future time you would wish me to present a more formal discussion of these issues, I would be very pleased to cooperate.

[January 15, 1976]

From Marc H. Hollender, M.D.:

Here are a few quick answers to the questions you posed in your letter.

1. Yes, definitely. Anything powerful enough to be a force for good can also be a force for evil.

2. One example of a negative force would be the fostering of regression and dependence in a person who then clings to the therapist. At that point therapy becomes a way of life instead of an aid to living. I know of no way to definitively separate the patient who holds together because of strength derived from a therapist and the patient who has been infantilized and crippled by a therapist. It is my impression, however, based on clinical consultations I have done, that some therapists promote regression and dependence and the result is most destructive.

3. The answer to 3 is contained in 2 above. I would only add that therapists who do not encourage patients to make treatment a way of life but who do little or nothing to head off such a use of treatment may also be responsible for negative results.

[November 28, 1975]

*   *   *

Your focus on the negative effects of psychotherapy has stimulated a number of ideas. For one thing I have taken note of the variety of dangers I pointed up in my book on psychotherapy. There are more instances than I had previously realized.

For example, I pointed up the fact that "positive transference presents a special danger—the danger that it might be used for Pygmalion-like purposes." Another example: A patient not only felt like a child in relationship to· the therapist but she was placed in the child's position in relationship to him. I commented, "Direct gratification interferes with self-understanding and change and should therefore be avoided."

[February 1, 1977]

From Donald J. Holmes, M.D.:

I shall reply to your questions one by one:

1. Yes, in my opinion there can be negative effects produced "as a result of psychotherapy or related interventions."

2. I think that by definition a worsening of a patient's symptoms would constitute a negative effect, or the production of new—not previously existing—symptoms. To me, the most reliable indication of a negative effect having been produced would be the patient's complaint, the complaint of those closest to him and most concerned about him (of course this can be very biased), and my own judgment about the patient's progress, or lack thereof. These are essentially the criteria that I would be most apt to rely upon in estimating whether or not a patient has become worse as a result of therapy, along with any relatively objective indicators as to how well he is getting along in his life, on the job, in school, in his relationships, and so on.

3. I think the one factor most likely to be responsible for the production of a negative result in psychotherapy is in the therapist's inadvertent overemphasizing those things about the patient which he (the therapist) sees as "sick" and underemphasizing the patient or client's personality assets, or strengths. (Such an attitude on the therapist's part can have a very powerful and lasting influence on the susceptible patient, and this unfortunate result can be

produced very effectively by verbal, nonverbal, and combined signals sent from therapist to patient.)

There may be a few charlatan-types who would do something like this on purpose, chiefly to increase their income. Most of the time, however, I believe the therapist does this unconsciously and with the unconscious motivation of enhancing his own personal *and* professional self-esteem by comparing himself much too favorably with the patient whom he sees as weak, helpless, and in need of a great deal of help from the wise, powerful, and "super healthy" expert.

If you are by any chance interested in a more expanded version of my view on this question, you might want to get into my textbook a little bit. This is called *Psychotherapy*, published by Little, Brown and Company, 34 Beacon Street, Boston 02106, in 1972.

Your work sounds most interesting and I would be interested in your findings. And thank you for your interest in my opinion.

[March 4, 1976]

From Frederick H. Kanfer, Ph.D.:

My delay in responding to your letter concerning the problem of negative effects is due to the fact that I was out of the office when your letter arrived. It was also a difficult letter to answer without some time to think about it.

To handle the question you ask would probably require some research and a paper. However, I want to make some comments because I have mused about this question on many occasions. Unfortunately, time does not permit me to do more than give you some relatively spontaneous thoughts.

Yes, I believe that patients can get worse as a result of therapy. The evaluation, of course, depends on the criterion for improvement. By getting worse I mean that the client can be prevented from seeking more effective help elsewhere, can be led to overlook preventive measures that would avoid a future problem, or can be treated without success and with a result of decreasing confidence in psychological treatment. In extreme cases, I have also seen deaths due to failure to recognize medical problems.

Clearly, the behavior change over time can never be attributed solely to therapeutic intervention, since other life events continue to influence the patient. However, indications that a particular treatment results in behavior change that aggravates the situation might be a clear criterion for negative therapeutic .results. For example, implosion sessions that result in increased anxiety, or assertiveness training that leads to worsening of interpersonal relationships, or encounter sessions that increase feelings of alienation or depression might all be examples.

Among the many factors associated with a negative effect might be the therapist's attempt to accomplish excessively demanding goals or proceed too rapidly toward a change. From my emphasis on giving clients full responsibility for change, encouragement toward strong dependency on the therapist may result in negative effects on termination.

A presentation of insight, or confrontations or assessments of a patient's weaknesses without following it up with opportunities for improvement and change or working-through can represent a negative effect. Selection of an objective for treatment which is either abstract or not agreed upon by the client might be another factor leading to negative effects.

I would be glad to hear what other ideas have come in and will look forward to seeing the product of your work.

I was glad to have an opportunity to be of help, however little. With best personal regards.

[January 30, 1976]

From Jane W. Kessler, Ph.D.:

I am answering your letter "off the top of my head" in order to be sure that it does not go into my procrastination file. Obviously my frame of reference will be psychotherapy with children and adolescents and the related work with parents, teachers, and physicians.

The major pitfall in working with children is that the therapist will introduce new conflicts. If the therapist is markedly more permissive or delves into "family secrets," the child may find that he is in a loyalty conflict or that his new behavior (such as verbal expressions of aggression against the parents) gets him into difficulties. These difficulties may be so severe that the parents precipitously withdraw the child from treatment and then the child is probably "worse off" than before. This would be a negative effect of psychotherapy but the indicators would be hard to assess.

Perhaps it would be easier to assess the indirect effect on parents. If the parents feel more alienated from their child, or more helpless in their task of child-rearing, as a consequence of the child's therapy, these would be negative effects. Similar effects might be observed with the child's teachers. It is important that child therapists be as empathic with parents as with children and sometimes this is very difficult.

Of course there are potential negative effects associated with what I would consider mistakes in psychotherapy but I presume that your group is not so concerned with these. I would indeed be interested in your ideas as these might suggest additional observations on my part. Incidentally one might consider "no change" a negative effect with children since it can be assumed that children normally change some simply with maturation and age! I have occasionally observed that child therapists may be reenforcing infantile anxieties or defenses with their sympathy and understanding which leads to a "no change" result.

[January 10, 1976]

From Donald J. Kiesler, Ph.D.:

1. Is there a problem of negative effects, i.e., can we legitimately speak of a patient getting worse as a result of psychotherapy or related interventions? Patient outcome uniformity myth—"worse" in which ways? For which patients? Maybe some patients do, and some don't.

2. If so, what would constitute a negative effect? What are the indicators of a negative effect? By what criteria would one judge a patient as having become worse as a result of therapy? Same comment. Would have to specify for patient problems or homogeneous groups. More generally increase in depression; symptom frequency, intensity, or new ones; self-report that things are worse. But all these general indexes need to be qualified when talking about a particular client or homogeneous group of clients.

3. While any therapy outcome is obviously a function of many factors, which factors would you prominently associate with, or consider responsible for, a negative effect? Therapist poor-relationship factors, so-called "countertransference," "bad" advice, imposition of therapist's values.

From Peter H. Knapp, M.D.:

I am thoroughly convinced, after almost 30 years as a practicing psychotherapy teacher and researcher, that it is definitely possible to speak of a patient getting worse as a result of psychotherapy.

Let me start with some examples: During military service at a center for the hard of hearing, where we were interested in conversion deafness, a young psychiatrist hypnotized a farm boy, "cured" his deafness, only to find him wandering around three weeks later hallucinating about the experience, quite psychotic.

Some years later, I recall a resident who misread some of the psychoanalytic literature about "satisfying masochism" and ended up in a very sado-masochistic relationship with a young woman with many primitive personality features, screaming and yelling, utterly unable to pull herself together and function. For almost ten years she followed him around town shouting imprecations outside his office, insisting that he had ruined her life. Today she might well have fallen into the hands of a lawyer and be suing for large amounts on the basis of malpractice. In any case her own malfunction was obvious.

In the late 1940's we were just beginning to learn about the psychotherapy of patients with severe psychosomatic disease, particularly ulcerative colitis. We saw numerous instances of patients who were encouraged to express their emotions. They got enormously involved with therapists, poured out beautiful material, and became steadily worse. Several of them died. Lindemann soon called attention to this kind of ill-advised intervention and insisted upon the need for sensitive supportive therapy with such sick individuals.

A subtler instance: A recent graduate of our residency program began treating an attractive, unhappily married young woman, who soon, under the pressure of her attachment to him, began talking of divorce. He was unhappily married, too, and I believe definitely urged her to act out some of his wishes. In any event she did get divorced, but remained in a state of isolation and slipped into alcoholism. She was stuck there by the time I heard about the case. Though the therapist had done nothing overtly improper, he had urged an impulsive and destructive course of action upon her.

Another example of a negative effect is the insensitive handling of suicidal risk. I recently saw a young psychiatrist who got locked into a protracted moralistic argument with an obsessional, smiling, depressed woman, who had made two serious suicidal attempts following a catastrophic loss some months earlier. The therapist refused to recognize the fact that this woman was seriously depressed; instead he looked at her as an argumentative, stubborn woman who would not make a "contract" with him. When she failed to keep an appointment, he was prepared to write it off as a part of her obstinate pattern. His supervisor insisted on going out to the home and breaking the door down, where the woman was found in a deep stupor as a result of a barbiturate overdose.

Another example, not from my own specific field of endeavor: A woman with hysterical leg paralysis was treated by a particularly crude and forceful form of behavior modification, partly bullied, partly tricked into walking in front of a class of students. She walked out of the hospital, and returned that night with both radial arteries slashed in a major suicidal attempt.

One could go on with many examples. To generalize, I would say that we can infer a negative result when symptomatic worsening, destructive behavior patterns or "regressive" and maladaptive personality features, emerge as what seems to be a direct consequence of therapeutic intervention, and are not met with effective counter measures by the therapist. The case is particularly damaging when they do not even seem to be recognized. Our criteria are not more final than they are for improvement. We must rely on fairly coarse estimates as to when a definite change in the direction of a person's life has taken place. There is little doubt about anecdotal instances, like the dramatic ones I mentioned to you. (Needless to say one must distinguish carefully from cases who are extremely sick to start with and who in spite of what makes a careful distinction between such instances and cases who start out with a history of progressive decline, which continues despite what seems to be, by all known standards, good treatment, and from those who are kept going by treatment, even though it seems interminable.)

Thus I believe iatrogenic worsening is a definite reality. Although I cannot speak from direct experience, I also believe that it is not too different from similar worsening reported as a result from intense encounter groups experiences.

In the individual psychotherapy, with which I am most familiar, I think that the result usually comes about by an unfortunate matching of unconscious elements in the therapist with those in the patient, so that the therapist manages to ignore and/or to live out deleterious patterns. A corollary would be that training deficiencies, which may be quite subtle, prevent him from getting the guidance necessary to change these patterns.

I have dealt with only extreme examples. If one looked carefully at other therapeutic encounters, one might see many instances of some imperfect matching, some insensitivity, some quasi-destructive angry reactions on the part of the therapist, which have definite, far-reaching detrimental effect. These considerations have, I feel, great relevance from some of the issues you addressed in your recent paper in the International Journal of Psychiatry. As a profession, we have been reassured by the old principle of primum non nocere—as S. Fisher put it—that is, we have felt that what we do is at least not harmful. In most cases that is probably so. Patients are highly adaptive and well defended. If we try forcibly to deprive them of symptoms or confront them prematurely with a major conflict, they usually manage to deny, substitute, evade, etc.; and they usually preserve more or less the balance they had originally. Likewise therapists, intuitively for the most part, let well enough alone, close their eyes, wittingly or unwittingly or otherwise skirt around many dangerous or destructive issues. Incidentally I would expect that that is what you would find with your "wise college counselor dyads"—namely, a good deal of mutual regulation of distance and avoidance of serious trouble spots.

But when you have therapists who are committed ideologists, determined to break down symptom barriers, to extort full disclosure, or "to walk barefoot through the Id" (as Doug Bond once put it)—I am not sure that we are dealing with something so foolproof.

Obviously what we need are more searching questions about the various learning teaching strategies of different therapists and therapies, and more impartially collected data about what really happens. The latter within a descriptive framework first, leaving aside for the time being complexities of evaluating "health" and "improvement." That is why your letter of inquiry is so important, and why your article and the research you are involved in is so important.

[February 20, 1976 (revised July 1, 1976)]

From Heinz Kohut, M.D.:

The letter in which you ask me for my views about negative effects of psychotherapy has been lying unanswered on my desk for all too long. The reason for my hesitance in replying to it is twofold: I know both too little and too much about the topic concerning which you are collecting the views of people in the field of psychotherapy. I know too little because in the circumscribed sense of your inquiry I have not given sufficient attention to the problem you raise in order to give you an answer that would satisfy me. I know too much because I am at the present time putting the finishing touches on a book *(The Restoration of the Self)* that deals with the question of the termination of analyses and the problem of defining the concept of psychological cure. But perhaps I should just give you the simplest possible answer on the basis of a non-scientific impression concerning my own psychotherapeutic experiences. Looking back over about twenty-five years of practice as a psychoanalyst, I can think of no case in which I could clearly say that I have harmed the patient directly. There was one suicide in a woman who did not live in Chicago and who was not clinically depressed as far as anybody in her environment could see. (I only saw her once or twice a month.) And there was, very early in my career (I was still a student at the Institute) an analysis that ended when the young patient (a man, age 21) became diffusely anxious and had dreams indicating the disintegration of psychological structure. I heard later that he had been doing fairly well for about a year after the end of the analysis, but that he then (in another city) had become schizophrenic and was chronically hospitalized. And, finally, there is the analysis of a training candidate, a 35-year-old man, who seemed more or less balanced when he started the training analysis with me. After about six months I had to discontinue the analysis because instead of tackling his problems via insight, he began to act out wildly. I heard later that he has been drinking heavily ever since the analysis ended. But I also learned (from his wife; a physician) that he had been drinking heavily before he entered analysis—a fact which he had hidden from the admissions committee of the Institute and from me. Have I harmed these three patients? Would they have fared better had I not undertaken treatment with them? I don't think so. It is possible that my increased understanding of narcissistic disturbances and of the factors that lead to the disintegration of the self would make me now more capable of handling such cases—but to acknowledge this fact is not the same as saying that I then harmed these people.

Once more my apology for being so tardy with my reply.

[March 4, 1976]

From Leonard Krasner, Ph.D.:

This is in response to your inquiry about my views on the problem of "negative effects" in psychotherapy. I believe that a major cause of growing concern about this issue on the part of therapists is the gradual shifting in theoretical model that is now taking place, particularly among psychologists. The shift is away from a "medical" model to that of a "social-educational" model.

I believe that this shift is taking place subtly and unobtrusively with some therapists, sharply and avowedly with others, and of course many are not shifting at all and remain with the hard core "illness" model.

Working within the medical model issues of the patient getting better or worse are comparatively easy in that the aim of the therapist is the restoration to a hypothetical state of "health." It is true that an individual could become "sicker" during the therapy process. In fact some theoretical orientation would even argue that it is necessary to get "sicker" in the process of "getting well."

As alternative theoretical models develop, the issue of changing virtually every behavior becomes one of "What are the consequences of changing this specific behavior both for this individual and for the others in his life?" Each change is now value-laden with possible positive or aversive consequences for the client, the people in his life, and for the therapist. Issues of negative effect must now be considered within this broader issue of values (what is good behavior for an individual and for society). Hence issues of possible negative effects become far more complex for everyone considered. In effect they may well be the key focus of discussion and decision making between the therapist and the client.

[December 15, 1975]

From Robert Langs, M.D.:

Thank you for your inquiry regarding the critical issue of negative effects in psychotherapy and related forms of therapy. This is certainly a problem that all psychotherapists and psychoanalysts have considered, yet it is one regarding which little definitive research has been done. I therefore welcome both your investigation of the subject and the opportunity to comment briefly.

As for your question as to whether there is indeed a problem of negative effects, it appears quite certain that a patient can suffer an intensification of symptoms—or develop new symptoms—as a result of a psychotherapeutic experience. There is no conceivable guarantee that a given psychotherapist will consistently intervene in a valid or helpful manner; further, one can anticipate specific situations in which a patient will, despite every helpful effort, show a deterioration in regard to his symptomatology—e.g., the negative therapeutic reaction. It might be advisable to classify negative effects along the following lines: those that are immediate, acute, hopefully temporary, and possibly, at times, even necessary for an eventual positive therapeutic outcome can be termed *ongoing negative effects*. The second major grouping, which clearly overlaps the first, would refer to the accumulation of such isolated negative effects into a distinct and lasting negative outcome to the psychotherapy. Such a result would characterize the treatment at the time of termination and might be termed *negative outcome effects*; these may prove chronic or may remiss after termination. Investigation may well reveal both similarities and distinctions between these two aspects of negative effect.

Your second question, as to the criteria for negative effects, raises many complex issues; the development of operational criteria would indeed prove difficult. Stating the issue broadly, I would consider a negative effect to be any failure in symptom relief or the appearance during the course of therapy of any new emotionally based symptom—psychic or psycho-somatic—which proves relatively irresolvable. Of course, transient negative effects may occur in sound therapy, and even during the course of a valid therapeutic experience, life circumstances and a variety of intrapsychic and somatic factors may lead to emotional deterioration; we therefore need basic criteria for ascertaining the underlying basis for symptom exacerbation. In this respect, it is my clinical impression that careful attention to the latent content of the patient's associations, studied in the context of the symptoms problem, could offer a reliable clinical means of detecting the underlying factors—especially as they pertain to the therapeutic interaction. It is here that an extensive utilization of what I have termed the *validating process* would prove essential; any formulation of the unconscious basis for an exacerbation in symptoms must be carefully validated from the patient's associations and the therapist's subjective reactions. I would place special stress on the importance of the search for these unconscious factors and on indicators that relate to indirect communications from the patient that permit more than a surface assessment.

The main factors in the negative effect clearly lie within the therapeutic interaction, and may stem from difficulties within either the patient or the therapist. In sorting out these elements, the therapist must undertake an in-depth study of the material from the patient, and of the conscious and unconscious interaction between the patient and himself; here too there must be a stress on the use of the validating process and a thorough search of the latent content of both the patient's associations and the therapist's subjective reactions. While it is quite possible that the responsibility for such negative effects may reside primarily within the patient, my own clinical observations would lead me to emphasize the role of unconscious countertransference difficulties within the therapist, as these are communicated to the patient through interventions and failures to intervene. Further, I refer here not only to the therapist's verbal interventions—e.g., his incorrect interpretations—but also to his technical errors in the management of the ground rules of therapy—the framework. This latter dimension has been quite neglected and constitutes a significant factor in negative therapeutic effects.

Finally, for my own clinical research and review of the literature, which was, in part, designed to identify the sources of negative therapeutic effects in both psychoanalysis and psychoanalytic psychotherapy, I refer you to two recent books: *The Bipersonal Field* and *The Therapeutic Interaction*. In the first work, both unconscious countertransference problems and pathological interactions such as therapeutic misalliances are extensively explored in the context of negative therapeutic effects. In stressing interactional sources of symptom exacerbation in the patient, I've coined the terms *iatrogenic syndromes* and *interactional neuroses* in order to specify the therapist's contributions to the patient's illness. I have also pointed out that in the alleviation of such negative effects any pathological contributions by the therapist must be rectified before interpretive efforts can modify such symptoms through insights and positive introjective identifications within the patient.

I hope that this brief response is of some help to you, and I look forward to hearing further from you as you own work progresses. I will also be pleased to elaborate upon these initial thoughts if they seem of interest to you.

[January 17, 1976]

From Arnold A. Lazarus, Ph.D.:

In answer to your specific questions, I offer the following observations:

1. We can legitimately speak of a patient getting worse as a result of therapist's interventions.

2. Negative effects seem to follow several different pathways. Some people may become more anxious, more depressed, more guilt ridden, more confused and less self-confident. In others, the negative effect is not so much an exacerbation of symptomatology as a hardening in their negative attitudes toward future help. These individuals typically get turned off to the entire mental health profession. Yet another outcome is the way in which some therapists foster their patients' dependency, teach them to become preoccupied with intrapsychic phenomena instead of solving their problems, and lead them to view themselves as "sick" or "abnormal."

   I am not addressing gross problems of mishandling. We all know of therapists who use coercive means, especially in groups, to invade their patients' privacy, and those therapists who exploit their dependent clients and obtain sadistic pleasure by so doing. I am focusing more upon seemingly responsible practitioners who never deviate from the specified ethical norms but who nevertheless harm rather than help many of the people who consult them.

3. One factor that seems prominently associated with a negative effect is the use of labeling. There are far too many people who have been labeled "schizophrenic" (or "homosexual," or "hysterical," etc.) and for whom this unfortunate label becomes either an excuse and/or a reason for repeated failures and bizarre conduct. (I am not

including under "negative effects" the mass of individuals who are simply not helped—rather than harmed—because therapists have used incorrect techniques, or given poor advice, or have missed the essence of the problem.)

I am enclosing a xerox copy from a recent popular book of mine which underscores some additional factors. As you can deduce from the questionnaire, I have some clear-cut notions regarding therapist characteristics that tend to prove helpful or harmful.

I am most interested in hearing your ideas as well as other clinicians' notions on this very important topic.

[January 15, 1976]

From Robert P. Liberman, M.D.:

Regarding your letter enquiring about negative effects in psychotherapy, I would like to make the following points:

1. Establishing the existence of negative effects should ideally require more than a single or few measures of the patients' behavioral or affective state prior to treatment. Continuous measures, as are obtained during baseline observations in behavior therapy programmes, would be a more reliable means of determining whether treatment brings about negative effects.

2. There is the problem of certain treatment methods making patients temporarily "worse" as a condition of their making a recovery. A good example of this is the exposure or flooding treatment for compulsions and phobias. The patient is exposed to the anxiety-provoking situation, and after temporary rises in anxiety and discomfort, experiences symptomatic relief and cessation of avoidance behavior.

3. I think, from my own clinical and research experience, that negative effects do occur in behavioral therapy. Some of the causes of this are:

a. The need for stable baselines in conducting experimental, single case treatment. At times, patients deteriorate while being observed during the baseline period. This is particularly true where patients are taken off medication, and who suffer from a psychotic disorder.
b. In a similar vein, conducting reversal designs necessitates producing negative effects in order to demonstrate the causality of treatment effects.
c. Establishing goals that are too difficult or large, and moving too quickly to reach goals (versus gradually shaping between goals) can produce negative effects.
d. Negative effects can also be brought about by inattention to relevant influences, such as the family system and other environmental reinforcers.

[January 24, 1976]

From Morton A. Lieberman, Ph.D.:

I will address the three questions you raised regarding the problem of negative effects in psychotherapy and related forms of therapy.

My data source is from the numerous psychotherapy patients for whom I have been in supervisory responsibility, as well as from some pilot work I did last year while at the University of Wisconsin. Yes, I think that we can legitimately speak of patients getting worse as a result of psychotherapy. On the basis of research material (resident-run groups) the simple-minded approach of using the target problem complaint model yielded numerous patients who appeared to be doing worse. There is sufficient correspondence between this kind of self-reporting and incidents such as hospitalization, leaving school, and other "disintegrator effects" that are suggestive. Obviously, it's difficult to know without more complex research designs whether such patients would have moved in similar directions without intervention. However, I am persuaded on the basis of tying in the frequency with which some patients were reported in particular groups and not in others to believe that there is some contribution of the therapeutic process itself.

The factor that stands uppermost in my mind for patients getting worse is inappropriate placements, in particular therapeutic arrangements. A recent clinical example where a young woman who might be classified in the old diagnostic nomenclature as an infantile person clearly began to go downhill because she was put into a group that functioned at a much different level than she could tolerate. In some way, I realize that I would consider negative results in therapy to have occurred for this woman if she had remained the same or gotten slightly worse. I think the point, though difficult to demonstrate, would be that in a different treatment context, with the right kind of therapy (in this particular instance, a real mothering figure who was not afraid of physical contact) this woman would have stabilized.

What I am raising, although realizing the complexity of it in a research design, is that I am not sure what the zero point should be for measuring positive and negative change. I think we've blithely assumed that no change is the appropriate zero point, but I have some philosophical misgivings about that and would probably move it in the direction of the positive side. Such a move would clearly result in the increase of frequency what we as therapists see as negative change as a result of therapy.

[no date]

From Lester Luborsky, Ph.D.:

1. Is there a problem of negative effects? Answer: My reply is based heavily on the experience with the 80-case study we have just completed. However, even though it's completed I don't have the results in a form that bears precisely on the question you raise. My impression is that the patients in the low end of the improvement spectrum are mainly non-improvers rather than people who got worse. My sample is patients in psychotherapy who range anywhere from border-line and above. In that population the main effect at the low end of the distribution of improvement is that the patient didn't get what he wanted and was very disappointed and hurt, and possibly angry, but major worsening effects are not clear. There may be a small percentage of patients who get grossly worse but in our sample there were no cases of this sort.

2. The factor which most typically makes for a negative effect is the actualizing and experiencing of the conflictual relationship theme which tends to occur in the relationship with the therapist as the treatment proceeds. When the therapist does nothing to help this or may even fit in unwittingly with the patient's expectations, a negative effect is likely. (Ms BJ, patient no. 6 in the sample of non-improvers, is a good example of a patient's treatment in which nothing was done to counter the actualizing of the expectations involved in the core conflictual relationship theme.)

[December 16, 1975]

From Michael J. Mahoney, Ph.D.:

Thank you for your letter. As you may have expected, I am intrigued by your project regarding negative effects in psychotherapy and the criteria which would be used to evaluate it. The ethics of psychotherapy comprise a large part of my own clinical teaching here at Penn State, and I would indeed like to be kept informed of your progress on this very important theme.

It seems to me that an adequate analysis of the problem will require at least three sub-explorations:

1. At what point does logic (reason, data, etc.) enter into the argument? That is, given the current consensus by axiologists that there are no universal moral imperatives, everyone must make a "leap" to some basic (albeit subjective) premise (such as "human suffering is bad," etc.). The recent Humanist Manifesto II is the best attempt I have seen so far.
2. Who decides the status of psychotherapy outcome (client, therapist, MMPI, behavior rating scales, etc.)? This gets into the thorny issue of psychotherapy as a service—is its prime goal then the "satisfaction" of its customer?
3. In light of the behaviorists' insistence on *behavior change* as the sine qua non of therapeutic success, it should be easy to demonstrate that there are instances where the absence of that change (and the absence of aspiration toward change) could be defended as more "successful" outcomes. (That is, I would argue that there are instances where the client is best served by being aided in *accepting* rather than futilely trying to change, untoward life circumstances.)

Unfortunately, I don't think I have any inside tracks on resolving this issue, but I heartily commend your broaching it, and particularly your efforts to raise consciousness of it among therapists and psychotherapy researchers.

[January 20, 1976]

From David Malan, M.D.:

This is a reply to your letter asking about negative effects of psychotherapy. I have done a lot of thinking about this since then, and my thoughts follow:

1. In what I write I am concerned entirely with negative effects from dynamic psychotherapy of an "uncovering" kind.
2. I am absolutely sure that there are such effects and that they are relatively common.
3. I do not agree with Allen, who in all his writings implies that negative effects are always due to bad therapy.
4. On the contrary, it is in the very nature of dynamic psychotherapy to stir up conflict and hence quite possibly to make the patient worse in the initial stages. This is an absolutely natural phase of all deep-going psychotherapy, and I would say tends to occur at one stage or another in almost every analysis.
5. The hope is always that once the patient has faced these conflicts, he can resolve them and come out the other side much better.
6. There are many therapies and many types of patient with whom this doesn't happen, and the patient may well be left worse off as a consequence.
7. It is the task of anyone selecting patients for psychotherapy to assign them to a form of therapy appropriate to the nature and degree of their disturbance.
8. It is a particular task to try to exclude from very deep-going psychotherapy those patients who have not the strength to bear it.
9. It is the failure to match therapy to the patient's disturbance that is most likely to lead to negative effects.
10. One could give a very long list of those effects, which all consist of intensification of the patient's disturbance: (a) depressive breakdown; (b) suicide; (c) psychotic break-

down; (d) severe regression; (e) destructive or self-destructive acting-out.

11. With those effects already mentioned are those that occur outside the therapeutic relationship. There are also those that occur within it, such as: (a) severe dependence on the therapist; (b) unresolvable positive or negative transference; (c) delusional transference, etc.

I have a long list of therapeutic disasters that have occurred, either in my private practice or in patients that I have known about at the Tavistock Clinic. These include many psychotic breakdowns, e.g., a woman who apparently suffered from an ordinary character problem who one day announced in the group that Dr. Malan and she were deeply in love with each other and intended to get married but she would continue as a co-therapist as long as she was needed! She eventually turned up at my home, convinced that I would marry her and was astonished to find that I already had a wife and child. Another example of a therapeutic catastrophe is an Irish girl whose boyfriend died suddenly of a coronary not long after a serious quarrel with her. She had an appalling family history, with signs of dementia and alcoholism probably due to schizophrenia in at least three members of her close family. She was living only in a bed-sitting-room and had nobody in this country but a married sister to support her. My hope was that we could deal in brief therapy with her feelings about the traumatic loss of her boyfriend, but the inexperienced therapist rapidly got involved in her dependent transference, and she committed suicide. A third example is of a man of 24 complaining of a single fugue-like experience. He quickly revealed that he was a borderline psychotic, and we took him on in the full knowledge of what the consequences would be like. He is not a therapeutic disaster, because I think we assessed him correctly, but during the course of three years of treatment he has had to be admitted to hospital as an in-patient or day-patient at least six times. His forearms look like marshalling yards with the number of times he has slit them with a razor and had to be sewn up again. On one occasion he had brought up a bottle full of his own blood to his therapist. He has made several suicidal gestures with tablets. We were well aware that this kind of thing would emerge during therapy, but felt that both he and his therapist were strong enough to bear it all, and so far our faith has been justified.

Yes, I would very much like to share your thoughts and those of other colleagues about these problems, which I have thought about deeply over a number of years.

[January 13, 1976]

*   *   *

In the initial stages of therapy, and indeed sometimes in the latter stages, patients apparently "get better" and want to stop treatment. Analysts are all trained to regard this as usually being a "flight into health" and they interpret it as such and may succeed in keeping the patient in therapy. It is quite clear that sometimes this is not a flight into health and that even if it is a patient is sometimes able to make use of it as a point of growth. Keeping the patient in therapy may bring back his symptoms without the final outcome of resolving them. This is yet another way in which the patient may be harmed by therapy.

[July 7, 1976]

From Isaac Marks, M.D.:

1. Whether there is a problem depends on definition. Sometimes during exposure treatment patients experience transient severe anxiety and mild depression during, or for a day or two after, the session. This does not militate against

great improvement in outcome at the end of treatment and follow-up.

Occasionally improvement in a patient's behavior leads to social repercussions, e.g., when an obsessive man lost his chronic rituals, his fiancee said he no longer needed her and left him. He then had a minor grief reaction which soon cleared up and he got another girlfriend instead, remaining ritual-free at two-year follow-up. I would not call this a negative effect, but rather a social repercussion of change, which can occur with any treatment, e.g., the removal of congenital cataracts at adult life can produce serious personality disturbances and even suicide. This is not because the cataract serves any purpose for personality function but simply any major change in life style can have consequences for good or ill, and need to be coped with.

2. I would only regard as a negative effect a lasting deterioration in a patient directly attributable to therapy. This can be difficult to judge. The so-called encounter group "casualties" of Lieberman, Miles and Yalom, I would not regard as examples of negative effect, because their data suggested that clients were disturbed well before they joined the encounter groups and they may well have had the same course without the experience.

3. A stormy course after treatment is probably best predicted by a stormy course before treatment. Whether this is relevant to negative effect is dubious. Asking about negative effect is as unconstructive as asking about positive effect. One has to specify the problem being treated and the precise criteria for outcome during, at the end of, and subsequent to treatment, and the treatment methods employed. I doubt whether meaningful generalizations can be made across the board for negative effect talking about all patients with all forms of psychotherapy.

I would be glad to hear about the progress of your work and other people's comments on the subject.

[December 4, 1975]

From Judd Marmor, M.D.:

I shall answer your three specific questions briefly:

1. There is indeed a problem of negative effects as a result of psychotherapy, as any experienced clinician can document from his clinical experience.

2. Negative effects can be the obvious ones of an exacerbation of the symptoms that brought the patient into treatment in the first place, or, they may be more dramatic in the form of a psychotic break, a suicide or suicidal attempt, or, less frequently, an overt active aggression against either the psychotherapist or some significant other. A more subtle negative effect that is frequently encountered is the development of an undue dependency on the therapist, which may be fostered by specific elements in the psychotherapeutic technique. Still other subtle effects might be various forms of "acting out" during the course of psychotherapy. One other effect that I have sometimes encountered is a utilization of a psychotherapeutic experience (e.g., having been psychoanalyzed) to rationalize feelings of smugness, superiority over others, or utilizing their "insights" to aggressively comment on other people's behavior.

3. Any therapy outcome is a function of many factors. Off the top of my head, a few that come to my mind are: techniques that foster undue dependency on the therapist, interpretations that are so predominantly "transference-centered" that they distort or minimize the impact of reality factors in the patient's life (by this I mean interpretations that put everything that goes on in a patient's life and behavior as being the consequences of his relationship to the therapist only), seductiveness on the part of the therapist, lack of genuine interest or concern on the part of the therapist, destructive or critical interpretations (particularly if they are made before a genuine trust and rapport has developed between the patient

and the therapist), lack of warmth on the part of the therapist,
etc. One could enlarge this list almost indefinitely and I dare
say you have already considered most of these yourself.

[December 11, 1975]

From Joseph D. Matarazzo, Ph.D.:

The question you ask in your letter is an important one. In
my own practice I have considered two behavioral effects as
indicators of "negative effects" which arise from psychotherapy. These are: (1) suicide; (2) ego disintegration resulting in
an unexpected psychotic episode.

I have had an occurrence of about 5 suicides in my 20-plus
years of psychotherapeutic practice and definitely feel each
was a negative effect. I cannot, of course, attribute the suicide
to psychotherapy per se inasmuch as I never did a controlled
study (unless you want to say that my many hundreds of other,
nonsuiciding patients were such a control group). In all
candor, however, I believe my psychotherapy was a factor in at
least one of these—a young male homosexual, age 17, whose
identical twin had suicided a year earlier.

Interestingly, I cannot recall an instance of the second type
of negative effect in my own practice. This no doubt is because
I have never practiced an intensive, depth probing, psychoanalytic or psychodynamic type of therapy. I did, incidentally,
during my internship provoke a psychotic episode in a young
14-year-old inpatient while I was giving him the Rorschach.

One other negative effect that I remember occurred a year
ago. During a four-hour initial consultation with a 57-year-old
alcoholic executive and his wife I suggested that he allow me to
hospitalize him at our local Raleigh Hills Hospital for
Alcoholism. He countered that he could quit on his own. I
recommended against this and he countered he would think
about it and return in a couple of days. Unbeknown to me and

his wife he went "cold turkey" just as he left my office with none of the medical tapering off interventions we would have used at the hospital. Unfortunately at 2:00 the next morning he went into a withdrawal "fit" and suffered a brain syndrome with total memory loss that is still present today. I don't know where you will rate this last example as it was the result of his reaction to our initial consultation and thus before psychotherapy had begun.

[December 8, 1975]

From Philip R. A. May, M.D.:

It seems to me that any treatment that is likely to make patients better is also likely to make patients worse if it is used in the wrong way, in the wrong case, at the wrong time or in the wrong dosage. I would certainly regard acting out, sexual involvement with the therapist and sustained dependency as toxic effects.

You will appreciate that I cannot support my opinions with experimental data. It seems to me that psychotherapists should take seriously the question of toxic effects and delimit the situations in which techniques are used at the wrong time or in the wrong amount or with the wrong patients. Also delimit the type of patient that is at risk for particular types of toxic effect.

In this, I would think that psychotherapy researchers could learn a great deal about methodology from the type of research that is done on drug toxic effects.

[December 8, 1975]

From Paul E. Meehl, Ph.D.:

I have not thought as much about negative effects of psychotherapy as I should have, mainly, I think, because I vacillate between a belief that it is too trite and obvious to warrant spending much time on, and thinking that it is so subtle and complicated that the time would be wasted. But since you say that you will take any comments, however brief, and don't require that the conjectures or impressions be scientifically documented, here are mine. (I number sections isomorphically with the three numbered paragraphs in your letter.)

1. I believe that we can legitimately speak of a patient getting worse as a result of psychotherapy, and I am reasonably convinced that I could point to instances, including some in which I was the therapist. I even have an instance from my own experience—which was, alas, one of the supervised psychoanalytic cases I treated—who *maybe* did the oft-mentioned and widely feared (but not, I think, frequently encountered?) business of "blowing up into a schizophrenia" when she started with a psychoneurosis. I never had much guilt feelings about that case, even assuming, doubtfully, the causal hypothesis is correct, because my supervisor had interviewed her and had treated her husband, the husband was himself a clinical psychologist and a seasoned psychotherapist, and all four of us (that is, supervisor, supervisee, husband psychologist, and the patient herself) perceived her as a hysteroid personality, and actually a good candidate for high density, horizontal, transference-interpretive kind of intervention. She improved markedly in several dimensions, but then (after some 300 couch hours) began to act pretty "strangely" in ways I need not go in to. Then she had a serious automobile accident involving objective danger to life (herself and child) plus a pretty severe whiplash injury with some neurological sequelae. (Accident not purposive—a truck ran into her while she was

stopped for a red light.) That gives me and my supervisory analyst an "out" because, as you probably know, some neurologists think that whiplash injuries are mysteriously associated with micropsychotic episodes having paranoid residuals. My experience with this condition is too limited to entitle me to have a judgment. Anyway, she deteriorated into first a paranoid and then an almost hebephrenic-like schizophrenic condition, and the last I heard was still in one of the Minnesota State Hospitals, some 15 years after I was treating her. A bad scene!

2. I would count as a negative effect of psychotherapy anything "adverse" which can be plausibly inferred to have been produced, exacerbated or potentiated by the psychotherapy. I assume away evidentiary questions, although you don't explicitly say to do that. As is my custom in respect to term "adverse," I would simply make a list of those things about the patient's subjective experience, social impact, overt behavior, or medical symptoms that are either opposite in direction to the explicit or implicit therapeutic contract—that is, the presenting complaint of which he wishes to be relieved—or which involve antisocial, medical, or broadly "competence" dimensions *when they reach the extremes*, even if he doesn't "complain" of them. Thus, if a person loses the ability to make money when he is a businessman, or suffers a decline in sexual potency, or develops an ulcer, or becomes overtly criminal, I would count any of these as an adverse effect. These indicators I would prefer not to call "indicators" (despite your language and that being one of my own favorite words, when I am talking psychodiagnosis and genetics) because, as I argue against Gottesman and Shields in my chapter at the end of their book on schizophrenia, the word "indicator" suggest to me the notion that one is employing the so-called indicator as a sign or symptom of some other trait or dimension. When we are doing psychodiagnosis or genetics I believe that is a correct description of the methodological situation. But when we are

talking about psychotherapeutic improvement it sometimes is but, in my opinion, it often is not. Gottesman and Shields, for instance, talk about "indicators" or "measures" of *severity*, and they treat this notion as though severity were some type of MacCorquodale-Meehl hypothetical construct (like a gene or germ or superego lucuna or fractional anticipatory goal response r_g), whereas I don't look upon severity as being that kind of entity at all, and therefore I avoid words like "symptom," "sign," or "indicator" that even suggest it is such an inferred latent H. C. variable. I have no reason for postulating that there *is* a valid concept of "overall mental health" or "overall therapeutic benefit." Analogously, I do not postulate such a homogeneous entity or factor for physical health. Psychotherapists and psychotherapy researchers have frequently got hung up—at times I think I can detect a whiff of this even in your thinking, but I won't hassle that—with the notion that we have to put together some kind of a "composite index of overall improvement" in order to study outcome. There is nothing wrong with such an idea provided one is clear about it being a mixed empirical and axiological problem, like cooking up a price index to evaluate what is happening in the economy. If there is no latent or underlying "entity" comparable to a germ or a gene or a neurophysiological construct like Hull's reactive inhibition (I don't believe there is such a thing, but that is not the point) then the question, "What is the *best indicator of this construct?*" cannot properly arise. So that in medicine, for instance, if we find that the patient's anti-pain medication relieves his pain but makes him feel a little "snowed," we don't worry about how to concoct a "health index" for him that will validly weight these two indicators; we simply make two separate empirical statements to the effect that (a) codeine relieves his pain but (b) it also makes him a little dull. It is then up to him and his doctor and his family— ultimately the patient himself—to decide whether avoiding pain is worth becoming a little dull. Nor have I picked a particularly far out example here, as you know. All sorts of medicines and surgical procedures and hygienic restrictions of activity (don't play tennis, don't make love too often, don't smoke cigarettes, don't drink whiskey, don't stay up late at night, don't spend so much time chasing a buck, and so on and so forth) involve certain adverse consequences or are intrinsically somewhat unpleasant to the patient, and a large part of the practice of organic medicine consists in leaning on recalcitrant patients for their own good. Despite the important differences between the medical and psychotherapeutic (or social-psychological) models, I cannot see a fundamental difference in this respect, whether one speaks explicitly about a so-called therapeutic contract or not. The point is that the question of the empirical correlation of so-called indicators of mental health or adjustment or whatever should be carefully put so as not to prejudge a theoretical inference about a latent or underlying pervasive causal entity that "gives rise to" the medical symptoms or psychological traits or whatever, which latter are then used with some appropriate statistical weight as a basis for inferring the state of the latent variable. I don't, of course, mean on my side to prejudge the question by dogmatically postulating that there *is* no general psychological health dimension that can sometimes be meaningfully talked about. It's just that I would not want my semantic habits to prejudge this either positively or negatively. And I am myself inclined to doubt that there is such a thing, except in the rather weak sense of general mental health as when we say that Jones doesn't have much stickum in the ego, or Smith has lots of trouble gratifying his intense needs in ways that are socially acceptable, and the like. To Freud's simple (and largely adequate, as I see it) formulation that mental health consists of *lieben und arbeiten*, I would be strongly inclined to add freedom from severe reality distortion due to impairment of the cognitive ego functions, freedom from a self destructive tendency to engage in behaviors that are strongly punished by the society, and freedom from the production of medical symptoms that are psychologically mediated, including organic lesions that are psychologically induced or exacerbated. I think we can all call to mind individuals whose ability to love and to work is relatively unimpaired (unless one sets up a super idealized model of perfect experiencing and performing in those areas) who nevertheless have psychosomatic symptoms, or get in trouble with the law, or have crazy ideas. So I would rather include the ability to work, to give and receive love, to be free from crazy ideas (about oneself or other people or the world in general), to be free of psychosomatic symptoms, and not to get in trouble with the cops. If these qualitatively diverse things happen to be correlated, that's all right; but it wouldn't lead me to conflate them into one index, any more than the fact that the various MMPI scales are correlated leads me to prefer eliminating the profile in favor of a single index of "MMPI health," although psychologists have done this, and for some purposes it may be all right.

You can see that I would have trouble with the third sentence of your second question if I took it to mean more than providing a list like the above, or—at most—a list like the above in which the patient's and society's values are somehow expressed as a value weight in the utility function. And of course, as pointed out by Truman Lee Kelley way back in the 1920s in discussing how to use factor analysis and how not to use it (that is, before the generalized multiple factor business had been invented, although Kelley was adumbrating Thurstone himself at that time), the psychometric *theorist* is often interested in something different from what the industrial psychologist or educational and military psychologist has to worry about, namely, what are the weights that we want to attach to certain things quite apart from questions about their empirical correlations or their inferred "validities" as "indicators" of a latent or historical (causal-H. C.) entity. So that a "therapy improvement index" might crudely add some measures of the above six components on the basis of the therapeutic contract or some other kind of evaluation of their "importance," and these weights might not correspond very much—might conceivably be even negatively correlated—with the weights that would be obtained by doing a cluster or factor analysis of the empirical changes in the domain listed as a result of successful or unsuccessful psychotherapy.

3. On this one I guess I really don't have much helpful to suggest. Never having done any research in this area like yourself, I have to rely on anecdotal impressions and clinical experience, and we know how dangerous that can be in matters of this sort. Let me list the main kinds of counterproductive consequences of psychotherapy as I think I have discerned them in my own practice or in colleagues, friends, neighbors and students who have talked to me at length about how their psychotherapy went, or—a very biased kind of basis of inference—patients of mine that I have helped who came to me after an unsuccessful trial with some previous therapist. It goes without saying that this latter group must correspond to some unspecifiably large or small group of people who had adverse effects from seeing Meehl and who subsequently went on to see somebody else who benefited them. Since I tend to assume that the kinds of mistakes that we make are somewhat characteristic of each of us as a psychotherapist, I consider it unlikely that the ways in which I made the patient worse by my gentle ministrations would be of the same sort, by and large, as the ways in which those previous therapists had made the patient worse and then the patient was helped by me. Here are the main ways that come to my mind in which a psychotherapeutic intervention can worsen the patient's condition:

a. *Loss of hope:* I believe strongly that one of the most important things involved in psychotherapy (as in organic medicine and, for that matter, life in general) is hope. I have seen some evidence, and I certainly believe it clinically, that one of the main differences between the patient who merely has suicidal thoughts at times and one who is in grave danger of making a serious suicide attempt is that the truly suicidal risk has suffered (a) massive, (b) pervasive, (c) continuous, and (d) recalcitrant loss of hope. I think that the loss of hope is one of the differences between a psychotic and a neurotic depression, and as you know there is some statistical support for that clinical impression. But that's not the kind of case I'm thinking of, it merely illustrates the background notion about hope in a dramatic way. When a patient finally comes to the point of seeking professional help for his functional incompetence or subjective distress, and goes and spills his guts to a psychotherapist and takes time and money to do it, it means, even among most intellectuals, a certain amount of ego threat, from having to admit failure to cope on his own, and the whole business about labeling oneself as "mentally aberrant" and the like. Then when the patient finds, despite what he perceives as his own cooperative behavior in paying the fee and showing up and talking and so forth, that he doesn't get any better, this result is experienced by many people as a *nearly catastrophic removal of a background source of hope*, an "ace in the hole" that they had carried around (sometimes for years) from reading books or talking to friends who had gone into psychother-apy successfully. Such a person has to say, "What a psychiatric basket case I must be! Here I am paying out my money and coming to this shrink who has diplomas on his walls and seems to know what he's doing and came highly recommended by my friend George L. Fisbee and who has apparently cured all kinds of people of my acquaintance, and he doesn't seem to be able to help me. I must be a real mess, I'm a hopeless case, I might as well go jump off a bridge because I'll never be any better." Notice that this particular one, which I have run across in a number of people of my acquaintance and patients who, in some cases, had gone for *several years* without further help-seeking effort after they had failed with some psychotherapist in this community, does not require that the therapist bungle or goof or do anything less than optimal, let alone anything extremely bad in technique or theory. I mean by that if psychotherapy is not the treatment of choice for a particular patient, the loss of hope can occur, presumably equally forcefully and dramatically and discouragingly, as it would if the therapeutic failure was based upon inappropriate patient-therapist matching or patient-theory matching or patient-technique matching or whatever.

b. *Battered self-concept:* I am sure you will agree with me that in addition to having hope about the future, one of the things human beings need to be reasonably healthy and happy is a belief in their own worth and love-ability. I have seen people, again some of them being patients of mine and others friends who have talked to me about therapeutic experiences, in whom the self-concept had been reduced rather than increased by psychotherapy, including psychoanalytic therapy where the therapist made interpretations without the requisite skill in timing, tact, "buffering" and so on. Thus, for instance, I have a friend who is a psychiatrist and who was in analysis with an internationally known analyst whose name you would immediately recognize, who kept banging away at certain interpretations of the patient's hostility (I myself never was convinced that it was that important in his personality makeup), the clumsy "You say that because you want to kill me" kind of hard-assed interpretation of negative transference stuff. So this very bright, very warm, very sophisticated (but, I will admit, extremely neurotic—I think possibly schizoid, never have made up my mind about him) young psychiatrist told me that every time he lay down on the couch he felt more than anything else like the man in Kafka's *Metamorphosis*. He also told me a couple of stories about extra-analytic social interactions with this analyst in which, assuming that my friend's account was accurate in substance despite some distortions on his part, were extremely clumsy and I would say crudely aggressive. Of course the interesting thing to

somebody with my type of psyche is that I can't imagine
myself going for hour after hour after hour over a two-year
period to somebody that made me feel like Kafka's man.
That my analyst was an individual duly accredited by an
analytic institute who had published papers on theory of
technique and whose name was known to me before I ever
came into analysis with him, none of this would affect me
much after I had heard, say, a dozen crude, tactless,
insensitive and aggressive interpretations. But my friend,
despite his brains (part of the problem was the same as the
patient in Lillian Roth's story about the ordeal of Dr.
Blauberman, namely, that the analysand had some thirty-
plus IQ points on his famous analyst) could not say, "My
analyst is a schlock." Whereas I would have concluded that
whatever his merits for other patients he was not suitable
for me and the hell with it. I asked my friend this question,
but he was so beaten down by the analyst's constant
interpretations of hostile transference, etc., he said that he
was still operating on the assumption—after two years
mind you—that it was mainly something wrong with him
and not something wrong with his analyst.

But here again, as in my loss of hope category, it is not
necessary to postulate that the battered self-image effect is
always, or even mainly, attributable to poor therapeutic
technique or an unfortunate "personal style" by a therapist
who might be theoretically (and in some narrow sense
"technically") adequate. I believe, as I think a reading
between the lines indicates Freud believed, that there are
things worse than lacking self understanding! In one of the
papers published shortly before World War I, Freud said
explicitly that there are people whose situation is such that
it is better to leave well enough alone, that they are doing
better with whatever symptomatic or character neurosis
they have than they would probably be doing without it. A
good friend of mine, a social psychologist now deceased,
told me once about his experiences with a psychotherapist

in the Twin Cities to whom I had referred quite a few people with good results and who was a broadly psychoanalytically oriented therapist who had personal analysis and so forth, although he did not call himself a "psychoanalyst." I knew this therapist personally and socially, and also had served on a couple of committees with him and had a high regard for him as a human being and as a clinical practitioner. And as I say, I had good feedback on quite a few people I had referred to him over the years. But my social psychologist friend, who got on well with him as a person and who believed that in some ways he had been helped by his contacts with him, said that on balance he was not sure that it had been profitable because, as he put it forcefully, "I have come regretfully to the conclusion, which goes against my grain as a psychologist, that sometimes it is better for people not to know too much about themselves and their relationships to others, especially their families." I have never seen any really convincing theoretical argument which shows that it is *always* a good thing to "have insight" to what one is, what one is doing, how one's wife or children or parents feel about one, how one feels about them, and so forth. As a compulsive cognizer and what Fr. Malachai Martin would call "an Intellecter," I naturally lean this way. But I can't prove it, I've never seen anyone else do a good job proving it, and the more I reflect upon it the less obvious it appears to me that it's *always* a good thing to "know all about one's own mind and one's interactions with significant others." So again, while it's no doubt *on the average* a worse thing if the patient's battered self-image becomes worse because his therapist entered the field as a way of expressing his own aggressiveness in sublimated ways and the sublimation doesn't come off too well; or even if the therapist is skillful and the technique in some sense appropriate for the kind of patient; it still may be the case that psychotherapy of an uncovering or broadly expressive sort can be for some people counterproductive, by acting adversely upon their self concept. The idea that it is possible to become completely relaxed and accepting of *anything* about oneself and that, if this miracle hasn't taken place, we still need to have some more psychotherapy is an idea which I do not find either theoretically plausible or supported by clinical experience.

c. *Wrong focus:* This category is perhaps harder to justify as being literally a mode of adverse influence, because it operates negatively not *per excessus* but *per defectum.* By focusing on whatever the therapist is (I assume here incorrectly) emphasizing with his queries, reflections, and interpretations, the patient has a lowered probability of coming to focus upon something else which, if it were attended to and dealt with in a problem solving way, *would* have been more effective. Somebody might say that it is unfair to blame the psychotherapy in a case of this kind. On the other hand, by analogy with what I believe economists usually refer to as "opportunity costs" (meaning that you can't spend limited resources on X if you are instead expending them on Y) it does not seem overly harsh to me to say that the therapy has had a bad effect, if we begin by postulating that the patient had a non-negligible probability of arriving at a correct focus but that the psychotherapist deflected him from what he might otherwise have, sooner or later, come to pay attention to. An example of this would, in my judgment, be patients with a drinking problem. I have known persons who sought treatments with strongly dynamically oriented or Rogerian therapists, each of whom downgraded the *causative* significance of alcohol abuse (in generating multiple occupational and family problems in the patient and also by contributing rather directly to the patient's maintenance of a chronic level of anxiety, depression, or lowered self-esteem, the latter often based quite directly upon the patient's objective awareness that he had said and done bad things under the influence of booze), because the therapist took the traditional view that "The drinking is merely a symptom, we have to get at the true underlying psychological cause," and the alcohol abuser—as any non-doctrinaire experienced therapist surely knows—is all too ready to avoid talking about drinking as such and finds it a good deal more comfortable to talk about his battle-axe mother or his cold wife or his authoritarian father or whatever the hell, instead of the fact that he is in the tank. The first thing to do in treating an alcoholic or a problem drinker is, I am convinced, to get him to see loud and clear that his main problem is drinking and that, for whatever genetic or biochemical or early conditioning or whatever reasons, he ca·mot drink "just like other people" and ought to quit. Another example: Consider a graduate student or professor who wants to talk about his self-image instead of facing the fact that he procrastinates in carrying out his professional work, finishing his thesis, taking his Ph.D. prelims, and the like. You know me well enough to know that I don't underestimate the power and pervasiveness of intrapsychic conflicts and unconscious processes and latent themes and so forth on producing "symptoms" or "character traits" such as over-drinking or work procrastination or sexual avoidance or whatever. On the other hand, a graduate student who wants to be a college professor and whose self concept involves professional achievement and earning a living in academia, is in my opinion going to have a hard time feeling comfortable about himself if he doesn't get off his ass and finish writing his Ph.D. thesis so he can get a job as a teacher and researcher. Similarly, a person who feels guilty because he beats his wife or goofs off on his job because he drinks to excess is not *likely*, no matter how many hours he spends exploring the wonders of his mind in therapy, likely to start feeling much self-acceptance. I have known quite a few people, as I daresay you have, who have spent many hours in intensive psychotherapy and who have in fact learned a good deal about themselves (and I don't mean just "verbal parroting" of interpretations, I mean really learning something about their feelings and characteristic modes of defending and avoiding, and so forth) who are still pretty ineffective or unhappy individuals, in large part because they are persisting in overt behavior of a destructive or ineffective kind. For such persons it would require some kind of massive brainwashing for them to stop feeling unethical or incompetent, for the simple reason that they are *in fact*, by any usual standards of ethics or of vocational, financial, family and sexual performance, doing things that are wrong, or inept, or both. If a person is a free loader or a marginal economic unit or an inadequate lover or an academic failure or a drunk or a passive saboteur in the work group, he will, unless he has unusually successful narcissistic rigid defenses or a sociopathic gene, usually feel pretty dissatisfied with himself as a human being, and this self-evaluation is, alas, realistic.

Nor does it have to be a matter involving antisocial conduct or deficient performance. It can simply be a matter of what the patient slowly learns to pay undue attention to, so that his problem solving behavior is deflected or constrained to the extent that he comes to accept the therapist's erroneous focus. I think, for instance, that strongly "family oriented" psychotherapists often do damage in these matters. I know of a man who spent around 15 years acting as kind of a psychiatric nurse to a borderline psychotic and extraordinarily castrating and malignant wife, because some mushhead family therapist had brainwashed my friend into believing that he had by his neurotic behavior "made his wife the way she was." The wife is a borderline schizophrenic with several diagnosed schizophrenias in the family tree (including one who spent some 40 years of her life under more or less continuous psychiatric care in and out of hospitals, one who died in a state hospital diagnosed as a schizophrenic, one suicide in a mixed schizophrenic-affective episode, and several others whom I have met socially or on the campus who, while not psychotic, are all in my view a little bit crazy). My friend is not the least bit schizophrenic or manic depressive, although he does have some neurotic character traits, but has at no point since I first met him 30 years ago evidenced *anywhere near* the severe psychopathology that the wife has always had. He walked around for several years feeling guilty for having "made his wife this way," until I finally pounded it into his head (in a series of informal nonprofessional conversations) that there was no good evidence that he had made her that way but that she was always pretty looney and that the main trouble with her was that she was cursed with having inherited a bunch of crazy genes. Subsequently another psychiatrist with whom the wife was in treatment agreed with me but also did some damage by telling the husband that while his wife was a rather severely mentally ill individual and probably would have been more or less aberrated much of the time regardless of whom she had married, he went on to say that if the husband abandoned her she would probably decompensate, become severely psychotic, and perhaps commit suicide. So he spent another five years or so *relatively* free of the guilt that the first psychiatrist had dumped on him for making his wife crazy, but nevertheless feeling that he was obligated to stay in the marriage because otherwise she would fall apart completely. He was, however, unable ultimately to do this. One night, after a vicious verbal and physical assault by her, he packed his bags and left, never to return. He is now happily married to another woman. He looks back wondering why he spent 15 years functioning as a kind of psychiatric aid with no gratifications of either sexual or affectional kind—especially since his first wife is functioning as adequately as ever without him! (Just as I predicted, because she never should have been a wife and mother to begin with.) In my judgment the first psychiatrist caused this man to waste quite a few years feeling guilty for something he had no objective reason to feel guilty about, and the second one, while aiding and abetting my propaganda against that unwarranted notion, nevertheless did some damage of his own by making a clinically unjustifiable forecast about the wife's probable psychosis. So I think this pair of professionals darn near did the fellow in.

One of the reasons I am attracted to RET (despite the fact that as a mode of treatment it becomes pretty boring after a while, at least for me) is that I know people who have had many hours in psychotherapy and who have uncovered and worked through a lot of stuff of the traditionally emphasized kind, and who may well have profited considerably by this, but who have become so focused on the wonders of their psyche and its internal connections that they have lost all disposition to examine their ethical and philosophical commitments, including what Albert Ellis would call irrational postulates about life. Traditional psychodynamically oriented therapy has a tendency, once the patient "gets the hang of it," to downgrade the work of the intelligence and to classify almost any rational examination of either external reality or value commitments as being mere intellectualization, something suitable for a seminar in philosophy or ethics or whatever but not useful as a means of improving one's behavior or subjective state. It seems to me there is something wrong with a psychotherapy which can leave a high IQ and well-read person, after hundreds of hours, in a state where he feels it obligatory, deeply axiomatic, an implicit hypothesis which he cannot (as Poincaré says) abandon *since he doesn't even know he holds it*, to be liked by everyone or sell more stock than anybody in the office or to publish two brilliant papers a month or whatever crazy idea is bugging him. Of course all of this depends on what role we assign to primary value commitment and to cognitions as dependent versus independent variables. Freud said that the voice of the intellect, while low, is persistent. But as I read the evidence, people have almost as much trouble directing the intelligence at unquestioned life postulates which are screwing them up as they do directing it at a nondefensive understanding and experiencing of their own impulses. This might not matter much if nontherapeutic experts, authorities, gurus, seers, or general "wise men" were classified by most educated persons as mere resources when in mental trouble. But in our day the professional psychotherapist has replaced the wise man, the priest, the guru so that most persons who are the sort who will seek psychotherapy in the first place are rather likely to assume that if there are any guru type issues involved in their psychological difficulties, those will be handled as part of psychotherapy. I incline to think that Albert Ellis is right in arguing that they are often *not* adequately dealt with in traditional psychotherapy, because such value questions are likely to be approached as mere derivatives of something else that is the real source of the problem.

I would be somewhat inclined to add another category labeled something like "cognitive bafflement," except that I suppose its countertherapeutic effects can be largely subsumed under one of the preceding. But I'm not quite sure about this. Enough for now, except to amend my list of "mental health" criteria by adding another item, "adequate hedonic capacity." The ability to experience pleasure should be added to relative freedom from abnormal nonreality based subjective distress (e.g., chronic, frequent, or exaggerated emergency affects of fear and rage, or of depression). Unlike many psychotherapists, I don't usually conflate these two, because of my views on hedonic capacity as a variable orthogonal to the others and whose deficiency can result in exaggerated amounts of fear and rage or depression rather than the usually assumed opposite direction.

[January 16, 1976]

From Neal E. Miller, Ph.D.:

There is a problem of negative effects:

1. Distraction from a more effective form of therapy—ranging from failing to get a necessary operation to remove a brain tumor to failing to get a more effective drug or form of psychotherapy.
2. Getting worse as a result of the intervention.

   a. One example is the negative therapeutic effect discussed in Dollard and Miller, *Personality and Psychotherapy* (McGraw-Hill, New York, 1950), and on page 351 through the reference to Makyo at the end of page 352 of my chapter, Applications of Learning and Biofeedback to Psychiatry and Medicine in *Comprehensive Textbook of Psychiatry/II* (A.M. Freedman, H.I.Kaplan, and B.J.Sadock, editors). Williams and Wilkins, Baltimore, 1975, pp. 349-365.
   b. Another example is symptom substitution, which while it does not always necessarily occur, sometimes certainly can occur if a symptom that fulfills an imperative need is blocked without providing any alternative solution to the problem.

I believe that recent data which Parloff at NIMH can put you in touch with shows that some of the faddist encounter groups produce approximately 30 percent getting worse while standard psychotherapy makes some but comparatively few people worse.

Sorry I don't have the time or experience to go into your other questions more thoroughly, but I do believe possible negative effects are an important problem.

[February 10, 1976]

From John C. Nemiah, M.D.:

My answer to your questions will be brief and limited to one or two observations that I feel are important. I hope that you have also written to Peter Sifneos, who has thought far more systematically and studiously about the problems of psychotherapy.

My first thought is that one must define "psychotherapy"— or, perhaps better, "psychotherapies," since, to state the obvious, there are many psychotherapeutic approaches, and what is useful for one patient may prove harmful to another. In other words, it is essential to make a careful diagnostic assessment of each patient, with particular attention to his ego functions, in order to determine what kind of psychotherapy is indicated.

More specifically, I feel that psychoanalytically oriented insight psychotherapy, which has been so widely taught for so many years, although helpful and the treatment of choice for many patients, can be actively harmful when applied to many borderline patients, or those with psychosomatic disorders. In the borderline patients it tends to promote the development of a regressive transference that leads to angry acting out, as well as manipulative and suicidal behavior. Many psychosomatic patients find the focus on their potential fantasies and feelings incomprehensible, and if they do not soon give up the therapy in disgust, they may suffer an exacerbation of symptoms.

Obviously these brief observations are derived from clinical impressions and are not the result of any kind of systematic study of the harmful result of psychotherapeutic interventions—studies that are hard to come by. For that reason, what you are proposing to do could be tremendously helpful to all of us. I shall be interested to hear of the progress of your work.

[January 14, 1976]

From Martin T. Orne, M.D., Ph.D.:

Thank you for your letter. The issues you are addressing are as important as they are difficult. It certainly is time for someone to bite the bullet and seek to address these matters empirically. I wish you luck!

As you are aware, each of the questions you pose could well be the basis of a monograph and, at the very least, merit lengthy discussion. All I can do at the present time, however, is respond with somewhat random comments and associations.

To the extent that we can speak of patients getting better as the result of psychotherapy, we must certainly be able to speak of their getting worse as the consequence of such intervention. Unfortunately, the problem of defining getting worse is at least as difficult as the problem of defining meaningful criteria of improvement. Probably it is even more difficult since it is possible to arrive at some picture of what the patient hopes to achieve in treatment and use that as a means of assessing the outcome (the target symptom approach). Obviously this has drawbacks but it has proved to be useful in several studies. On the other hand, the patient who gets worse does not usually do so in terms of the target symptoms. For example, the patient with recurrent incapacitating pain of unknown etiology responds to psychotherapeutic intervention with a considerable lessening of the target symptom; by the same token the patient becomes progressively more paranoid, sufficient to require occasional hospitalization and significantly interfere with functioning over many periods; the patient with low back pain of a functional nature, seeking and obtaining suggestive help leading to the relief of pain but precipitating a severe depression, etc. Anecdotal case reports of this kind abound. One can always argue that these problems would have occurred even without the intervention, but then such an argument can always be given for improvement which is often tenuously linked with the patient's treatment. In the final analysis, I think the only approach to this problem is to assess the patient's functioning, not in terms of a quantitative checklist but in terms of ability to enjoy work, love and play and to successfully cope with the usual stressors of life.

The obvious problem is that it can be argued that we are merely recording random fluctuations and adjustments. Unfortunately, to document that this is not the case it becomes necessary to predict when a patient will get worse with certain kinds of intervention; however, a systematic study of this kind is simply not feasible. Probably the best one can do is try to assess the kinds of problems that are more likely to deteriorate with psychotherapeutic intervention. The single most important aspect in any assessment of outcome is an adequate knowledge of the natural history of the patient's difficulties— some clear idea as to the degree of normal fluctuation over time. As this information becomes available, a Campbell-type quasi-procedure might be considered.

In my view it is possible to predict which kinds of symptoms serve useful needs in an individual's overall adjustment. If these symptoms are somehow undercut and the patient does not develop alternative coping mechanisms, it is possible to predict worsening of his overall adjustment. In my view it matters very little whether these symptoms are interfered with by behavioral, suggestive, or interpretative means. I see the issue in terms of the resources available to the individual to cope with external and internal stressors. The usual kind of assessment does not focus on the functional value of psychopathology. Not only would such an emphasis be useful in helping to assess possible negative effects but it would also facilitate any psychotherapeutic approach to the patient.

As I indicated earlier these problems are extremely interesting. I have not myself been involved with these issues for some time because of my interest in short-term therapy on the one hand and the use of suggestive techniques on the other. Certainly individuals with focal symptoms when they get worse in response to therapeutic efforts often show new symptomatology. On the other hand, there is, of course, another group of patients who are basically decompensated borderline individuals. Here it becomes possible to precipitate a frank psychotic episode by pushing too much, by getting closer to the patient than he can comfortably tolerate, establishing a close relationship and threatening his continuation, and similar maneuvers. A study of these issues can probably be carried out in any good outpatient clinic which serves as a training ground for well supervised residents. The reason why such a setting is useful is not because there are more difficult patients but because it would provide the context in which they could be recognized and studied for everyone's benefit.

I will look forward with interest to your efforts in this area. I wish it were possible for me to be of more help directly since you are dealing with one of the core problems of our field. As it is, however, I will need to be content with hearing about how things progress. With best regards,

[December 2, 1975]

From James O. Palmer, Ph.D.:

I do find it a little bit difficult to separate your three questions, as answering one does seem to lead into the next. I would answer your first question possibly, i.e., I do believe we can legitimately speak of a patient getting worse as a result of psychotherapy or related interventions. This negative effect would probably demonstrate it behaviorally in the increased symptoms or the presence of new symptoms. However, the problem then arises as to how to distinguish between negative effects and no effect. Thus, a person might become more emotionally disturbed despite psychotherapy, rather than because of it. In order to understand whether or not the increase in symptoms was the result of psychotherapy or not, it would be necessary to review in detail the therapeutic process preceding such a negative change.

A negative outcome of therapy is probably the function of any one of a number of factors or even more likely, a combination of many factors. My first thought is that the errors may be made originally in the diagnostic process which too many therapists skip over. That is, if the therapist has an inadequate or erroneous appraisal of the patient's problems and methods of coping then the wrong or inadequate therapeutic process might be applied. (This presumes that we know which therapies fit which problems.) Thus, for example, if the therapist did not realize how close to schizophrenic the patient might be and instead thought the patient to be largely neurotic, an "uncovering" therapy might be instituted which would serve only to open up the schizophrenia. The second major error I commonly encounter among my students is a too rigid adherence to one kind of therapy or the other. Thus, if the therapist tended to use the same techniques with all patients, behaving as if this particular therapy were a panacea, some patients who needed other kinds of treatment would be at best neglected and thus might grow worse. A third factor in therapeutic failures and negative effects often arises from poor handling of the countertransference. I must admit I am using a psychoanalytic term here, but I mean it to cover all the patient-therapist relationships of any kind of therapy, especially those where the therapist may not be aware of other kinds of motivations in oneself than the welfare of the patient. Nearly every patient makes the therapist a little angry, a little tense and a little sad. We often underestimate these feelings and some therapists, particularly those using primarily behavior modification techniques, may ignore the therapist variables altogether. However, our patients are quite sensitive to our reactions. A fourth major factor, which again I fear is too often neglected by psychotherapists, is the failure to deal with the social milieu in which the patient exists. Such a failure often results in wiping out any therapeutic gains, especially when we are dealing with children, but may be equally disastrous in treating adults. Thus we have learned over the past several decades to deal with whole families and to see the disabilities of children as part of the family social group. After several decades of treating children and adults as if they lived purely inside of a therapist's office, we have come full circle to the kind of combination of psychotherapy and social work that I was taught working under Jean MacFarlane. Thus, I think a psychotherapist should be a practicing sociologist. This does not mean that the therapist has to make the interventions into the patient's environment that a caseworker might do at times, but rather to be conscious of the environmental stresses themselves and to be able to help the patient to evaluate them realistically. This latter error might be called the error of devoting therapy entirely to the inner man. Thus, if we help persons to know themselves better, they may still be so inner-directed as to fail to face the stresses in the real world around them.

Thank you again for inviting my comments. I'll be delighted to hear the results of your inquiries and to see your book.

[January 28, 1976]

From Gordon L. Paul, Ph.D.:

I do believe there is a problem of negative effects in psychotherapy, usually as a result of therapists failing to appropriately assess the client problems and circumstances, failing to establish good working relationships, or coming on "too strong" with specific advice or tasks.

[December 15, 1975]

From Arthur J. Prange, Jr., M.D.:

I have no doubt at all that psychotherapy can do harm, but this would be no easier to demonstrate than my companion conviction that it can also do good. I suppose one would use the same instruments in both cases so long as they are "bimodal." (One sees an analogous problem in drug research when a scale only admits degrees of improvement.) If psychotherapy can't do harm it is the only therapy in medicine so blessed.

I suppose that psychotherapy most often does harm when the therapist allies himself with id (uncovering) mechanisms when this is inappropriate. I think it happens in adolescents quite often. Beyond this, I think that psychotherapy, like surgery, can be meddlesome. The difference is that surgeons have always recognized the possibility and psychiatrists have not. Psychotherapy always sends the message "you're not OK," so it starts a little below baseline.

[January 21, 1976]

From John M. Rhoads, M.D.:

I do believe that there is a problem of negative effects. Some patients are definitely made worse, by my observation, through psychotherapy.

Negative effects may take a number of forms. Perhaps the most commonly observed is an increase in symptoms, corresponding perhaps to heightened resistance or defensiveness. This frequently occurs in psychotherapy as the result of premature or inaccurate interpretations. Another negative effect might be a change in the nature of the illness for the worse. An example of this might be a patient, let us say, with some symptoms indicating a somatization, who through psychotherapy changes the pattern of response from one which, if not carried to extremes, elicits at least some sympathy, to a paranoid reaction released by successful interpretation of the affect bound up in the symptoms. Since paranoid behavior is much less acceptable to those around the patient, it would appear to be a negative effect both to them, and ultimately to the patient. I have observed on several occasions psychoses precipitated in a borderline patient by overeager interpretation or by blocking (on an inpatient service) to use of symptoms as a means of "binding" the latent psychosis.

Still another type of negative effect I have observed takes place when the patient loses confidence in the physician. This may not only make the patient's illness worse, or at least not make it any better, but may make it very difficult if not impossible for the patient to seek help from other sources or from other therapists.

In the last few years I saw two patients who were treated by "implosive therapy," both of whom I would regard as borderline types, who had psychoses precipitated by this type of treatment. Clearly what was at fault here was the failure to adequately diagnose the patient's ego weakness.

Perhaps the most pernicious negative effect can be precipitated by countertransference in the physician. These usually result either in rejection of the patient with its damage to what is usually an already shaky self-esteem mechanism; or an exploitation of the patient—as exemplified by seduction by the therapist. We had an episode a year or so ago which hit the newspapers in a neighboring community, though the papers had the full story. This was an incidence of a female patient who committed suicide at a remote rural cabin belonging to a psychiatrist. This man had first entered into a sexual liaison with the patient, then had rejected her. I regret to say that while this was general knowledge, nothing ever came of the matter either legally or through the licensure board since there seemed to be no way to provide any evidence that would stand up in court.

[January 31, 1976]

From Howard B. Roback, Ph.D.:

Thank you for inviting my reaction to your important questions on negative effects in psychotherapy. I hope my reply will be of some usefulness for your purposes.

1. I believe strongly that almost all treatment modes, be they pharmacologic, psychotherapeutic or surgical are capable of both positive and negative effects. The concept of iatrogenic conditions (i.e., an illness caused or made worse by the physician) is not a new one, but admittedly is seldom discussed in the psychotherapy literature. However, it would be naive to think that some patients are not made worse by their psychotherapeutic experience.

2. It is extremely difficult in most instances to make the determination of psychotherapeutic malpractice. For example, there are a large number of psychotherapeutic techniques in which standards for evaluating their usage have never been devised. In addition, the determination of a negative effect is an extremely complicated task. It involves initially a comprehensive understanding of the patient; this would include his premorbid personality, his present "condition," and expected symptomatic fluctuations prior to the prescribed treatment taking effect. This would prevent a confounding of expected variations in the condition (e.g., a manic outburst in a case of bipolar depression) with a negative treatment effect. Also, it would be important not to confuse a patient's demonstrating his "craziness" (either verbally or nonverbally) to his therapist after learning to trust him as a negative treatment effect. This could well be a positive sign.

With the above in mind, I would consider deleterious changes in a patient's cognition, perception and/or behavior that resulted from some factor, or set of factors, related to the treatment experience as constituting a negative effect.

However, I would add the proviso that in psychotherapy it is not uncommon for patients to go through periods of heightened anxiety and depression as they confront issues that had previously been avoided. These changes I would not consider as negative treatment effects as they are most often temporary "dips" which serve as a springboard for further improvement. On the other hand, if they become enduring, then the therapist may well have misjudged the patient's resources for facing these important issues.

3. I believe that the most *prominent* factors leading to negative treatment effects are therapist variables (including "poor clinical judgment," technical errors, and breakdowns in therapist-patient communications). You will undoubtedly receive numerous illustrations of technical errors and therapist-patient misunderstandings so I will not burden you with more. However, I believe that there is a segment of therapists who are responsible for many of the negative effects in psychotherapy due to the "poor clinical judgment" factor. These are therapists who are unable to utilize their intellect and acquired knowledge in therapeutically productive ways. For some, personality needs (e.g., needs to control and dominate; underlying problems with sado-masochism and voyeurism; gimmicky and faddish, etc.) seem to dominate their decision-making processes. That is, clinical decisions are based on their own personality needs (although perhaps theoretically rationalized), rather than on the patient's therapeutic needs. Thus, negative treatment outcomes would be expected with this group of clinicians.

Less prominent factors leading to negative outcome would be patient related (such as distortions; omissions and falsifications in his communication to his therapist leading to improper treatment) and perhaps treatment setting factors (breakdown in communication about treatment between nurses and physicians on an inpatient service, etc.).

Hans, I would appreciate learning more about your ideas in this area as your work progresses.

[January 14, 1976]

From Leon Salzman, M.D.:

There are negative effects of psychotherapy, more easily identified when it is practiced by unscrupulous and inadequate non-professional healers. However, they also occur when the therapist is experienced and well-trained. Specifically, those individuals who have no background in the healing sciences and whose training is exclusively psychodynamic, maintaining the psyche-soma dichotomy do, I believe, serious damage in failing to recognize the psychosomatic aspects of human functioning.

1. Yes, many elements in the psychoanalytic process tend to fix obsessional symptoms, since the process of therapy tends to be an obsessional ritual itself. This occurs when the therapist is rigid, inflexible, insecure, and essentially a technician following rules of procedure. Such rigidity also tends to crystalize and support the psychodynamic concepts of determinism where the focus of difficulty lies with parents, society, others, and not within the individual's own resistances to change. The failure to acknowledge the role of will, intention and personal involvement in one's neurotic problems prevents change, since the patient comes to expect it from the outside sources and agents. This leads to the endless and interminable therapeutic experiences. For change there must be intentional commitment as well as insight. While this is given lip service to in some therapies, it is yet to become a working principle. In spite of years of experience and the enormity of intelligent practitioners, psychoanalytic training still focuses on the interpretation as the key factor in change. This,

I believe, does damage to the individual's lack of autonomy, responsibility, and esteem, and ultimately, to the state of dependency on outside authoritative figures. There are many such elements in the psychodynamic process that still support and encourage the authoritarian nature of the process because it can be effective in producing change (EST is a marked example).

2. What constitutes a negative effect? (a) Excessive dependency manifested by exaggeratedly long therapeutic relationships; (b) failure to change, while verbalizing insights and formulas for living; (c) substituting drugs and anxiety-relieving devices for more meaningful change in life style; (d) participation in group organizations such as EST, Transactional groups, marathon groups, etc., for excessive periods of time and substituting mystical activities (Yoga, movement therapies, etc.) in extreme forms for valid life movements. This is a widespread tendency that encourages belief in the irrational as a comfort and to avoid a more painful confrontation; (e) exaggeration of somatic difficulties when their presence was the basis for initiating therapy; and (f) extension of phobias and restriction of activities rather than broadening activities.

3. It is my belief that negative effects are due to: (a) limitation of psychotherapeutic knowledge and skills. The total picture of human behavior and its neurophysiological and biochemical correlates has yet to be established; (b) false assumptions of omniscience of the practitioner; (c) sociological factors; (d) poor training facilities and the development of delivery systems which do not require the maximum background in the biochemical and psychological sciences.

I am interested and would be glad to participate to whatever degree is possible.

[December 7, 1975]

From Robert L. Spitzer, M.D.:

I believe that negative effects in long-term outpatient psychotherapy are extremely common. I believe that I personally am acquainted with several instances of it. There are many people who are attracted to the patient role who find it irresistible to regress during psychotherapy of a special sort who might otherwise do rather well in the absence of long term psychotherapy.

[January 23, 1976]

From Leonard P. Ullmann, Ph.D.:

First and above all, I do not think of psychotherapy and other interventions as a single thing, but rather have to ask what, for whom, under what conditions, etc. Further, as a radical behaviorist, I measure behavior; this does increase feedback, and is the basis for the answers to your questions as below.

1. Yes. For example, there may be reinforcement of an inappropriate response such as reinforcing sick-talk; going too rapidly on a hierarchy; and certainly at the start of an extinction program one may observe an increase in irrelevant behavior (e.g., when starting work with temper tantrums).
2. An increase in overt changeworthy behaviors or decrease in prosocial ones.
3. Two things. The major problem for behavior therapists today is the use of techniques as techniques rather than models. That is, technician application in place of understanding and thoughtfulness. These people "do behavior mod" as if it were a pill to be given (e.g., Marks,

Gelder, and other English types, and many U.S. psychiatric types).

A minor problem is that of moving too fast or too slow; not a major problem if there is therapist response to the observations; a bad problem if, as above, there is not such response.

[December 1, 1975]

From Robert S. Wallerstein, M.D.:

I have your letter with your questions concerning the problem of what you call "negative effects" in psychotherapy. As you would guess, my reaction is that it is a big and important question, but how can I possibly address it within a letter? We've had a number of occasions to get together in the past to talk about the issues of common concern in the area of psychotherapy and I'd be more than delighted to do it again, specifically around the questions you ask in your letter.

But in lieu of that, or anyway in advance of that, let me state very briefly (since once I try to elaborate, it would become a major paper) that, yes, of course, we can legitimately speak of people either not being helped by psychotherapy or being worse off. I suppose the most obvious kind of example would be the people who have psychotic ruptures (which sometimes are enduring) after or with ill conceived psychotherapy and also, of course, with what you call "related interventions." The criteria that I would use in relation to negative effects would be coordinate with or identical with the criteria used to assess positive effects, whether these be questionnaires, rating scales, clinical judgments, etc. (depending on the researcher).

In regard to your third question, obviously we live in a multi-causal world. There would be some interaction between the propensity of the patient towards a psychotic decompensation, for example, and the less than optimal or even the misguided handling by the therapist.

Let me stop at that point and leave the rest for when we can talk together. And in regard to your comments in the last paragraph of your letter, of course I would be interested to be kept apprised of how this endeavor works out.

[December 5, 1975]

From Irving B. Weiner, Ph.D.:

I appreciate your including me among the people to whom you are addressing questions about negative effects in psychotherapy. In thinking about the questions you pose, I realize I could answer each at some length. I also realize, however, that much of what I would say would only duplicate ideas you already have or will hear from other people to whom you are writing. Hence I decided I would answer the questions from just one perspective—not necessarily the perspective I consider most important or salient, but one from which I may be able to make a relatively unique contribution to the ideas you are collecting.

Along with my interest in psychotherapy, I have an equally strong and abiding interest in effective psychodiagnosis. From the point of view of someone who believes firmly in careful diagnostic evaluation as requisite for effective psychotherapy, and who believes further that conceptually oriented utilization of psychodiagnostic instruments plays a useful role in such evaluations ... let me proceed to give some admittedly specialized answers to your questions.

1. There is definitely a problem of negative effects from psychotherapy or related interventions that occur when treatment is planned without sufficient regard for the patient's or client's personality structure. Especially striking in this

regard is the ill-conceived utilization of uncovering or insight oriented approaches with people who have borderline or psychotic personality organization. People tend to fall apart in such circumstances, and the fault lies neither with the specific or nonspecific features of the treatment situation themselves, but rather with an inadequate prescription for psychotherapy.

2. Viewed from the perspective I am taking, a negative effect in psychotherapy would consist of personality decompensation or decline in level of personality integration. Such declines in level of personality organization during psychotherapy would appear on and could be effectively measured by a variety of psychodiagnostic instruments. Using the Rorschach as an example, Holt's measures of adaptive and maladaptive regression have proved effective in predicting response to psychotherapy and in monitoring its course. The same can be said for Exner's use of the "experience base" and "experience potential" as outlined in his recent book. A number of other conceptually sound Rorschach indices of ego functioning are available and can be used effectively to measure both improvement and deterioration during psychotherapy.

3. Continuing with the diagnostic perspective, the factor responsible for a negative effect in psychotherapy would be identified as the wrong choice of treatment approach. Unfortunately, it is not easy to label a treatment as poorly chosen when the data show no change or modest change and one wishes to argue that some other treatment would have produced marked change. It is also necessary to face the fact that a person who becomes worse during psychotherapy may have been going downhill rapidly before the treatment was begun and may, by virtue of receiving it, have been spared from becoming even more disturbed or disorganized than he did during the therapy. Nevertheless, I feel there is no lack of instances in which sensitive commissions have realized that (a)

a patient is getting worse in psychotherapy and (b) this decline could have been avoided if more care had been taken in evaluating the patient prior to beginning the therapy, in order to select a treatment approach suited to the patient's personality style and level and adequacy of personality integration.

Having been dictated extemporaneously, these answers to your questions may not read as clearly or cogently as I would like. However, I did want to get a response to you promptly, and I did want to take the opportunity to stress the important role that I think psychodiagnosis can and should play in planning and evaluating psychotherapy. You can count on my continuing interest in your project.

[January 16, 1976]

From Walter Weintraub, M.D.:

I am responding briefly to your letter about the "negative effects in psychotherapy and related forms of therapy." I shall leave unexamined the very important questions of what you mean by "related forms of therapy," "related interventions" and "negative effects."

I believe that one is better off speaking of negative effects "associated with" rather than "resulting from" psychotherapy. There are roughly two kinds of negative effects to consider: (1) those generally harmful to the patient; and (2) those harmful to the attainment of the goals of therapy, which may or may not include harm to the patient.

Some "negative effects" associated with psychotherapy are obvious and would be so considered by most everyone: suicide, the emergence of psychotic symptomatology or the development of a severe manic or depressive state requiring hospitalization, ECT, drug therapy, etc.; homicide or other extremely violent acts; the erosion of solid interpersonal relationships; the development of work inhibitions; a decreased ability to experience pleasure in one's activities and relationships; the development of addictions, etc.

"Negative effects" resulting in termination of therapy before the attainment of mutually agreed upon goals may or may not be associated with obvious harm to the patient or client. The so-called "transference cure" in psychoanalysis would be an example of a positive outcome from the patient's point of view and a negative one from the analyst's point of view. The same effect can be viewed by the therapist as negative or positive depending upon the strategies and goals of therapy. Thus, rapid reduction of anxiety and disappearance of symptoms will be welcomed in brief psychotherapy but not in long-term psychotherapy. Therapists working with "target symptoms" may be indifferent to the emergence of other negative effects in therapy. For example, a young clinical psychologist with whom I am acquainted treats obese clients by behavior modification and measures her success solely by the amount of weight lost. I do not believe that she would consider suicide a failure so long as the weight loss was maintained to the end.

Certain effects may be regarded as negative by some and positive by others depending upon the impact of the patient's behavior upon them. Examples of these effects would be termination of relationships, increased ability to experience hostility, changes in lifestyle, etc. As for factors associated with negative effects, I would distinguish those probably caused by events external to therapy and those seemingly due to psychotherapeutic errors in strategy and technique. Among the latter, I would include: (1) inappropriate contractual arrangements between therapist and patient; (2) imprecision in the formulation of therapeutic goals; (3) attacking defenses of fragile patients; (4) inability to maintain minimum professional distance and, particularly, sexual exploitation of the patient; (5) breaches in confidentiality; (6) prolonging therapy when an impasse has been reached; (7) inadequate preparation for termination.

This is my first reaction to your request, "off the top of my head," so to speak. The topic is a fascinating one.

[January 20, 1976]

From Otto Allen Will, Jr., M.D.:

I am replying to your letter in which you refer to your study of possible negative effects in psychotherapy. My responses in what follows are somewhat "off the cuff," but I have given some unsystematized thought to the subject during my professional years. Now that you are getting at the problem in a more systematic fashion, I shall like very much to hear from you something about your progress.

1. I do think that there is a problem of negative effects. I have repeatedly said in lectures, and so on, that a patient can get "worse" as a result of psychotherapy. It seems to me that psychotherapy cannot in any sense be "neutral." As in any other human relationship, the psychotherapeutic one is likely to bring about some changes in the participants. Some of these changes may be useful and some harmful. I think it may be necessary to attempt to define what some of these changes are. For example, one must consider what he may think of as "the overall" effect on personality; this would be in contrast to some aspects of personality which may be adversely effected, whereas the total personality change is considered to be positive.

2. I think that certain undesirable obsessional processes may be increasingly refined, rather than altered, during the course of treatment. The patient in such case might substitute a number of intellectualized "insights" for other obsessional thought processes. This would be, in my opinion, a negative effect. It is also possible for a patient to become increasingly paranoid during the course of therapy. The development of such paranoid ideation may go unnoted until the appearance of a delusional system. This development would be more

difficult to alter than the earlier condition for which treatment was sought. Another example of a negative effect would be the patient's growing discouraged with any form of human relationship because of his feelings of discouragement about treatment itself. In the examples given, I think that each patient will have further estranged himself from intimate human relationships.

3. I think that strict adherence to a therapeutic technique without due regard for the individual characteristics and needs of a patient may lead to such a preoccupation with technique that undesirable changes are unnoted—or the patient is labeled unsuitable for treatment. I also think that the failure to bring into the open the details of the actual relationship between the patient and the therapist will encourage the development of a negative effect.

All of the above is rather casually stated, which fact does not reflect any failure to appreciate the value of the research. I hope you will keep me in touch with its progress.

[December 4, 1975]

From Lewis R. Wolberg, M.D.:

1. Patients do get worse as a result of psychotherapy done by a bad therapist as a consequence of a traumatic relationship (see page 60, 2nd Edition *The Technique of Psychotherapy*).

2. A negative effect could take multiform shapes. Increase of symptoms, escaping from therapy, a hostile or other negative attitude toward the therapist (2nd paragraph, page 1109 of above).

3. See chapter on "Failures in Psychotherapy," p. 1106. Chief difficulty: incompatibility of personalities of patient and therapist.

[February 16, 1976]

From Joseph Wolpe, M.D.:

1. Yes, a patient may get worse as a result of psychotherapy or related interventions.
2. The indicators of negative effect are: (a) exacerbation of suffering, usually in terms of intensification of anxiety and related reactions; and (b) spread of anxiety to new areas of stimulation that had emanated from the psychotherapeutic interaction.
3. The main factor in making a patient worse is the arousal of great anxiety in him. I have found this to have been done in a great variety of ways. A patient who had a fear of falling began also to have a fear of insanity and hospitals when a therapist told her that she would find herself in a state hospital if she did not respond to his treatment. The secondary fear was more intense than the primary and had lasted for two years when I saw her. Other patients are made worse by being told such things as they are sexually attached to their mothers, that they wish they belonged to the opposite sex, and that they are somehow basically abnormal, on the basis of an inability to achieve orgasm, for example. In the latter kinds of case, the terrifying message need not always be conveyed directly, but by innuendo.

[December 2, 1975]

From Benjamin Wolstein, Ph.D.:

Just a brief note to say that I would be pleased to join you in the sort of study you outline in your letter. I have, of course, been interested since my earliest associations with psychoanalytic therapy in finding ways to consider the questions you raise, and, over the years, have developed some tentative working ideas, in terms of a structure of psychoanalytic inquiry I've been working at since the middle 1960s expressly to account for the wide interpretive plurality of therapeutic experiences that arises from a common, singular matrix of observations and definitions, postulates of transformation, and explanatory theory.

To make my views of the structure of psychoanalytic inquiry more directly relevant to the questions you and your group are pursuing, however, I shall want to hear about the different views as they develop.

Let me say, in closing, that I look forward to contributing what I can, and hope that your project becomes a stimulus to further clarification of the basic issues involved.

[November 30, 1975]

From Irvin D. Yalom, M.D.:

I have done a great deal of thinking about negative effects in psychotherapy. I'm sure you are probably familiar with my article on "Casualties in Encounter Groups," which is somewhat condensed from the chapter on "Negative Effects of Encounter Groups" in the book *Encounter Groups: First Facts* (Lieberman, Yalom, and Miles 1972). I have thought about the concept of negative effects in a number of informal contexts. I have seen a large number of my group therapy patients at various stages in therapy be more uncomfortable, more distressed, than when they began therapy. To a large extent this is to be expected in the normal course of psychotherapy.

However, with time limited groups or encounter groups, many of the groups may end these particular intervals when the patient is not afforded the proper time to work through the issues that are confronting him at that point.

I've recently finished a large project in which thirty-five patients in long-term individual psychotherapy were sent to a weekend group experience. (There were a total of three groups, each with pre-group conditions. The patient either went to a gestalt group which was designed to arouse affect, or to a control meditational group.) We are still analyzing data, but our findings so far seem to confirm that of the twenty-three patients who attended the gestalt groups, there were two who seem to have had serious negative effects of the experience. This, despite the fact that they had the benefits of continuing to see their therapist in long-term individual therapy immediately subsequent to the weekend.

[December 31, 1975]

From Clifford Yorke, M.D.:

I am writing to acknowledge your letter to Miss Freud. I do not think that we can be very helpful. We are mainly concerned here with problems of psychoanalytic therapy and it seems to us that the best safeguard against adverse effect is a thorough diagnostic assessment. We think that where this is carried out effectively, an inappropriate "prescription" of psychoanalysis might more often be avoided, and a form of management or treatment more appropriate to the case recommended. To this end we employ, as a routine in our diagnostic assessment, Anna Freud's "Developmental Profile." You probably know this well. It is described in her book *Normality and Pathology in Childhood*, as well as in the Psychoanalytic Study of the Child. As for adverse factors in analysis, we would distinguish from other possibilities the negative therapeutic reaction as described by Freud in *The Ego and the Id* where the patient apparently gets worse in spite of apparently thorough working-through, but usually improves with appropriate technical measures. Our own view would be that effects which really are adverse *might* develop from inappropriate techniques—for example the use of defence analysis in psychotic patients. This view differs of course from the Kleinian standpoint.

Lastly, my own feeling is that where analysis is concerned, it is not necessarily so much a question of adverse response as a waste of time, skills, resources, money and often of using inappropriate therapeutic techniques or applying too rigidly a particular model to all cases.

[January 21, 1976]

From Joseph Zubin, Ph.D.:

There are several underlying assumptions in my thinking on the problem which I should postulate first.

1. All mental disorders (including schizophrenia) are not continuous and persistent, but episodic, and most, if not all, eventually disappear even without therapeutic intervention.

2. The individual's permanent characteristic is not the disorder, but his vulnerability to the disorder (like an allergy).

3. Life event stressors (both endogenous and exogenous) are necessary to trigger an episode in a vulnerable individual and the lower the vulnerability of an individual, the greater the impact the stressor must have to elicit an episode.

4. Once the episode is over, the patient returns to his premorbid level unless the therapeutic intervention interfered with his return.

5. The last point is where your letter enters—Does the therapeutic intervention ever interfere with the return to the premorbid level?

6. Perhaps the best known principle in prognosis and evaluation of outcome is that good premorbids most always do well (returning to their premorbid good level) while poor premorbids do poorly.

7. The good outcome of the good premorbid is no surprise.

8. The poor outcome of the poor premorbids may result from two possibilities:

   a. The poor premorbid also returns to his premorbid status, but because this status was insufficient to cope with life's exigencies adequately, the end of the episode is not seen in him, and he is mistakenly regarded as unimproved, or still in his episode.
   b. The poor premorbid may actually be worsened by the episode.

The problem can be clarified, as I see it, by examining a group of good premorbids who failed to recover to see what factors interfered—this is the group that you are apparently concerned with. Similarly poor premorbids who happen to defy the law of return to premorbid level, and actually improve on their premorbid status, should be studied to see what factors helped in their recovery.

Perhaps we should separate out for clarity, two issues:

1. The return of the patient or client to his premorbid level.
2. Improving the coping level and competence of the poor premorbid so that he can cope better than he was able to do during his premorbid existence. This, however, is not therapy in the usual sense, but rehabilitation—which transcends the usual boundaries of goal directed therapeutic endeavor. Rehabilitation is the attempt to improve people's usual coping ability and competence regardless of their previous mental status (whether they had an episode or not) so that they can be more productive, happier, etc. This is not necessarily a part of the usual therapeutic intervention when a person has an episode of illness.

So much for the general problem as I see it.

More specific problems arise from the patterning of the various criteria we utilize in the evaluation of outcome. The criteria based on self-evaluation on the part of the patient, evaluation on the part of the therapist, family, social network, system of delivery of health care (relapsing into hospitalization), economic system (employment) etc. are probably not linearly related into a composite. It would be well to find the typology of outcome in its various clusters for these criteria. Then we might discover that there are some patterns in which a person declines on some measures (say economic ladder) but is the better off for it in the other factors.

Some investigators include relapse as a criterion from improvement, tending to denigrate improvement which is followed by a relapse. From the point of view of the vulnerability model, relapse is not a criterion of outcome. Relapse would not enter into our criteria since relapse is dependent on degree of vulnerability, and we are ill-equipped to reduce vulnerability except temporarily by means of drugs. Of course, we can use depersonalization or other types of behavior modification to reduce the stressor value of life events which formerly triggered episodes, but this does not reduce the essential vulnerable nature of the person (except to the contingencies which have been desensitized).

If we ever get a handle on vulnerability itself, we could classify therapeutic intervention into long term vs. short term effectiveness. The short term interventions would merely hasten or bring about the end of a current episode and have no effect against relapses in the future. The long-term interventions would tackle the problem of prevention of future episodes. At first, the efficacy of long term interventions could be studied only empirically and retrospectively by examining individuals who do not relapse and in whose case the intervention was crucial, i.e., individuals of the same premorbid status who benefited from the intervention (had no relapses) while their peers who were not treated similarly failed to benefit. Once the characteristics of the benefiters are established, prognostic indicators predicting no relapse (reduction in general vulnerability) could be found and used in future interventions. This, however, is still far in the future, since thus far, we have been unable to determine how to reduce vulnerability except temporarily with drugs.

The omnipotent view of therapy in being able to improve adjustment in general regardless of the presence or absence of psychopathology is beyond the scope of therapeutic intervention today.

To measure general adjustment (aside from propensity to future episodes) is a question which is beyond the usual scope of evaluation of therapeutic intervention. It can be studied, but is not part of the problem of therapeutic evaluation. It entails life value systems and philosophic problems beyond the usual scope of therapy.

Another problem that is no doubt well known to you is the problem of transfer of training from the clinic or therapeutic session to life. . . .

I have omitted any reference to psychotherapy vs. the other options open to therapeutic intervention, but this is a totally different issue than the one you intended.

Please keep me informed of your progress.

[December 1, 1975]

Author Index

Subject Index